Good Practice
Communication Skills in English for the Medical Practitioner

Teacher's Book

Marie McCullagh
Ros Wright

CAMBRIDGE
UNIVERSITY PRESS

CAMBRIDGE UNIVERSITY PRESS
Cambridge, New York, Melbourne, Madrid, Cape Town, Singapore, São Paulo, Delhi

Cambridge University Press
The Edinburgh Building, Cambridge CB2 8RU, UK

www.cambridge.org
Information on this title: www.cambridge.org/9780521755917

First published 2008

Printed in the United Kingdom at the University Press, Cambridge

A catalogue record for this publication is available from the British Library

ISBN 978-0-521-75591-7 Teacher's Book
ISBN 978-0-521-75590-0 Student's Book
ISBN 978-0-521-75593-1 DVD
ISBN 978-0-521-75592-4 Audio CD Set

Contents

Introduction to the Teacher's Book

Welcome note

Whether you are an experienced trainer or this is your first time teaching medical English, the Teacher's Book that accompanies *Good Practice* seeks to provide you with the essential tools and background necessary to empower you in the medical English classroom. The potential implications of a badly managed patient encounter are considerable, and the outcome possibly fatal. As such, an understanding of the psychology required in patient management and the rationale behind effective communication skills is imperative; it is necessary for you to be aware of the implications of the training, as well as the approach employed. While your learners will not expect you to be capable of giving an accurate patient diagnosis, they will tend to have more confidence in a trainer who has an understanding of the relevant concepts involved in medical communications skills. Consider this rather as a meeting of two experts – your role being that of expert in the field of communication skills and the English language. For more information about the course, see the Introduction to the Student's Book.

What are the special features of the Teachers Book?

Background provides you with an overview of each unit, setting out the aims and offering relevant background information related to the patient interview.

US versus UK English sections at the start of each unit give a list of the different British and American English terms that appear in the unit or the audio script.

Rationale offers you an explanation of the pedagogical rationale behind each activity and helps you justify its purpose to your learners.

Teaching guidelines give you indications as to how you might teach the activities, depending on the size and dynamic of your group. Additional activities are also included. Please note that these do not include guidelines on classroom management.

Answer key appears alongside the relevant activity as an easy-to-use guide.

Language Notes supply you with additional information regarding the lexical and grammatical points covered in each unit, including notes on intonation patterns and pronunciation.

Recommended reading gives you a list of titles/extracts written by experts in the field of patient communication skills specific to the unit that you might find useful should you wish to read around the subject.

Readings for discussion are extra materials in the form of authentic articles from a variety of sources, including medical journals and core textbooks for medical students. These are related to the theme(s) covered in the unit and can be used for further discussion.

How might *Good Practice* help you prepare your learners for medical examinations?

Good Practice can help you prepare your learners for the oral components of accreditation exams (USMLE, PLAB, etc.), where clinical knowledge *and* communicative ability are measured. The patient-centred approach, functions, language, and skills featured throughout the course are all highly relevant, and the scenarios portrayed in the DVD clips closely replicate the simulated clinical scenarios (*stations*) they are likely to encounter.

Introduction to communication

At the end of this introduction, learners will:

- recognise the different elements that make up communication
- understand how good communication benefits the patient interview

Background

The purpose of this unit is to give learners an overview of what communication involves and of its importance to the doctor–patient interview.

Defining communication

Learners begin the unit by considering the communication process and giving their definition of communication. The most important point to bear in mind is that communication is a two way process: the sender of a message should not assume that their message has been received and interpreted in the way they intended until they have had some form of feedback from the receiver.

Elements of communication

Five main skill areas are introduced in the unit: verbal communication, non-verbal communication, voice management, listening, and cultural awareness. A jigsaw metaphor is used to show how these fit together. Various exercises are designed to raise awareness of good and bad practice in medical communication.

Importance of communication

A key point in this unit is making it clear that communication skills training is not just an add-on option to their medical training; it is key to the whole practice of medicine. Quotations from key medical texts are provided to help underline this.

Lead in

Rationale: to raise awareness of different models of communication

- Tell learners to read the quotation and then ask them to discuss in small groups what the author means. (Answer: Often people regard communication as something that is done consciously; however, we are communicating all the time without realising it.)
- Ask learners to think of an example of communication which follows the transmission model and one which follows the interactional model.

> **a** The author means that communication takes place at a sub-conscious as well as conscious level.
>
> **b** Examples of transmission model: being paged in a hospital; where a doctor gives instructions to a patient who has not fully understood and does not ask for clarification
>
> Example of interactional model: in the patient interview where the doctor takes steps to check that the patient has understood the message

Discussion: Defining communication

Rationale: to elicit how learners perceive communication

1a • Ask learners to write down a definition of communication and share it with a partner.

- **Suggestion:** Write any key words that come up from their definitions on the board.

1b • Ask learners how their definition compares with the quotation.

2 • Ask learners to look at the jigsaw. The jigsaw represents five component parts of communication. The first component is given: verbal communication. They should suggest what the other components are.

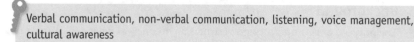 Verbal communication, non-verbal communication, listening, voice management, cultural awareness

Verbal communication

Rationale: to consider factors that determine what we say

3 • Ask learners to write down three factors which influence how we communicate with somebody.

The context (formal or informal), relationship of speakers to each other, gender, age, level of education, whether the other person is a native speaker or non-native speaker of English

4a • Learners should read the example from a patient interview and then underline the expression that has caused the misunderstanding of *cardiac arrest*. Then ask learners to suggest an alternative expression.

The expression that caused the misunderstanding was *cardiac arrest*. The doctor should have said *heart attack*.

Communication Skills

• Explain to learners that it is vital to have good control of communication strategies. By using communication strategies such as checking, clarifying, paraphrasing, summarising, the risks of being misunderstood are greatly reduced.

4b • Ask learners to suggest what the doctor should say to the patient when he realises that the patient has misunderstood his question.

The doctor should clarify what he means, e.g. he could say: *I'm sorry, that's not what I meant. I want to know if there is a history of heart attacks/disease in your family.*

Voice management

Rationale: to develop awareness of the aspects of voice that can influence meaning

5 • Ask learners individually to consider what aspects of voice can influence the verbal messages we send. Learners should compare their ideas with the rest of the group.

Intonation, word stress, speed, loudness of voice, pitch, pausing

▶ 0.1 **6** • Tell learners they will hear three different doctors saying the phrase *can you raise your leg as far as you can?* They should match the adjectives (bored, friendly and irritable) to the appropriate doctor. Play the recording (UK English).

Audio script >>

STUDENT'S BOOK **page 137**

0.2

> **a** 2   **b** 1   **c** 3

7 • Tell learners they will hear a doctor asking a patient the same question twice. Ask learners to identify which one they think sounds more inviting. Play the recording (US English).

Audio script >>
STUDENT'S BOOK **page 137**

> The second question is more inviting. The emphasis on *why* in the first question sounds as though the doctor is demanding an explanation, whereas the emphasis on the word *medicine* in the second question makes it sound more objective.

Non-verbal communication

Rationale: to develop awareness of how we communicate non-verbally

8 • Ask learners to write down as many ways they can think of in which we communicate non-verbally, and then to compare their examples.

> See Exercise 9 for ideas.

9 • Ask learners to match the pictures to the form of non-verbal communication that it demonstrates. The example 'slight movement' is given.

> **1** b   **2** h   **3** g(c)   **4** f(e)   **5** c(g)   **6** e(f)   **7** a   **8** d

10 • Refer learners to the different forms of non-verbal communication from Exercise 9. Ask learners to position them along the line provided, in terms of how easy/difficult they are to control.

> There is no set answer to this. However, generally speaking, some of them are more difficult to control than others, though this can be improved through awareness-raising and practice. The following tend to be easier to control: environment, clothing and accessories, eye contact, proximity, orientation, touch. The following tend to be more difficult to control: posture, facial expressions, movement.

11 • Now ask learners why it is important to observe and respond to non-verbal cues.

> It is important because non-verbal cues allow verbal messages to be delivered more accurately and efficiently by reinforcing the verbal message.

Active listening

Rationale: to develop awareness of the difference between hearing and listening

12 • Ask learners to comment on the difference between listening and hearing. Ask them what barriers prevent us from hearing a speaker and what barriers prevent us from listening to a speaker.

1 Hearing is passive, but listening is active.
2 Barriers to hearing: external noise, if the speaker mumbles, speaks very quickly, has a strong accent, stresses words in the wrong place.
3 Barriers to listening: thinking about what you are going to say next, day-dreaming, filtering out only certain words that you want to hear, making a judgement in advance that prevents you from listening objectively, predicting what the speaker is going to say.
4 Suggested answers
- Showing you are prepared to listen, i.e. not giving the impression that you are in a hurry.
- Listening to verbal cues, observing non-verbal cues.
- Showing your understanding by making utterances, such as *uh-huh*, or using phrases like *I see, Right,* etc.
- Using communication strategies, e.g. clarifying, to show that you are following what the person is saying, summarising what the person has said.
- Using appropriate body language, e.g. eye contact, orientation (the way in which you position yourself in relation to the speaker).
- Pausing before you ask further questions.

0.3 **13a** • Contextualise the dialogue: Tell learners they are going to listen to a doctor eliciting information from a patient. Learners should identify what is wrong with the patient. Play the recording (UK English).

Audio script >>
STUDENT'S BOOK **page 137**

The patient is concerned that the antibiotics he has been taking for a chest infection are not working.

13b • Ask learners to comment on how accurate the doctor is in obtaining information from the patient and to consider how effective the consultation has been.

Accurate insofar as he collects information about the condition which the patients has been diagnosed with. However, he does not attend to other possible conditions. Overall, the consultation is not as effective as it could be, as the doctor has not explored the patient's concerns completely. He has not given any reason why the patient has had to take three different types of antibiotics, or any real counter to the fact that the patient does not feel better. There is the possibility that the patient will not continue the course of antibiotics. In addition, there are signs that the patient may be suffering from depression or anxiety (symptoms are: fatigue, sleeping badly or too much, significant change of appetite, low self-esteem and lack of hope for the future). By failing to observe, or choosing to ignore this, the doctor is reducing the effectiveness of the consultation, as the patient is likely to return.

Cultural awareness

Rationale: to develop awareness of the importance of cultural factors in communication

14a • Ask learners to think about and write down three elements that make up 'culture' and three distinctive elements of their own culture.

1 Language, religion, beliefs, values, customs/habits, festivals, art, literature, music

14b • Learners compare their responses with a partner.

14c • Ask learners to read the definition of *culture*. They should then identify two cultural factors that set doctors apart as a professional group.

> High levels of personal responsibility, high status, clear code of ethics, specific body of knowledge and use of language, need for evidence/logic

15a • Ask learners to read the text and then discuss what kind of cultural background and bias a doctor, as an individual, might bring to his/her work.

> Class, ethnicity, national culture, political beliefs, religious beliefs, influence of media

15b • Invite learners to share any personal experiences where lack of cultural awareness resulted in a misunderstanding, in either their personal or professional life.

16a • Ask learners to read the case study. They should circle any elements that surprise them or are different from their way of thinking.

16b • Learners should then discuss their responses with a partner and describe how they would have reacted to the case.

17 • Ask learners to look at the completed jigsaw. Ask them why they think cultural awareness appears in the middle of the jigsaw.

> It is in the middle because all communication at all levels is culture bound.

Benefits of good communication

Rationale: to develop awareness of the benefits that good communication brings

> **Quotation** (Silverman, Kurtz and Draper)
> • This quotation neatly summarises the benefits that good communication can bring. It is important for learners to realise that good communication does not just mean being pleasant and caring to the patient; it also means being efficient and accurate at eliciting information.

18 • Ask learners to indicate whether the outcomes contribute to the effectiveness of the consultation in terms of accuracy, efficiency or supportiveness.

> **1** S   **2** E   **3** S   **4** A   **5** E

Piecing it all together

Rationale: to reflect on their level of communication skills, in light of what they have covered in the unit

19 • Ask learners to work in small groups. They should outline what they perceive to be their current strengths as communicators and those areas which they feel the need to improve.

Recommended reading

• If you would like a little more information on this topic, we suggest you read the following:
Maguire P and Pitceathly C. *Key communication skills and how to acquire them.*
BMJ 2002; 325: 697–700

Reading for discussion

• Go to page 146.

Unit 1 Receiving the patient

LEARNING OUTCOMES

At the end of this unit, learners will be able to:

- greet a patient and put them at ease
- introduce themselves and their role
- ask the opening question and set the agenda for the interview

Background

Establishing rapport

Being able to establish rapport with the patient is the crux of the whole interview; indeed, the way in which a doctor receives a patient can make or break the consultation that follows. A doctor needs to treat their patient with respect, of course, but establishing rapport within the first few minutes is also about how doctors greet the patients and introduce themselves, ensuring that they have clarified their role, making sure patients are comfortable and even that the seating arrangement is appropriate (see audio 1.1).

Opening question

The next step is to understand the issues the patient wishes to address or the reason for their visit. The doctor's opening question needs to require more than simply a *Yes* or *No* answer so that the patient will express his/her story. It should be a question that opens up the discussion, e.g. *What would you like to discuss today?* or *What brings you here today?* The patient will then produce his/her opening statement. Note that a follow-up visit might start with *Am I right in thinking you have come about your routine check up?* but could then follow with *Is there anything else you would like to discuss today?* to ensure that all avenues are covered – the patient may well wish to bring up other issues.

Opening statement

The opening statement is when the patient reveals the issues he/she wishes to discuss. Interrupting the opening statement (which is something many doctors do) means that fewer complaints are elicited and vital signs and symptoms may be missed, possibly resulting in misdiagnosis. Instead, doctors should use active listening skills to determine the salient points of the statement in order to set the agenda for the consultation, using the verbal and non-verbal patient cues (looking upset, sounding frustrated, etc.) that determine both the physical and emotional state of the patient.

Setting the agenda

Setting the patient's agenda, as opposed to carrying out the doctor's agenda, is important. Based on the salient points of the opening statement, the doctor must decide on a schedule or structure to the encounter, e.g. *Shall we start with ... and then we'll come back to the problems you've been having with ...?* Doctors should not forget to obtain the patient's agreement on the agenda, e.g. *... if that's OK with you?*

William Osler (1849–1919)

The celebrated 19th-century physician from Ontario, Canada, Osler, known as one of the most influential physicians in history, is still quoted today by many experts in medical communication skills. He believed students learnt best by doing and that clinical instruction should begin and end with the patient. Quotes from Osler include: *Medicine is learnt by the bedside not in the classroom* and *Care more for the individual patient than for the special features of the disease.* For more information, see www.medicalarchives.jhmi.edu/osler/biography.htm

US versus UK English

UK	US
be sick	vomit / throw up
collect the kids	pick up the kids (audio 1.2)
consultant	MD (Medical Doctor)
diarrhoea	diarrhea
GP (General Practitioner) (audio 1.3)	PCP (Primary Care Physician)
hospital ward	hospital department

UK	US
locum	I'm covering for Dr ...'s practice
playing up	acting up / giving me trouble
registrar	resident
student doctor	medical student
surgery / consulting room	doctor's office
waterworks (audio 1.3)	plumbing

Lead in

Rationale: To highlight the fact that the simplist form of contact with the patient can be the most effective means of establishing initial rapport

- Give learners a minute to think about the quote before getting them to share their thoughts as a group.

> Osler's quotation is highly relevant, even today, especially as many doctors are still not engaging in the most basic of relationship-building skills with their patients. This initial contact with the patient is vital. Doctors who don't take the time to greet their patients risk alienating them from the outset. Patients may or may not understand much about their condition, but what they do understand and appreciate is warmth and empathy, which can so easily be conveyed by the doctor, can be reassuring, and will eventually facilitate the encounter.

Putting yourself in the patient's shoes

Rationale: to remind learners what it feels like to be a patient and to draw on their own experience as a patient

1
> **Suggested answer**
> Patients are likely to be more frightened than the doctor (even during a first consultation) or to think their condition is more serious than the doctor says. They may even be afraid of the doctor. Patients may be even more anxious in a hospital because: of the unfamiliar environment; they don't know the doctor; it's busy and noisy; they might have to wait longer.

2a
- Ask learners to think about the experience from the patient perspective. Encourage them to put themselves in the patient's shoes – not necessarily an easy task but vital if they are to embrace the patient-centred approach.
- You might want to ask learners to visualise themselves in the role (of patient) before completing the questionnaire; it might help some to 'get into character'.
  OR
  Ask learners how often they visit the doctor, when the last time was they visited the doctor, or how they felt about the experience.

- **Suggestion:** If you haven't already done so, complete the questionnaire yourself along with your learners.

2b

Quotation (Bickley)

- Ask learners to read the quotation and then ask them to give suggestions as to how to best receive the patient.

Suggested answers:

Smiling, eye contact, handshake, tone of voice, sitting forward, being prepared to receive the patient, giving them your full attention, etc.

Think about

Rationale: to assess their own skills at this stage, considering their own experience of establishing rapport with a patient in English

3a
- Some learners might not have experience of doing this in English. They should evaluate their current level of competence as they see it; it is a kind of self-assessment.
- Be aware that learners tend to overestimate their competency.

3b
- At this stage there are no right or wrong answers; the activity serves as a Needs Analysis for the unit for you and the learners. Learners are likely to be less competent in terms of the pragmatics of spoken communication.

Establishing initial contact (non-verbal and verbal communication, cultural awareness)

Rationale: to develop learners' understanding of the importance of the physical setting, and the doctor's ability to establish initial contact with the patient

- Start by asking learners to describe a doctor's office that they know well.
- Ask learners what they think would be the best seating arrangement in the office.

▶ 1.1 **4a**
- Contextualise the dialogue: tell learners they are going to listen to a communications expert talk about the importance of seating arrangements in a consulting room (UK English).

  Audio script >>
  STUDENT'S BOOK **page 137**

- Play the recording. Reassure learners that on first hearing they might not understand everything, but they'll get a second chance to listen.

Seating arrangement 1.

4b • Ask learners to predict the answers before listening in detail.
  • Play the recording again.

> **1** Because the patient is more relaxed and therefore more forthcoming if the seats are placed at right angles to each other, and the doctor is not behind a desk.
> **2** c
> **3** Because you don't want to be so far away from your patient that you can't hear them or that they feel you aren't interested in what they're saying; neither do you want to make them feel threatened by being too close.

4c • **Suggestion:** Ask learners to mark out the distance in the classroom and then ask them Question 1.
  • Emphasise that this is just one opinion and that they can disagree – it might depend on cultural factors.

> **2** c
> **3** To ensure that he/she is on the same level as the patient, e.g. by pulling up a chair to carry out the encounter. He/She shouldn't lean over the patient, as this might be intimidating.

▶ 1.2 **5a/b** • Contextualise the dialogues: Tell learners they are going to hear two patients talking to friends about a recent encounter with their consultants; accounts are given from the patient perspective (UK English).

Audio script >>

STUDENT'S BOOK **page 137**

  • Point out to learners that the criteria used to analyse the consultants' skills to establish a rapport are the same as the 'Think about' in Exercise 3. Also point out that they don't need to worry about the Examples column the first time they listen. Play the recording.

> **Consultant 1 (outpatients)**
> **1** needs improvement (didn't acknowledge patient or ask her to sit down)
> **2** needs improvement (didn't greet patient)
> **3** needs improvement (sounded bored)
>
> **Consultant 2 (ward round)**
> **1** fairly competent (took his time with patient, but stared at her and didn't suggest more private place for interview)
> **2** competent (polite / shook hand)
> **3** competent (not mentioned, but can assume was appropriate, as patient described him as having a lovely voice)

5c • Encourage learners to give their own advice based on what they have already covered.
  • Encourage learners to give explanations for each point of advice, as if giving feedback to a medical student.

Quotation (Bickley)
• Ask learners to read the quotation and then ask them what they understand by the expression *undivided attention*. Then ask learners to what extent they think it is possible to make up for poor initial contact later on in the encounter.

Greeting and putting your patient at ease (verbal communication)

Rationale: to develop linguistic competency in establishing rapport with a patient

▶ 1.3 **6** • Contextualise the dialogues: Tell learners they are going to listen to three doctors welcoming their patients (UK and US English). Play the recording.

Audio script >>
STUDENT'S BOOK **page 137**

> **1** GP's surgery (Familiarity – use of first name with patient might indicate the doctor already knows the patient.)
> **2** specialist's office (This is a referral for further investigation.)
> **3** hospital ward (The doctor introduces himself as being the registrar on the ward this evening.)

7a • **Suggestion:** Ask learners how they feel when they meet someone for the first time and that person automatically calls them by their first name.
 • Ask learners to fill in the table, giving each objective a heading. This will serve as a reference.

> **Suggested answers**
> Objective 1 Greet the patient and obtain his/her preferred form of address (unless already known).
> Objective 2 Introduce yourself and clarify your role.
> Objective 3 Explain the purpose and agenda of the interview.
> Objective 4 Obtain permission for special circumstances (e.g. for another doctor to attend, to take notes).

 • Remind learners that in some cultures, obtaining a patient's preferred form of address is not necessarily considered; it is assumed the family name will be used.
 • Ask learners what doctors should also consider when using a patient's name. Out of respect, doctors should not assume a woman is married nor that a patient wants to be called by his/her first name – or indeed surname (this may create too much formality and even hinder relations).

8
> **1** With some patients, the use of the phrase *have a little chat* might encourage patients to talk; it lessens the formality and makes them feel more at ease.
> **2** The verb *chat* for some patients reduces the seriousness of the situation, so it should be avoided if the doctor has to break any kind of bad news, for example. The doctor needs to try to gauge his/her audience.

 • **Suggestion:** With a monolingual group, reinforce the rationale behind the use of the verb *chat* by eliciting the translation and asking learners to what extent it would be appropriate to use (the translation of) this verb in their own language during a patient interview.

▶ 1.4 **9a** • Contextualise the dialogue: Tell learners they are going to listen to the beginning of a patient encounter (UK English). Refer learners back to the box in 7a. They should tick the objectives in the order they hear them. Play the recording.

Audio script >>
STUDENT'S BOOK **page 138**

> The doctor achieves all the objectives in order (1, 2, 3, 4).

9b The doctor also makes sure the patient is at ease by asking if she is comfortable / would like another pillow.

Communication Skills

- Point this out to learners and then ask them to stand up and mingle. Ask learners to introduce themselves to three different members of the group, practising this sentence.

10 • **Suggestion:** Brainstorm two or three different scenarios for your learners to work with before they practise. The group should be able to come up with these based on what you have already covered.

Conveying warmth (voice management)

Rationale: to develop awareness of an appropriate tone of voice and its importance in enhancing rapport with the patient in English

- Refer learners to the Introductory Unit, to Thompson's quotation about voice management on page 10. Ask learners to visualise how a doctor might convey warmth through his/her voice.

▷ 1.5 **11a** • Contextualise the dialogue: Tell learners they are going to hear two versions of two different patient encounters (UK English). They need to decide if the doctors sound welcoming or unwelcoming.

Audio script >>
STUDENT'S BOOK **page 138**

Encounter 1, Version A: welcoming
Registrar is lively and friendly.
Encounter 1, Version B: unwelcoming
Registrar speaks in a monotone.
Encounter 2, Version A: unwelcoming
Dr Patel is abrupt and doesn't respond to the patient's frustration at having been kept waiting.

Encounter 2, Version B: welcoming
Dr Patel apologises for the situation.

- **Suggestion:** Ask learners to comment on the attitude of Dr Patel. Ask them what the difference is between the way he responds to the patient in Version A and how he responds in Version B. Play the recording.

11b In English, the rising and falling intonation, speed, pitch and tone of the voice determine if a voice is welcoming or not.

Language Note:

Showing a welcoming voice
It is imperative that a doctor is able to convey a positive welcoming attitude when receiving their patient.

A welcoming voice is shown through a moderate pitch and speed, and a gentle rise and fall intonation pattern.

Registrar: Good evening. Ms Finley, isn't it?

Registrar: I'm Dr Cameron. I hope I'm not disturbing you.

- **Suggestion:** Discuss the possible outcomes of inappropriate tone of voice / intonation; e.g. the patient is made to feel nervous and uneasy, and may not feel he/she has the trust of the doctor; as a result the patient may not divulge all the issues he/she had wanted to discuss, which could lead to misdiagnosis, etc.

▶ 1.6 **12a** • **Suggestion:** Ask learners to come up with a context for each greeting before listening to the recording.

Audio script >>
STUDENT'S BOOK **page 138**

- Tell learners that tone of voice / intonation is dependent on context.

> **1** Specialist visiting patient in a hospital ward. (This is the most likely answer as the doctor refers to the patient's consultant.)
> **2** Woman coming to surgery / clinic. (A six-month check-up might be in the case of a patient with a particular condition that needs checking regularly by his/her GP, e.g. dermatological conditions.)
> **3** Patient attending appointment at surgery/clinic. (In the UK, patients can either be called in to the doctor's consultation room by the doctor him/herself or sent to the room by the receptionist, depending on the size of the practice.)
> **4** Doctor calling in next patient at surgery/clinic.

- Point out that in the UK, *clinic* means a place where a group of practising doctors are located in the same building; in the US it means *doctor's office*.

Cultural awareness

Point out to learners that eye contact may not be acceptable with some of their patients. They need to learn how to be able to read their audience.

13 • Tell learners they will now have a chance to consolidate what they have covered so far in the unit. They will role-play the initial introduction to an interview in each case. Tell them you will be giving feedback.
- **Suggestion:** Put the following on the board as a reminder – 'Eye contact', 'Tone of voice', 'Setting', 'Proximity', 'Facial expression'.
- Give feedback to learners on the above points.

Think about

Rationale: to assess learners' current understanding of the opening question and how it is formed in English

14a • Remind learners that with 'Think about' activities it is not a correct answer that is important, but the process they go through – they will have the chance to develop their skills in the activity that follows.
- Be aware that some learners may not fully understand the concept of the opening question, having not come across this in their training (see 'Background' at the start of this unit), or may not know how to form one in English. Tell them they will be looking at these in more detail in Unit 2.

14b

> The doctor's opening question invites the patient to explain the reason for his/her visit. The question needs to be sufficiently open and not exclude non-medical concerns the patient may have. From the response, the doctor will be able to set the agenda for the interview.

14c • Write both opening questions up on the board. Look back at the questions learners suggested in Exercise 14a and decide on the suitability of these two, as a class.

> *So, what's the problem?:* This could be perceived as very negative. It assumes the patient has a problem (or what could be perceived as a problem) and that what the patient fears (with or without reason) could be a problem.
> Some learners might have given this as the suggested answer for 14a. It is grammatically correct, but learners might not realise the negative connotation behind the use of the word *problem*, especially in a medical context. (It could be a negative transfer for learners with a Latin-based first language.)
>
> *What's up?:* This may come across as being very rude and is too colloquial a register for this context.

• Point out there are many different types of opening question, depending on the situation (see next exercise).

Asking the opening question (verbal communication)

Rationale: to highlight the need for different opening questions, depending on the situation

15a • **Suggestion:** Go through one or two of these first, as a group.

> **Suggested answers**
>
> **a** 2, 5, 7, 9
> **b** 2, 4, 6, 7
> **c** 2, 4, 5, 6, 7, 9, 10
> **d** 2, 3, 5, 9, 10
> **e** 1, 2, 5, 7, 8, 9

15b
> **Suggested answers**
>
> **1** Doctor refers to the patient's GP, so the most likely answer is (e).
> **2** This question is a very general question that a doctor in any situation would use to open up the discussion in a patient-centred approach.
> **3** (d) is the only possible situation, as the doctor refers to a baby, and carers of newborns are required to attend surgery for routine check-ups.
> **4** The patient might have been given a course of tablets on a previous visit and is on his/her follow-up visit to the surgery (c) or he/she has been hospitalised and is being followed up on by the registrar/doctor during the ward round on a course of treatment (b).
> **5** Only (b) would be an inappropriate situation for this question, as the doctor would already know why the patient is in his/her care if currently in the ward.
> **6** As for question 4.
> **7** Only (d) would be inappropriate, as the doctor is asking about the patient's health (and not that of a baby).

> 8 As for question 1.
> 9 Only (b) would be inappropriate, as this question assumes the doctor is not aware of the patient's reason for visiting. A doctor/registrar during a hospital round would know the reason for the patient being on the ward.
> 10 The doctor could quite possibly be referring to a small child or a baby, and so either (c) or (d) would be appropriate. The doctor appears to know the child and therefore (c) is possible.

▷ 1.7 16a • Contextualise the dialogue: Ask learners to think back to the encounter they listened to with Mr Mahoney (from Exercise 11) and say what they remember about it. Play the recording.

Audio script >>

Audio script >>
(STUDENT'S BOOK **page 138**)

>
> 1 *Any improvement in the arthritis since I saw you last?*
> 2 Recurring headaches
> 3 It was not the most appropriate opening question, as Dr Patel assumes Mr Mahoney wants to talk about his arthritis and doesn't allow for Mr Mahoney's own agenda. This type of question is therefore limiting and doesn't encourage the patient to express him/herself in his/her own words. The doctor shouldn't assume anything.

16b
> *Am I right in thinking you've come about the arthritis?*

Language Note:

> ### *Am I right in thinking you ... + present simple OR present perfect*
>
> Point out to learners that there is no difference in meaning between the use of the present simple or present perfect in this construction.
>
> Example: *Am I right in thinking you're here about your arthritis? / Am I right in thinking you've come about your arthritis?*

• **Suggestion:** Brainstorm reasons for using this opening phrase, e.g. the doctor does not automatically assume the reason for the visit, but as the patient is known to him he acknowledges the possibility of the patient's need to talk about his arthritis. This form of opening question checks the reason for the visit and allows the patient to correct if necessary, thus ensuring a more patient-centred approach.

> ## Quotation (Silverman et al.)
> • Refer learners to the quotation to reinforce the previous activity (16b).
> • Ask learners to share instances of when they have followed their own agenda and not considered their patient's second agenda. Then ask how they managed the rest of the consultation. Did they feel their patient left the consultation having finally been able to discuss his/her own agenda?

17
> 3, 4, 6, 8, 10

(18) Unit 1 Receiving the patient

Out & About

Rationale: to encourage learners to notice native speaker usage and further develop their competence in posing the opening question

- Explain the rationale behind 'Out & About' activities, as this is the first one of the book (see Introduction to Teacher's Book, page 4). If time allows, discuss the benefits of this type of activity for language learning.

18 • Ask stronger learners to demonstrate possible body language used in their country and then ask other members of the group to do the same.

> **Suggested answer**
>
> In Anglo-Saxon countries, the following body language can be used to open the interview: open seating position (no crossed arms/legs), slight inclination of the head, sitting slightly forward, eye contact and a smile.

- Point out that some patients may not respond to this, and that it may need to be followed up with the appropriate opening question.

Setting the agenda (active listening)

Rationale: to train learners to activate their listening skills and achieve Objective 4 (see 7a), which opens the interview

> Well, yes, I'm sure you've got all this information, but … my <u>arthritis</u> has been playing me up a bit as usual – I'm having <u>difficulty sleeping</u> and I'm in some <u>pain first thing in the morning</u>. But it's the <u>headaches</u> that are really getting me down. They're so <u>painful</u>, sometimes <u>I've been sick</u> with them … literally. I'm starting to <u>have time off work</u> now because of them. <u>My wife's really worried</u>. She's the one that insisted I go and see Dr Patel …

Language Note:

[It's] getting me down = [It's] making me feel depressed

19 • Learners should have no problem picking out the important points – they will bring their medical knowledge to the task.
  - … *have time off work* and *My wife's really worried* indicate that the complaint is going beyond the illness itself and that the doctor needs also to consider these points during the interview.
  - Be aware that some learners may not pick up on the more social aspects of the opening statement at this stage. (Learners will cover these in Unit 4.)

20a **Suggested answers**
- Enables the doctor to hear the patient's story
- Prevents the doctor from making premature hypotheses and chasing down blind alleys
- Reduces late-rising complaints
- The doctor doesn't have to think of the next question (which blocks the listening capacity of doctor). The patient, who is mostly answering questions, tends to be more passive.

> - Gives the doctor an indication of the patient's emotional state
> - Enables the doctor to observe more carefully and pick up on verbal and non-verbal cues
> - Is helpful to patients for whom it is not easy to define problems – allows them time to clarify what they want to discuss
> - Signals the doctors interest in the patient

- Be aware that learners may not be able to offer all of these responses, especially if they are not used to the holistic, patient-centred approach (see Unit 2).

▷ 1.8 **21** • Play the recording.

Audio script >>
STUDENT'S BOOK **page 138**

 I can see it's the headaches that are really bothering you, so **if we can start by** looking at those. **We'll come back to** the arthritis later, if that's **OK with you.** Is there **anything else** you want to discuss today?

- After listening, elicit the significance of *if that's OK with you?* (i.e. doctor obtains permission to set the agenda in this way) and *Is there anything else you want to discuss today?* (i.e. doctor gives patient the opportunity to add other points for discussion if necessary). Both are examples of the patient-centred approach.
- Refer the group to the 'Language for setting the agenda' box.

22 • Tell learners they will now have the chance to practise setting an agenda.

Piecing it all together

- Explain the rationale behind 'Piecing it all together' activities (i.e. to get learners to reflect on their level of communication skills in the light of what they have covered in the unit). If time allows, discuss the benefits of this type of activity for language learning.

23a/b • Take time to monitor each pair to check they are able to set up the role-play correctly, especially as this is the first one of the book.
  - Tell learners you will give them feedback on both positive and negative points of their verbal and non-verbal communication, their voice management, and their active listening skills.

Progress check

- Explain the rationale for the Progress check (see Introduction to Teacher's Book).
- Ask learners to go through the Progress check.
- Give learners some group feedback and indicate where they might need to improve.
- Give individual feedback to those who wish.

Recommended reading

- If you would like a little more information on this topic, we suggest you read the following:
Silverman J et al. *Skills for Communicating with Patients.* Oxford: Radcliffe, 1998 (35–55)

Reading for discussion

- Go to page 147.

Unit 2 The presenting complaint

LEARNING OUTCOMES

At the end of this unit, learners will be able to:

- encourage their patients to express themselves in their own words
- take an accurate history of the presenting complaint
- ask about the intensity and degree of pain
- use techniques such as facilitation, repetition and clarification

DVD clips 1 and 2

Background

Patient-centred versus doctor-led approach

Read the text in Exercise 1a to get a clear idea of the concept and the differences between the two approaches.

George Engel (1913-1999)

The US psychiatrist George Engel was known for his pioneering work on doctor–patient relations. He believed a more in-depth understanding of patients' problems could be achieved through a bio-psychological model that states that the working of the body can affect the mind, and vice versa. For more information regarding this model, see the *American Journal of Psychiatry*, vol. 137.5, 1980, http://ajp.psychiatryonline.org/

Presenting complaint

The presenting (or chief) complaint is the complaint with which the patient presents him/herself to the doctor's surgery or hospital emergency department. There can be more than one presenting complaint, in particular with elderly patients. Asking about the presenting complaint requires a series of questions in a particular order (see answers to Exercise 23).

Question types

- <u>Open questions</u> (*what*, *why*, *where* type questions) open up the discussion and encourage the patient to give a detailed response, allowing patients to express themselves in their own words.
- <u>Closed questions</u> require a one-word answer (*Yes*, *No*, or a specific piece of information), without encouraging the patient to express themselves in any detail).

When interviewing a patient in certain contexts (e.g. if they are suffering from respiratory problems, are highly stressed, or are in A&E), it is better to use a closed questioning technique. Used inappropriately, however, this question type can be quite restrictive. Nonetheless, good non-verbal communication can turn closed into open questions.

Doctors are encouraged to avoid the following question types:

- <u>Multiple questions</u> (several questions asked at the same time) can be confusing and stressful for the patient; doctors are advised to ask one question at a time.
- <u>Leading questions</u> are those that in effect put words into the mouth of the patient and 'lead' the patient towards a particular answer.
- <u>Tag questions</u> (an example of a leading question) tend to guide patients in their response. The 'tag' part of the question reinforces the question in a particular direction (*You're not sleeping too well, are you?*). Tests have shown that patients tend to be influenced to agree with the doctor's perceived point of view. (See Language Note below for information on form.)

Effective question technique

The 'cone technique' moves from open to closed questions. It ensures that the doctor obtains a picture of the problem from the patient's perspective by opening up the discussion. With the need to confirm specifics and narrow down the cause of symptoms, etc., the doctor then follows with more closed questions. It is important for the doctor to become more focused as the interview progresses, investigating specific areas that may not emerge from the patient's story.

US versus UK English

UK	US
reckon	think

Lead in

Rationale: to establish learners' comprehension and experience of patient and doctor-centred approaches to patient care

Language Note:

patient/doctor-centred/led

Point out to learners that *patient-centred* = *patient-led* and *doctor-led* = *doctor-centred*. They may come across both expressions in the context of the patient encounter.

- Be aware that some learners may not be fully familiar with the patient-centred approach, depending on the extent to which students have studied medical communication skills in their own country. However, it is not a problem at this stage – there are no right or wrong answers for this task. This task can be used to gauge your learners' current understanding of these two approaches.

A patient-centred approach to history-taking (cultural awareness, active listening, verbal communication)

Rationale: to reinforce the benefits and encourage the use of a more patient-centred approach, starting with the history-taking process

1a
- Contextualise the text: Ask the group what they know about George Engel and his approach to patient relations.
  - **Suggestion:** Tell the group to look at the sentences (a, b, c, d) and ask them which approach they think each belongs to: doctor-led or patient-centred. Ask them why.

> **1** b   **2** d   **3** a

1b

> Closed questions are questions where the response is either *Yes/No* or another one-word answer. When used appropriately, they can determine specific information. Used inappropriately, they can be quite restrictive. 'Inappropriate use' means the doctor is trying to control the encounter and not allowing the patient to express him/herself. Other kinds of questions are:
> - **open:** These questions require an answer of more than one word (as opposed to closed questions). They typically start with a question word, such as *who, where, why, when, how*, etc.
> - **multiple:** This is where several questions are asked at the same time, making it harder to focus on the answer required, e.g. *Does the itching always occur in the same place, and how bad is it?*
> - **leading:** This is where the question is phrased to elicit a particular answer, e.g. *Does the itching always start first thing in the morning?* (as opposed to *When does the itching start?*).
> - **tag:** These are a form of closed and leading question, characterised by the 'tag' at the end of the sentence. The tag is formed by the opposite form (positive or negative) of the auxiliary verb in the sentence (e.g. *have, do, must*, etc.) and the subject, e.g. *The itching doesn't bother you at night, **does it**?*

2 • Encourage learners to write in note form.

Doctor-centred approach	Patient-centred approach
• disease and patient were completely separate • tightly controlled • doctors take the dominant role • patients have limited participation • patients not expected to participate actively • patients' health is entirely in the hands of the doctor • doctors ask leading questions • impact of disease on patients' life barely considered	• patient is expert of his/her own disease • patient is the main source of information • holistic approach • social, physical and economic factors are important • doctors show more empathy • patients are more likely to comply with treatment • doctors are more responsive to patient cues
Question type(s): closed questions / leading questions	**Question type(s):** open questions

3 • The statistics may or may not surprise your learners, depending on what their previous experience has been with the holistic, patient-centred approach. Encourage those with a knowledge of this to share their experience with the rest of the group.

2 A&E department (emergency situations), patients with respiratory problems, patients with learning difficulties, etc.

3 Some patients prefer doctors to take the lead; difference in cultural attitudes may play a role; it also depends on the emotional/physical state of the patient as to whether he/she wants to / is able to participate so fully in the encounter.

4a • **Suggestion:** Complete the table yourself, rating your own GP or specialist. It might be interesting to share your experience with the learners so they can get a(nother) patient perspective.

Think about

Rationale: to assess learners' own skills at this stage, considering their experience of gathering information on the presenting complaint from a patient in English

5a • Some learners might not have much experience of doing this in English; they should evaluate their current level of competence as they see it, as a kind of self-assessment.

5b • Be aware that learners tend to overestimate their competency. Learners may also feel that their question style is appropriate, but this may not be the case in reality.

Using exploratory questions (verbal communication, active listening)

Rationale: to develop an appropriate and effective questioning technique when gathering information about the presenting complaint

Audio script >>

STUDENT'S BOOK **page 138**

▷ 2.1 **6a** • Contextualise the dialogue: Tell learners they are going to overhear part of an encounter between a doctor and her patient in the next cubicle. The patient is suffering from intermittent (irregular / off and on) high temperature (UK English). Play the recording.

> Dr Haines is more of a doctor-centred consulter, although there are some positive aspects to her approach. Rating: 2/5
> **Positive aspects:** friendly and polite; introduces herself
> **Negative aspects:** interrupts patient; asks too many closed questions; doesn't allow patient to express himself in his own words; asks tag, multiple and leading questions; confuses patient; answers for the patient; interrogative style

▷ 2.1 **7**

> 1 Do you still **have a temperature?**
> 2 How long have you had that, **a couple of days?**
> 3 Are **you shaking?** Are you having **night sweats?**
> 4 Do **you have any muscular pain?**
> 5 You're not suffering from achy joints as well, **are you?**

8

> 1 NO – Dr Haines doesn't allow the patient to tell the story from his own point of view, referring instead to his Patient Note. She interrupts the patient.
> 2 NO – As above. Also, she asks closed questions, where the patient can only answer *yes* or *no*, or tries to put words in the patient's mouth.
> 3 YES – She asks about muscular pain.
> 4 NO – She sometimes asks two questions at the same time, and this is not always clear for the patient.

• Encourage learners to discuss reasons for their responses in their small groups and then together as a whole group. Point out that they will be working on this in more detail in the next activity.

9 • Avoid giving too much information prior to the task; let the learners discover the language for themselves.
   • Reiterate that there may be more than one category for each.
   • Key: C= Closed, L= Leading, M=Multiple, O=Open, T=Tag

> 1 C   2 C, L   3 C, L, M   4 C   5 C, L, T

Language Note:

Question tags

A question tag can be added to the end of a statement to turn it into a question. Question tags are used to check information but, in the context of patient encounter, could be considered inappropriate, as they might guide the patient in a particular direction (see **Intonation in question tags** below).

The verb used in the tag depends on the verb in the statement:

A positive question is followed by a negative tag:

> *You did check his pulse, didn't you?*

A negative question is followed by a positive tag:

> *You haven't forgotten to contact the patient's parents, have you?*

Intonation in question tags

The answer the doctor expects from the patient can be shown through the intonation pattern employed:

(a) If he/she expects confirmation from the patient, intonation falls on the question tag.

(b) If he/she is less certain of the patient's response, intonation rises on the question tag.

- **Suggestion:** Put the following on the board and ask the group to brainstorm the tag in each case:

  You did check his pulse, _____ ?

  You haven't forgotten to contact the patient's parents, _____ ?

- Elicit the rule (as in the Language Note above).

- Ask a strong learner to read out the questions using the appropriate intonation pattern.

- Model intonation pattern (a) above on the examples taken from the audio (*You're not suffering from achy joints as well, are you?*) and ask learners what effect Dr Haines' question has on the patient. (The patient's going to want to answer *No*, as the question suggests this is one symptom too many. He will want to agree with the doctor.)

- Using the same question tag, model intonation pattern (b). Then elicit the rule for intonation patterns.

- Point out that it is important for learners to understand tag questions, as their patients will use them, but that they themselves should avoid using them.

▶ 2.2 **10a** • Contextualise the dialogue: Tell learners they are going to overhear part of another encounter between a different doctor and patient. This patient is also suffering from intermittent high temperature (UK English).

Audio script >>
STUDENT'S BOOK **page 138**

- Stress to learners (if necessary) the rationale behind concentrating on the language as opposed to the content in this dialogue, to enable them to make the comparison between this and the dialogue in the previous exercise. Play the recording.

> Dr Linley begins with an open question and encourages the patient to tell her own story. He then uses closed questions appropriately to obtain specific information. Rating: 4/5

11 • **Suggestion:** Put the uncompleted questions up on the board before listening and complete them as a whole group – it might help some learners to grasp the concept. Then play the recording to enable learners to hear the language for themselves.

> 1 How have you **been feeling?**
> 3 Any **other symptoms?**
> 5 Any **pain in your joints?**
>
> 2 Can you **tell me a bit more about it?**
> 4 **Whereabouts?**

12

1 YES (All of his questions)
2 YES (*How have you been feeling? / Can you tell me a bit more about it? / ... any other symptoms? / Whereabouts?*)
3 YES (*Do you have any muscular pain? / Any pain in your joints?*)
4 YES (*Any pain in your joints? / Do you have any muscular pain?*)

- Learners should now be starting to grasp the idea of the different types of question being employed in the patient encounter.

13

1 0   **2** 0 (literally closed, but rising intonation makes it open)   **3** 0 (see 2)
4 0   **5** C, L (used appropriately to obtain specific details)

- **Suggestion:** Go through this on the board to be sure that learners have grasped this concept, as it is essential to the patient-centred approach.

14

1 Dr Linley was the most successful in obtaining a history.

- **Suggestion:** Elicit learners' understanding of the different question types. By now they should be able to give an explanation of each, having been exposed to them. It is important that learners have grasped this information, as this is the crux of good interview technique.

2 The 'cone technique' moves from open to closed questions. It ensures that the doctor obtains a picture of the problem from the patient's perspective, by opening up the discussion. With the need to confirm specifics and narrow down the cause of symptoms, etc., he/she then follows with more closed questions. It is important for the doctor to become more focused as the interview progresses, investigating specific areas that may not emerge from the patient's story.
Open questions allow patients to express themselves and follow their agenda. The first complaint is not necessarily the most important or the only one. The consultation could go in a completely different direction, as doctors usually have their own agenda based on previous experience. Open questions also give doctors time to think about the next question and to listen to important points.
Leading questions are those that, in effect, put words into the mouth of the patient and 'lead' the patient towards a particular answer.
Multiple questioning can be confusing and stressful for patients. Better to ask one question at a time.
Closed questions asked in a facilitating manner can encourage patients to tell more of their story; good non-verbal communication can turn closed into open questions. With patients in certain states – respiratory problems / A&E / stressed – it is better to use closed questioning.
Tag questions tend to guide patients in their response – the 'tag' reinforces the question in a particular direction.

15a

1 C, L   **2** C, L   **3** C, T   **4** M   **5** C, L   **6** L, T

15b

Language Note:

Open questions using modals

Some learners may be confused about the use of modals when forming questions, e.g. *Can you tell me ... / Would you mind telling me about ...,* etc., where the literal answer would be *Yes/No.*

Remind learners these questions are in effect requests. They are open, not closed, questions.

15c • It's important for learners to understand the possible repercussions of certain questions, especially closed and tag questions; this activity highlights this.

1 **a** The parent may feel some amount of guilt at having bought the dog following the son's reaction.

    b The parent will feel guilty because he/she didn't go to see the GP sooner.

2 Doctors need to avoid making patients/carers feel guilty for their actions or appearing judgemental. Biased/'loaded' questions can make patients feel as though they are being judged.

Quotation (Silverman et al.)
• Discuss possible reasons for this with the group.
• Ask learners to share experience they may have (or a case study) of asking a closed question too early in the diagnosis.

Cultural awareness

• Tell learners that in some cultures (Asian cultures, for example) it is not the norm to challenge the 'expert's' – in this case the doctor's – point of view.
• Remind learners that the patient-centred approach is based on the concept that the interview is the meeting of *two* experts: the doctor and the patient, as expert of his/her own condition or symptoms (see 1a).

Describing the nature of pain (verbal communication, cultural awareness)

Rationale: to increase learners' awareness of adjectives commonly used by patients to describe pain

• Start by getting the whole group to brainstorm adjectives they already know to describe pain. This could be done in teams, depending on the group dynamic. Learners may well find they know quite a few already.

16 • **Suggestion:** Elicit the fact that pain, how we feel, and subsequently how we deal with it, is highly subjective.

1a Children are more likely to say the pain is greater.

  b Elderly patients especially tend to underestimate the level of their pain, often due to the fact that they have learnt to tolerate pain / don't want to bother the doctor, and are more stoical, etc.

  2 To enable the doctor to arrive at an accurate diagnosis. Different kinds of pain can lead to different diagnoses.

17b

Suggested answers

1 migraine (blinding headache)
2 urinary infection (burning sensation)
3 period pain (cramping pain)
4 chest pain (crushing sensation)
5 heart attack / angina (gripping pain)
6 headache (pounding feeling)
7 sciatica/toothache (shooting pain)
8 indigestion (stabbing pain)
9 pins and needles (tingling sensation)
10 tension headache (throbbing pain)

- Encourage learners to add a translation in their own language; this will serve as a reference for later.

18

1 The metaphors are related to DIY/tools.

19a • The visual analogue pain scale is a tool used to gauge a patient's perceived level of pain. The doctor will ask the patient to put a cross along the scale to indicate the level of pain they are feeling, between 'no pain' and the 'worst pain imaginable'.

Put a cross on the scale to show me how bad the pain is.

19b

The following are examples of other methods used to assess pain:
- Ask the patient to rate their pain on a scale of one to ten.
- Ask the patient if they have ever experienced a migraine, bad toothache or a broken leg and then ask them to compare the current pain to that.

Out & About

Rationale: to encourage learners to further develop their knowledge of colloquial terms outside of the classroom

Patient speak

Rationale: to bring learners' attention to patient usage of the qualifier *quite* when assessing the severity of their pain

20

-ish means 'quite'.

Exploring the presenting complaint (verbal communication, active listening)

Rationale: to better equip learners in their line of questioning for the presenting complaint

21a • Contextualise the dialogue: Tell learners they are going to hear a doctor taking the first part of a patient history from a patient suffering from recurrent headaches (UK English).

• Reassure learners that it is not a problem at this stage if their questions still need improving. You can give them time later in the session to go back and rework their questions, if necessary.

> **Suggested answers**
>
> a How do they compare to a migraine?
> b Whereabouts do you get these headaches?
> c How long do they tend to last?
> d How long have you had the headaches?
> e Are there any other symptoms?
> f Can you describe the pain?
> g What seems to improve the situation for you?
> h When do they come on?

Audio script >>
STUDENT'S BOOK **page 139**

▷ 2.3 22 • Play the recording. Give learners sufficient time to note the questions used by the native-speaker doctor. They may need to listen a couple of times.

• **Suggestion:** Ask pairs to concentrate on a couple of specific questions and then feed back to the rest of the group.

• Tell learners there are sometimes several different ways of asking these questions but what is important is that they come up with open questions here.

23a • Be aware that there is a logical order to the history-taking process as a whole, as well as a particular order in which to gather information for the presenting complaint. Learners should be able to draw on their own medical experience for this task. The questions in Exercise 21a should therefore be asked in a specific order.

Audio script >>
STUDENT'S BOOK **page 139**

▷ 2.4 23b
> f, b, a, c, d, h, g, e

24
> a 3 b 1 c 4 d 4 e 7 f 2 g 6 h 5

25a
> The eighth attribute involves understanding the beliefs or thoughts of the patient regarding their illness, worries about what the symptoms might mean, expectations about how the doctor might help, emotions that the problems might induce, etc. This is to validate the patient's viewpoint (an important aspect of the patient-centred approach) and involve the patient. Doctors may also find out extra information at this stage.

25b
> No

25c
> **Suggested answers**
>
> *How has this made you feel? / You say you've been worrying ...?* (asking about the patient's concerns)
> *Tell me what you think is causing this pain.* (asking about the patient's belief)
> *What do you think might be the best plan of action?* (asking about the patient's expectations)

Patient speak

Rationale: to widen learners' knowledge and usage of phrasal verbs to describe signs and symptoms

26a • This technique for learning vocabulary is similar to mind mapping, which your learners may have come across in their studies.

• **Suggestion:** Write part of the spidergram up on the board first and brainstorm a couple of examples before getting learners to work on the task themselves.

• **bring up** (*transitive*): vomit / be sick
  My little girl was coughing so much, she **brought up** some yellowish phlegm.
• **build up**: increase
  I've been having headaches – the tension **builds up**, and I feel as though my head is going to explode.
• **blow up**: swell
  You say your stomach **blows up** after meals – you have a bloating feeling – is that right?
• **clear up**: heal
  The eczema seems to have **cleared up**; the hydrocortisone must have done the trick.
• **clog up**: block
  His ears are a little **clogged up** with wax, which is why he's been having problems hearing recently.
• **ease up**: improve
  You'll probably find the pain will **ease up** when you lie down and relax.
• **flare up**: erupt, get worse
  Doctor, the rash has **flared up** again. I was wondering if I could have a prescription for some of that cream I had last time.
• **tighten up**: become tighter
  Ms Singh says her chest has **tightened up**; she's also having difficulty breathing.
• **throw up** (*intransitive*): vomit / be sick
  He **threw up** last night; he must have eaten something that disagreed with him.
• **shoot up**: rise dramatically, inject
  The pain just **shoots up** my arm; I don't know what I've done.
• **puff up**: swell
  Kieran's eyes keep **puffing up** – I think he's got conjunctivitis again.
• **play up**: cause a problem
  Dad says his arthritis is **playing up** again; he's had a lot of pain in his joints.
• **dry up**: dehydrate
  Every winter, my face really seems to **dry up**, especially my forehead – the skin is all flaky.
• **cough up** (*transitive*): eject from the lungs by coughing
  The patient **coughed up** a little bit of blood this morning, but seems fine now.

• **Suggestion:** Ask learners to find examples of these in the dialogues in Exercises 10 and 22 (see audio script 2.2 and 2.3 on pages 141 and 142 of the Student's Book).

26c • Point out to learners the importance of paraphrasing as a communication strategy when you are not sure of what your patient is saying.

Out & About

Rationale: to further develop learners' understanding of common phrases to describe symptoms

Clarification, facilitation and repetition (verbal and non-verbal communication, cultural awareness, active listening)

Rationale: to develop strategies to encourage patient participation during an encounter

- Be aware that most people have difficulties identifying conversational strategies even in their own language and don't realise their importance in maintaining a conversation on a general level or, in this case, encouraging patient participation.

27 1 c   2 a   3 b

- **Suggestion:** Ask learners to think about how these strategies might be achieved in their own language/culture and, if possible, to discuss their ideas with other learners sharing the same first language / culture.
- Encourage learners to also think about non-verbal strategies that could be employed. Come together as a group to feed back before going on to the next task.

28/29

Technique	Examples
Clarification	*Could you explain what you mean by 'pneumatic drill'?* *So, if I've got it right, ...* 2, 4, 12
Facilitation	*Go on ... , Uh-huh?* 1, 5, 6, 7, 8, 9, 10, 11
Repetition	*No?* 3

30 • **Suggestion:** Elicit the facilitation technique of 'silence' by role-playing the technique yourself, as per the description in the Student's Book. Then ask the learners to discuss how comfortable they would be using silence during history-taking.

 facilitation

- Point out to learners they will have an opportunity to put these strategies into practice in Exercise 33.

Facilitating the encounter (voice management, active listening)

Rationale: to encourage appropriate intonation to accompany facilitation strategies

▷ 2.5   **31a**

Audio script >>
STUDENT'S BOOK **page 139**

Language Note:

Intonation for facilitating the encounter

Intonation is significant when facilitating the encounter. It is important that the doctor encourages a response from the patient, and in order to do this he/she should employ a rising intonation pattern.

To check information or to respond to a patient cue (see Unit 8) doctors should employ an intonation that rises slightly to encourage the patient to elaborate (as in 32a).

However, intonation falls on the phrase *I see*, which is the exception to the 'rule'. (*I see* + rising intonation = *I understand*)

- Note that these examples are not in context; this will allow learners to really concentrate on the intonation pattern itself for each. Play the recording (UK English).

> 3 is the odd one out (in 1, 2 and 4, the intonation rises gently; in 3, the intonation falls on the word *see*).

2.5 **31b** • Play the recording again, a couple of times if necessary, to give learners the chance to master an appropriate intonation pattern for each.

32a • Elicit the appropriate intonation pattern for repeated words: the doctor's intonation should rise slightly on the repeated word *terrified* in the first instance only.

33 • Tell learners they will now have a chance to consolidate what they have covered so far in the unit.
- Give feedback if you feel it is necessary at this stage.

Piecing it all together

34 • **Suggestion:** Go through the Observer's checklist first before going into the role-plays.
- Tell learners you will also be feeding back to them on both positive and negative points of their verbal and non-verbal communication, their voice management, and their active listening skills.

Progress check

- Ask learners to go through the Progress check.
- Give learners some group feedback and indicate where they might need to improve.
- Give individual feedback to those who wish.

Recommended reading

- If you would like a little more information on this topic, we suggest you read the following:

Lloyd M and Bor R. *Communication Skills for Medicine*. London: Churchill Livingstone, 1996 (26–36)

Engel G.L. *The Clinical Application of the Biophysical Model*. The American Journal of Psychiatry. May 1980; 137:5

Reading for discussion

- Go to page 148.

DVD clips 1 and 2

- Go to page 160.

Unit 3 Past medical and family history

At the end of this unit, learners will be able to:

- request their patient's past medical history
- discuss the family medical history
- take effective notes during an interview
- write an effective patient note
- structure and summarise the interview

DVD clip 3

Background

Past medical history (PMH)

The past medical history (PMH) is the information regarding the patient's previous health prior to the presenting complaint. This involves: past illnesses, childhood illnesses (mumps, measles, chicken pox, etc.), immunisation, surgical procedures, accidents and injuries, pregnancies (for women), allergies (including food, medication, over-the-counter medication, hay fever treatments, etc.) and medication (traditional and alternative medicine). A complete PMH is taken when the origin of the symptoms is unknown (e.g. swollen glands) and could be attributed to any number of illnesses. However, quite often a doctor will be required to take a more focused PMH. This depends on the nature of the symptoms: if the patient has been in a road accident and is suffering a broken collar bone, then certain questions may not be necessary. However, student doctors are encouraged to practise taking a complete PMH when they begin their clinical training so as not to miss important information.

Family history

Obtaining a history of the patient's family members (generally three generations) is important for two reasons. Firstly, the patient may be suffering from a genetically determined disease (e.g. hypertension, diabetes, coronary artery disease, rheumatoid arthritis, colon/breast cancer) or single gene disorder (e.g. familial hypercholesterolemia, sickle cell anaemia, cystic fibrosis). Secondly, the patient's concerns about his/her presenting complaint may be related to the experience of other family members (someone in the family had similar symptoms and was diagnosed with cancer, for example). It is equally important to explain the significance of taking a family history by asking *Is there a family history of ...?*

Pedigree diagram

It might be useful to obtain the family history by compiling a Pedigree diagram (or family tree) with the patient (see example on page 40 of the Student's Book).

Patient note

The patient note is a record of each encounter carried out by the patient's GP and/or specialist and, it should be remembered, is a legal document that must be signed and dated each time it is updated. (In the UK / Ireland / US the patient has a right to see his/her patient note if he/she wishes.) There is a particular layout that should be adhered to for ease of access and the content should clearly communicate the history and physical examination carried out on the patient, facilitating clinical reasoning and conveying essential information to other consultants and healthcare providers. The patient note can also include diagrams which serve to indicate information regarding the findings of the physical examination. Only relevant points should be included on a patient note. Familiarise yourself with the layout of the patient note by looking at the example on page 39 of the Student's Book.

Standard medical abbreviations

Such abbreviations are commonly used but, if in any doubt, doctors are advised to write the information out in full.

US versus UK English

UK	US
carer	caregiver
GP surgery	family practice
jabs	shots
medication	medications
nappies	daipers

UK	US
paracetamol	Tylenol
Pyrexia of Unknown Origin (PUO)	Fever of Unknown Origin (FUO)
secondary school (audio 3.4)	junior high (11–13) / high school (14–18)

Lead in

Rationale: to open up discussion on family history and the problems doctors may experience during the history-taking process

- Ask learners to read through the extract and answer question 1.

> **1** Patient may be suffering from a genetically determined disease; patient's concerns about presenting complaint may be linked to the experience of other family members (e.g. parent died from same condition).
> It must be done sensitively. Explain the significance of taking the family history and the patient will realise its importance. Access to medical care, patient's family culture, economic/educational background and adopted status (in certain cases) may affect how much a patient knows about his/her family members' medical history.

- **Suggestion:** Brainstorm as a group possible genetic disorders and susceptibilities.
  Genetic susceptibility: hypertension, diabetes, coronary artery disease, rheumatoid arthritis, colon/breast cancer
  Transfer of single cell / single gene disorder: familial hypercholesterolemia, sickle cell anaemia, cystic fibrosis
- Now ask learners to discuss the questions (2a–c) in small groups.

> **2a** Patients may have greater difficulty recalling family history than their own PMH, especially beyond two generations. Recent events are obviously easier for them to recall.
> **2b** Patients may be estranged from members of the family who may hold the key to certain genetic diseases. There may be difficult family issues involved, and patients may be reluctant to discuss these.
> **2c** Similar to b, plus fear of genetic susceptibility.

Components of the past medical history (verbal communication, active listening)

Rationale: to develop skills to take a complete past medical history (PMH) in English

1a • Contextualise the dialogue: Tell learners they are going to hear part of a talk given at a medical conference on the pitfalls of taking the PMH (US English).

- Learners will usually know the logical order of these components (see Key).

▶ 3.1 **1b**

1 Past illnesses	**2** Childhood illnesses	**3** Immunisation
4 Surgical procedures	**5** Accidents and injuries	**6** Pregnancy
7 Allergies	**8** Medication(s)	

Audio script >>
STUDENT'S BOOK **page 139**

- Elicit possible pitfalls of the components before carrying out the next task.

1c • Remind learners that the information in the box is in note form. Play the recording.

1 **Past illnesses:** Patients may <u>forget some illnesses</u> but remember more recent ones; they can be <u>vague about the details</u>, even adults.

2 **Childhood illnesses:** Patients remember childhood illnesses if they were <u>traumatic</u> or <u>if they took a long period off school</u>, e.g. chicken pox, mumps, measles. Also ask about unusual illnesses.

3 **Immunisation:** Important information, especially for <u>children</u> and <u>women of child-bearing age</u> (toxoplasmosis/rubella). Patients don't <u>remember details</u>.

4 **Surgical procedures:** Some patients <u>understand little</u> about surgical procedures and some may not even know <u>the reason</u> for their hospitalisation or exploratory investigations.

5 **Accidents and injuries:** Be aware of repeated injuries in women (might indicate <u>domestic violence</u>) and the <u>elderly</u> (may need help or referral to social services). Repeated injuries might possibly indicate <u>drug</u> or <u>alcohol abuse</u>.

6 **Pregnancy:** Ask all <u>women of child-bearing age</u> about pregnancy and related problems. Difficult for some to discuss <u>abortion</u> or <u>miscarriage</u>.

7 **Allergies:** Patients may not think to mention <u>allergies</u> to <u>medication</u> and <u>food</u>, but will remember hay fever, etc. Presenting complaint may be a reaction to <u>food</u> or <u>current medication</u>.

8 **Medication(s):** Patients forget to mention <u>over-the-counter medications</u> and <u>vitamins</u>. Reluctant to mention <u>alternative</u> medicines and medication prescribed by another doctor.

Communication Skills

Refer learners to the image in the table on page 33 and ask what its significance is. Ask learners what they do to remind themselves to do things. Next, elicit the questions in the box by writing 'What about …' on the board and asking them to complete the question.

1d

1 Many patients find it difficult to recall exact details, names of conditions/diseases, as well as dates and surgical intervention. They sometimes choose not to remember traumatic experiences.

2 People tend to associate the word *drug* with illicit/addictive drug-using behaviour.

Think about

Rationale: to assess learners' own skills at this stage, considering their own experience of taking a PMH in English

2a • At this stage there are no right or wrong answers; the activity serves as a needs analysis for you and the learners. Learners are likely to be less competent in terms of the pragmatics of spoken communication.

Taking a past medical history (verbal communication, active listening)

Rationale: to develop a sound questioning technique relative to the past medical history

▶ 3.2 **3a** • Contextualise the dialogue: Tell learners they are going to hear Dr Tran interviewing Ms Martin about her PMH (US English).

Audio script >>
STUDENT'S BOOK **page 140**

• Highlight the fact that Dr Tran has already asked about the presenting complaint. Play the recording.

a 1, b 2, c 6, d 3, e 4, f 7, g 5, h 8

3b

He doesn't ask in the same order because he often allows the patient to control the interview and so some components are discussed when they come up naturally.

▶ 3.2 **3c/4b**

Dr Tran	Since this is your first visit to the practice, I'd like to have a more detailed picture of things. Could you tell me about any illnesses you **1 might have had in the past?** *Doctor asks about general health. Open question*
Ms Martin	I had my tonsils out when I was a little kid, I remember that. *Patient remembers being hospitalised as a child – often a traumatic experience for a child and so easier to recall.*
Dr Tran	**2 Any other** childhood illnesses?
Ms Martin	Don't remember, to be honest – my mother would know, I'd expect. Mumps, measles, that kind of thing, usual stuff. *Difficult to recall – responsibility was with the parents, and children don't necessarily remember which of these illnesses they suffered.*
Dr Tran	Regular childhood illnesses, then? [*pause*] And **3 how has your health been** in general since then? *Doctor tries to get back to the question of adult past illnesses.*
Ms Martin	No, no real problems, to tell you the truth.
Dr Tran	Good. So, have you had any operations, **4 apart from** the tonsils? *Doctor demonstrates he has been listening – mentions tonsils.*
Ms Martin	No, no. Like I say, I'm pretty healthy.
Dr Tran	**5 Any other** visits to the hospital? *Doctor needs to find out about accidents, injuries.*
Ms Martin	Yes, for the birth of my son, and, er, then a couple of years ago, I had to go in for some tests. *Question leads to pregnancy automatically.*
Dr Tran	Mm-hm? What kind of tests, Ms Martin?
Ms Martin	Don't remember exactly. *Could be that the patient doesn't remember – patients tend not to remember details of tests. She is uncomfortable – maybe she's blocking something.*
Dr Tran	**6 Can I ask you how old you were** when you gave birth?
Ms Martin	Yes, it was just before my 40th – celebrated it surrounded by diapers that year!
Dr Tran	Going back to those tests, Ms Martin, can I ask you to elaborate on those a little? *Doctor acknowledges joke. He reads the patient cues and decides to probe, but asks an open question – still not wanting to assume anything – he wants to get the patient's story.*
Ms Martin	Oh, those, well, er, I lost my second baby, a little girl apparently. *Patient possibly in denial having lost baby. Patient in mid-40s and possibly wanting more children.*
Dr Tran	I'm sorry to hear that. **7 I have to ask**, was she stillborn? *Doctor needs to confirm and so poses a closed question to have exact information. He acknowledges patient's distress and apologises as he asks the question (I have to ask, ...).*
Ms Martin	Yep. *Patient upset by the line of questioning.*
Dr Tran	I understand this must be a painful memory for you. [*pause*] Moving on, if we can. Are you fully immunised? *Empathises with the patient. Doctor wasn't able to ask PMH in the logical order, but was allowing patient to lead the encounter.*
Ms Martin	I'm sorry? *Patient has not understood the word* immunised.

Dr Tran	What I mean is, how **8 up to date are you** with your shots, Ms Martin? *Doctor rephrases using patient-speak: shot.*
Ms Martin	I think I'm OK. I had most of those when I was at school. *People associate shots with school age, not something they were responsible for and so don't necessarily remember the details.*
Dr Tran	**9 How about** tetanus? *Doctor needs exact information – closed question.*
Ms Martin	Uh-uh. [*shakes her head*]
Dr Tran	Now, nearly finished this part. Um, have you ever suffered from allergies? *Doctor asks focused, but not closed question to give patient options.*
Ms Martin	No, not that I know of. My brother always got hay fever, poor thing, but not me. *Patient is sure she's not allergic, but hasn't made the connection with food or medications.*
Dr Tran	Any food allergies? *Doctor needs to be sure – closed question.*
Ms Martin	Mm … Strawberries – weird, isn't it? *Patient may feel a little embarrassed by this – it's an unusual allergy.*
Dr Tran	And I suppose they were your favourite fruit, too? *Humour is appropriate here.* **10 Are you allergic** to any medications – some people are allergic to penicillin, for example? *Doctor gives an example of medication to which people commonly have an allergic reaction.*
Ms Martin	No.
Dr Tran	And finally, **11 are you currently on** any medications at all, Ms Martin? *Doctor avoids using the word* drug.
Ms Martin	Ah, yes. I was taking antibiotics, but didn't finish the course, didn't seem to be doing anything. I'm not on anything else. *Patient hasn't thought about over-the-counter drugs or alternative treatments.*
Dr Tran	Right. **12 Can I ask you what you were taking** them for? *Patient hasn't specified, and doctor needs more accurate details of medication.*
Ms Martin	Oh, I'd had a very bad cold and I couldn't shake it off.
Dr Tran	How about medications you buy **13 over the counter?**
Ms Martin	Ah … laxatives sometimes, you know, for the problems I've been having recently. Tylenol, occasionally.
Dr Tran	Some people believe in alternative medicine; is this something that interests you? *Doctor phrases the question by allowing patient to feel it is OK to discuss these options – even if doctor may be against use of alternative treatments / homoeopathic medicine.*
Ms Martin	No, no, definitely not. *Patient rejects usage.*
Dr Tran	Well, some people are turning to alternative forms of treatment, and so this is a question we have to ask, in case of any possible complications. *Doctor reconfirms need to ask the question and explains rationale for doing so – to validate in the eyes of patient his line of questioning.* OK. [*pause*] So, I'd like to sum up your history briefly to make sure I have all the details correct before we proceed … *Doctor summarises and allows patient to add or correct if necessary. Not all concerns are mentioned at the beginning of the encounter.*

4a • **Suggestion:** Go through and compile the commentary for the first part of the dialogue as a whole-group activity to be sure learners have understood what is required of them.
  • Ensure the class is divided fairly equally in terms of their choice of analysis; it is just as important that the patient's responses are analysed, as they have a bearing on the doctor and his questions and responses.

- **Suggestion:** Ask learners to take parts of the dialogue to analyse (in pairs, depending on the level of the group).

4b • For commentary, see answer key for 3c.
- An analysis is not expected of each and every stage of the encounter, but the table above shows fairly typical responses, how the doctor deals with them, and his line of questioning.
- Be aware that learners may not pick up on all of these points. Where necessary, elicit any missing commentary as a whole group after the presentations.

5 • **Suggestion:** Ask learners what role pausing has in general conversation. This should give them a general insight into how this communication strategy might be used. Then ask them how beneficial pausing can be when interviewing a patient. (See audio script for pauses 1–3.)

Language Note:

Pausing (1)

Pausing creates a reflective time for both patient and doctor, and can allow time for the patient to gather him/herself together following a question that brings back sad or painful memories, as in the example. Pauses are also used as a signpost to indicate the next series of questions.

Pause 1: used as a facilitating technique to encourage the patient's story (see Unit 2).
Pause 2: sign of respect; doctor acknowledges pain the patient appears to be feeling at mention of death of baby.
Pause 3: indicates doctor is about to summarise the patient's story; he uses it as a signpost.

Language to request the past medical history

Rationale: to develop linguistic accuracy when requesting the past medical history

Quotation (Marsh)
- Ask learners to what extent they agree with this quotation from Marsh and why (not).
- Then ask how this quotation would have been received by professors at the medical faculty where they studied.

6
The second opener is the most appropriate.

Language Note:

might have

Might have had is a modal past perfect. It suggests a weak probability.

In using the modal *might*, the doctor does not assume anything or suggest the patient has suffered any illness. The question *Could you tell me about any illnesses you might have had in the past?* therefore opens up the dialogue more than the same question without *might have had* (*Could you tell about any illnesses you've had in the past?*). This is a subtle use of language, but one that is important.

NB Use of the modal *might* does not indicate something that the patient might not know about.

7 • **Suggestion:** Start by asking learners to identify reasons why tenses are so important when taking the PMH. (Correct use of tenses helps to clarify an accurate timescale of the timing of the presenting complaint or course of treatment. Inaccuracy in terms of the timing of the presenting complaint could result in misdiagnosis, or in the case of medication, an overdose, etc.)

• Be aware that some learners (even at this level) may not be familiar with all of the different past tenses covered here, or they may simply be unfamiliar with the meta-language. You may need to work through a few simple examples.

Language Note:

Past perfect continuous versus past simple
He was injecting three times a day.
In US English, the use of the past simple is more common here: *He injected three times a day.*

8 • Check learners have grasped the usage of the different questions used by Dr Tran before they go on to the role-play.

• Tell learners you will be giving feedback on the accuracy of their PMH.

Taking a focused past medical history (verbal communication, active listening)

Rationale: an extension of the previous section, more appropriate to most medical situations

9
Patients a and c
A focused PMH would be taken in the following cases: A&E, patient suffering respiratory problems, asthma, road traffic accident, acute chest pain, patient having difficulty responding due to pain, etc.

• Encourage learners to give a detailed explanation as to why a more thorough medical history would be necessary for patients b and d. Allow your learners to bring their own knowledge to the classroom. Sore throat, diarrhoea and a high temperature are all very common symptoms and can be associated with any number of different conditions. As a result, a more detailed PMH needs to be taken.

3.3 10 • Contextualise the dialogue: Tell learners they are going to hear Dr Bhaskar taking the PMH of one of the patients in Exercise 9 (UK English).

• Play Part 1 of the recording.

Audio script >>
STUDENT'S BOOK **page 140**

Patient c

11a • Learners should be able to predict the questions once they have determined which patient is being interviewed.

3.4 11b • Play Part 2 of the recording.

Audio script >>
STUDENT'S BOOK **page 140**

Dr Bhaskar focuses on:
- **past illnesses**
- **surgical procedures** (illnesses and operations were asked about, but briefly)
- **medication**

Note: although he doesn't ask about pregnancies, the doctor asked about gynaecological issues, but not pregnancy exactly, to eliminate this area as a possible cause of the anaemia; the patient has since had a hysterectomy, so there is no need to go into any further detail. As this is a focused PMH, it is normal for the doctor to interview the patient in this way.

11c

1 Hysterectomy in 1999 due to fibroids, periods started at age 11, no other operations or illnesses, no abdominal pain, good diet, prescribed iron tablets for a week.

2 Doctor Bhaskar takes a very focused history, but it is an appropriate line of questioning. He starts with open questions, then uses the cone technique to determine exact information related to the symptoms. For more information on the cone technique, see Unit 2.

- **Suggestion:** Elicit the most appropriate line of questioning necessary to find the differential diagnosis for the cause of the patient's condition (family history, social history, etc.).
- Note that the 'cone effect' is the technique whereby the doctor moves from open to closed questions (see Unit 2).

Quotation (Marsh)
- Ask learners to read the quotation and ask them what it signifies.
  Suggested answers: It highlights the fact that sometimes questioning needs to be more focused than at other times. It reinforces the importance of using the 'cone effect' when questioning the patient.

Patient speak

Rationale: to familiarise learners with common expressions used to describe how they are feeling

- Ask learners how many of the expressions in the list they have heard before or, even, used themselves.
- **Suggestion:** Put the following on the board: *off-colour, under the weather, run down, low* and ask learners about the origins of these expressions.
- Ask learners what the problem is with a patient using these expressions to describe their health. (This kind of language – *off-colour, under the weather,* etc. – is very vague and doesn't tell the doctor anything about the presenting complaint or the PMH. However, they are very common. Some patients find it difficult to express themselves and need some coaxing.)
- **Suggestion:** If time allows, ask learners to come up with appropriate stress patterns for these expressions. Put the two examples below on the board and invite learners to come to the board and underline the stressed word in each. Example: *I've not been feeling <u>too great</u> lately.* / *He's not been <u>that good</u> these past few weeks.*
- Ask learners to replace the adjectives with others from the list (*brilliant, clever,* etc.) and try the same activity again.

12a

> You could ask an open question or use non-verbal communication strategies to encourage a patient to tell his/her own story:
> *Uh-huh?* + eye contact or lean forward
> *Could you tell me in a little more detail how you've been feeling / how you feel?*
> *In what way 'under the weather'?*

Signposting and summarising (verbal communication, active listening)

Rationale: to highlight these vital communication strategies and encourage learners to put them to use

13a

> change direction = *moving on*
> refer to an earlier point = *going back to*
> ask for more detail = *elaborate on*
> summarise = *to sum up*
> end = *finally*

13b

> **1** They give more structure to the interview for both doctor and patient.

- **Suggestion:** Ask learners to think about how they structure speech in their own language. Once they realise usage in their own language is similar, they will be more at ease using signposting in English.

13c • Ask learners to work in small groups and discuss why it is important to summarize before moving on to the next stage of the encounter.

> What patient says might be ambiguous; patient may have forgotten something; patient may have misunderstood a question; if he/she has told his/story to another healthcare professional, the patient may assume the doctor already has certain information; the patient may have given a non-verbal clue that suggested something unintended to the doctor; the doctor may not have heard certain things correctly, for example due to external noise; the doctor may have misinterpreted the patient's response or question.

14 • Depending on the level of your group, you may wish to go through one of the scenarios as a group and develop the PMH for the patient. Use the list of components in 3a as a guideline and then ask learners to work in pairs to carry out a PMH, reminding them to use signposting where appropriate. Encourage learners to also give a brief summary at the end of the enquiry.

Writing the patient note (written communication)

Rationale: to highlight the necessity for the patient note – as a legal document – to be clear and legible

15 • Reassure learners, if necessary, that they do not need to understand the content of this patient note – indeed, this is the reason behind doing this activity.

The content of the patient note summary is accurate, but as the entry is partially illegible, there are obvious difficulties for the next doctor who needs to make use of these notes. The fact that the patient is persuing 'in vitro' treatment is vital information, for example. Other vital information: the name of the patient, especially the spelling; the fact that the pain is in the right breast and not the left; the time delay (three days), etc. Hence hieroglyphics literally could have dire consequences.

Think about

Rationale: to assess learners' own skills at this stage, considering their experience of writing a patient note in English

16a • Some learners might not have experience of doing this in English. They should evaluate their current level of competence, as they see it, as a kind of self-assessment.
   • Be aware that learners tend to overestimate their competency.

Standard medical abbreviations

Rationale: to familiarise learners with the use of standard medical abbreviations

17a • **Suggestion:** Depending on the level, divide the class in half to add a competitive element. Give them one minute to complete the activity.
   • Learners will draw on their own medical knowledge to carry out this activity.

HTN	hypertension	r	right
M	male	GI	gastrointestinal
b	black	h/o	history of
yo	year(s) old	l	left
Neuro	neurologic	f	female
cig	cigarettes	FH	family history
CXR	chest X-ray	w	white
PMH	past medical history	ETOH	alcohol
MRI	magnetic resonance imaging	ICU	intensive care unit
Abd	abdomen	c/o	complaining of

17b • Refer learners to the complete standard medical abbreviations list at www.cambridge.org/elt/goodpractice if necessary.

A 25-year-old black male presents complaining of abdominal pains on his left side. The patient has a history of gastrointestinal problems. Past medical history: the patient had a car accident in 2001 and was in an intensive care unit for two months. Family history: the patient's father and mother are alive and well. The patient is a non-smoker and drinks on average 25 units of alcohol a week.

18a • Remind learners that this is an extract only.

1 Yes   **2** No   **3** No   **4** No

18d • **Suggestion:** Brainstorm findings together as a class before looking at the corrected version.
   OR
   Depending on the level of the group, ask the class to rewrite the patient note.

- Remind learners they can refer to the list of standard medical abbreviations on the website if necessary.

A full evaluation of the patient note would be:
- The doctor has not indicated the full date (no year) nor used 24-hour clock.
- She did not write the surname in block letters as required.
- She has not added the age of the patient.
- She has not signed the note and printed her name in block capitals. It is a legal requirement to sign each and every entry.
- Entries should be clearly spread out for ease of reading.
- Not all the headings are clear: *Previous* should be *Past medical history* or *PMH*; *Drugs* should be written as *Drug history*.
- The patient note has not been written in a logical order: Past medical history (PMH) appears before History of presenting complaint (HPC).
- The presenting complaint (PC), HPC and FH are not written clearly and concisely, making it more difficult to distinguish salient points.
- She also repeats information that should appear later on in the drug history.
- She does not always use standard medical abbreviations: AP and Ren are not standard abbreviations for Appendectomy (UK English: also Appendicectomy) and Renal disease (AP stands for Anteroposterior).
- She has not indicated that she has asked about allergies to medication (NKDA = no known drug allergies).
- She doesn't indicate the age at which the father died, which is more significant than the year of his death.
- She doesn't use standard abbreviation for alcohol (ETOH), although it is still clear.
- She doesn't use diagrams, but this is not appropriate here. They would be more useful later on in the Examination section.

A better version of the notes would look something like this:

St George's Hospital A&E	Unit N° Z29104	Surname (Block letters) First Name(s) D.O.B./age	MATHERSON Michael 19/10/69 38 years	
Date / Time	Clinical Notes (Each entry must be signed)			
10/05/07 18:25	**PC** Breathlessness			
	HPC Started 2/7 Onset gradual Slowly worsening Worse during night Wheezy and chest feels tight Salbutomol gives minimal relief H/o asthma			
	PMH 1992– Appendicectomy ° HTN / DM / IHD / Ep / Renal / An			
	FH Mother – A&W, asthma Father – died heart attack aged 61			
	DH Salbutamol 100mg No over-the-counter medication	Allergies NKDA		
	Social H Office manager Office clean, no dust No cig / ETOH – occasional <10 units/wk No pets Sexual history – not appropriate			
	Signed: *Annabella Davies* ANNABELLA DAVIES			

19

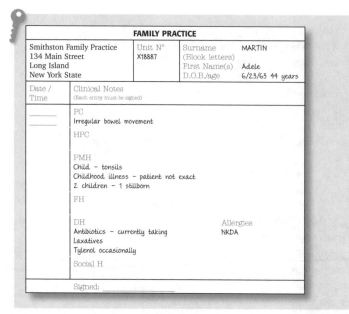

	FAMILY PRACTICE		
Smithston Family Practice 134 Main Street Long Island New York State	Unit N° X18887	Surname (Block letters) First Name(s) D.O.B./age	MARTIN Adele 6/23/63 44 years

Date / Time	Clinical Notes (Each entry must be signed)
_____ _____	**PC** Irregular bowel movement **HPC** **PMH** Child – tonsils Childhood illness – patient not exact 2 children – 1 stillborn **FH** **DH** Allergies Antibiotics – currently taking NKDA Laxatives Tylenol occasionally Social H
	Signed: _____

Taking a family history (verbal communication, active listening, cultural awareness)

Rationale: to familiarise learners with an effective questioning technique for asking about the family history

- **Suggestion:** Ask learners to discuss in small groups their own experience of taking a family history. How easy or difficult did they find it?

20 • The Pedigree diagram is a widely used tool, and as such many learners will know it, even if they have not yet come across the name in English. A Pedigree diagram resembles a family tree and represents the patient's family history. It usually indicates three or more generations, and the age and state of health for each member of the family. The patient is placed at the centre of the tree.

1 Colour blindness or Haemophilia A
2 Breast cancer
3 Neurofibromatosis (also known as von Recklinghausen's disease), dystrophia myotonica (muscle-wasting disease)

Out & About

Rationale: to give learners a comprehensive list of medical abbreviations, as symbols do sometimes differ

21 • Point out that the patient is indicated as ↗.

22 • **Suggestion:** Learners plot an imaginary Pedigree diagram if more appropriate.
  • Remind learners to make use of the form *might have* if necessary.

Piecing it all together

23b • **Suggestion:** Brainstorm this information as a group; learners should agree on the line of questioning before beginning the role-play.

23c • Emphasise that learners should be concentrating on the PMH, but that they could also look at the social history too.
  • Remind Student Bs they should take notes during the interview.
  • Tell learners you will give feedback to them on both positive and negative points of their verbal and non-verbal communication, their voice management, and their active listening skills.
  • Concentrate on giving feedback on the PMH but, depending on the level of your group, you may also choose to give feedback on their skills for obtaining a social history.

Progress check

• Ask learners to go through the Progress check.
• Give learners some group feedback and indicate where they might need to improve.
• Give individual feedback to those who wish.

Recommended reading

• If you would like a little more information on this topic, we suggest you read the following:
Enelow A et al. *Interviewing and Patient Care*. Oxford: OUP, 1996 (56–60, 66–67)

Reading for discussion

• Go to page 150.

DVD clip 3

• Go to page 162.

Unit 4 Social history and telephone consultations

LEARNING OUTCOMES

At the end of this unit, learners will be able to:

- enquire about their patient's social history
- employ good telephone etiquette
- ensure an effective telephone consultation
- summarise and check information

Background

Social history

The aim of this section is to establish a picture of the patient as a human being, and as such it is essential to the patient-centred approach. Social history is an umbrella term that includes the patient's **family life**, their **occupation**, their **environment** (where they live and the conditions in which they live), their **financial situation**, their level of **education**, and their **lifestyle** (tobacco, alcohol and recreational drug consumption; general fitness; rest and relaxation – holidays, sleep patterns, hobbies, etc.; and sexual practices). All of these factors have a potential bearing on the presenting complaint. Financial worries are renowned for causing stress, which could manifest itself in any number of ways (tension, depression, irritable bowel syndrome, etc.), while the level of education could give an indication as to the patient's perceived access/right to medical care. Look at audio script 4.1 for a summary of these factors.
NB: Asking about lifestyle is further developed in Unit 8.

General appearance

It is important for a doctor to be able to look beyond the appearance of their patient and avoid the possible assumptions that we all tend to make – a human failing from which doctors are not exempt. On the one hand doctors are told to avoid stereotyping while at the same time they are required to take note of their patient's appearance and read the clues. General appearance could give clues or indeed mask clues to the patient's well-being; for example, someone who is well-dressed and apparently without physical signs may be suffering from depression, or may have issues with alcohol, food, etc. The list is endless. Doctors also need to be aware of their own prejudices and learn how to avoid these causing problems in their interview technique or diagnosis.

Consultation by telephone

The telephone consultation is an increasingly popular means of communication between doctor and patient. This type of communication can be used as a follow-up on patients with both chronic and acute medical conditions, as well as for triage. There are, of course, some differences in this mode of consultation that the doctor needs to be aware of. The lack of visual clues has a direct impact on the exchange: the doctor is required to rely heavily on the patient's ability to describe their physical symptoms; neither can the doctor read the patient's non-verbal communication. Thus the doctor is forced to compensate by asking questions such as *You sound a little worried.* Look at the text on page 47 of the Student's Book for more information about the telephone consultation.

US versus UK English

UK	US
cleaner	housekeeper
The Council (audio 4.4)	Housing Office
council housing estate	low-income housing
fags (cigarettes) (audio 4.8)	cigs, smokes
	(*fag* is a derogatory term for a homosexual man in US English)

UK	US
Gaviscon (an antacid) (audio 4.6)	Pepto Bismol
holiday (audio 4.6)	vacation
... miss anything out	... leave anything out
off-licence	liquor store
surgery	doctor's office
telly (audio 4.3)	TV

Lead in

Rationale: to raise awareness of the learners' own personal prejudices and elicit the concept of 'social history'

- **Suggestion:** Write Tate's quotation up on the board before learners open their books.
- Ask learners what they understand by the quotation. Then ask them to look at the pictures and to elaborate on their initial understanding of the quotation. Ask them to what extent this changes their initial thoughts.

  OR

  Ask learners to look at the pictures first and note impressions one might make about these patients, stressing that this is not necessarily their own opinion; e.g. *the girl in black clothing is suffering from anorexia; the lady in her fifties is from an affluent background, showing no apparent health issues.*
- Note that each learner is likely to have a different perspective on the outward appearance of these people.

> The idea is that we shouldn't judge someone by their appearance; doctors are not exempt from this human failing. It is important that doctors avoid stereotyping their patients and making assumptions based on appearance, race, gender, sexual preference, etc. They should also remember that a patient's health is affected by social factors. In a holistic, patient-centred model of healthcare, it is impossible to separate the social factors from the medical condition or disease. They could all possibly play a role – on the general morale or appearance of the patient, if nothing else.

- **Suggestion:** Put up the words 'Social history' on the board and ask what learners understand by the term and the role it plays in the history-taking process (see Background on previous page).
- Ensure learners have grasped the concept of social history before going on to the next task, which will look at this section in more detail.

Think about

Rationale: to identify the different sections included under the umbrella of social history (unlike other 'Think about' activities, this serves as preparation for the rest of the unit).

- Elicit the headings as a group if necessary, depending on the level.
- Don't worry if the group is not able to brainstorm all the details; they will have the chance to note them in the next activity.
- Check the meaning of *sedentary* with your learners before continuing. Ask for examples of jobs that are essentially sedentary (e.g. office worker, machinist, etc.).

1a/b

Occupational
Sedentary or active work, unemployed (Unemployment is known to have an effect on morbidity rates.)

Environment
The physical environment, proximity to factories and farmland, condition of housing, toilet and bathroom facilities, stairs, number of rooms, number of residents

Financial issues
Well-known cause of stress and phychological well-being of the patient

Education
This can determine patients' potential access to medical information and how well informed they are in terms of medical care itself, as well as, for example, safe-sex practices, the dangers of smoking, right to health checks, etc.

Family
Number of immediate members, support networks

Lifestyle
Substance use: cigarettes, alcohol, recreational drugs; general fitness; rest and relaxation (holidays, sleep patterns, hobbies, etc.); sexual practices

---

Quotation (Bickley)
- Ask learners what they understand by the terms *source of support / coping mechanism*.
  Source of support = these can be formal (social services, church/religious groups, day centres, etc.) or informal (family, friends, neighbours, etc.)
  Coping mechanism = the way someone deals with a situation
- Ask learners to what extent they agree or disagree with Bickley.
- Ask them what kind of formal sources of support are available in their country of origin.

▶ 4.1 **2a**
- Contextualise the dialogue: Tell learners they are going to hear part of a seminar discussion at a university (UK English).
- Encourage learners to take notes in English, so replicating a seminar situation. Play the recording.

Audio script >>
STUDENT'S BOOK **page 140**

2b
- Allow learners time to think about these questions before asking them to present their answers to the rest of the group.

- Be aware that learners not used to the holistic, patient-centred approach might also not have realised the link between the physical illness and the social history of their patient (see Unit 2).

Occupational health (verbal communication, active listening, cultural awareness)

Rationale: to develop linguistic skills when asking about the different aspects of occupational health

3a • Learners will draw on their own knowledge of medical issues to carry out this activity. (They may not choose the right answer for the first point, however.)

▶ 4.2 **3b** • Learners listen and check their answers (US English).

Audio script >>
STUDENT'S BOOK **page 141**

4a

4b Learners will again bring their medical knowledge to the task; they should not have a problem coming up with examples for this.

5a

5b • The questions below are all quite general but could all be asked of a cleaner.

Possible questions for gathering information about occupational health:

- What type of work do you do?
- Please describe your work.
- Have you ever worked near any factories, shipyards or other potentially hazardous facilities?
- Has anyone in your household ever worked with hazardous materials that could have been brought home?
- Have you ever had environmental or occupational exposure to [asbestos/chemicals/lead/fumes]?
- Are you exposed to any hazardous materials in your workplace?
- Do you ever have any contact with toxic products / glues, fumes, etc.?

- Point out that doctors need to ask about household members, as this could also have a bearing on the patient's illness.

▶ 4.3 **6a** • Contextualise the dialogue: Tell learners they are going to hear a GP taking Mary Steven's social history (UK English).

Audio script >>

STUDENT'S BOOK **page 141**

- Encourage learners to take notes of the salient points, so replicating an interview situation. Play the recording.

1 Presenting complaint: mild asthma attacks
2 Place of work: hotel
3 Other pertinent information: patient only suffers attacks at home, no exposure to toxic products at work, no hazardous environment or fumes, kids' hobby: making model planes

6b

The GP asks the following questions:
What type of work do you do, Mary?
... if you could just describe your work for me?
And are you exposed to any toxic products at work?
*Has anyone in your household ever worked with hazardous materials that could have been brought home?** (environmental health question)
*Do you live near any factories that give off potentially hazardous fumes?** (environmental health question)
*How do you and the family spend your evenings, Mary?** (lifestyle question)

*These questions are not all strictly about 'occupational health' and will be dealt with later in the unit.

7 • Remind learners of the fact that patients don't always see the medical relevance of their social history. It is sometimes important to reassure a patient that particular questions are relevant to the interview, to give a rationale.
- Tell learners they will now have a chance to consolidate what they have covered so far in the unit. They will role-play the occupational health section of an interview.
- Tell learners you will be giving feedback after this activity, and that at the end of the unit they will have a chance to give peer feedback.
- **Suggestion:** Put the following on the board as a reminder: 'Eye contact', 'Tone of voice'.

Asking about lifestyle and environmental health (verbal communication, active listening, cultural awareness)

Rationale: to acquire a basic understanding of what is included in this section of the social history, further developing their ideas from the Lead in

8 • **Suggestion:** Ask each pair to consider one of the images in the Lead in and then present their thoughts to the rest of the group.
OR
Brainstorm ideas as a whole class.

• Be aware that in some cultures these are considered taboo subjects, and learners may only be used to dealing with same-gender patients; such issues would therefore be treated differently. It is important to gauge your audience.

• Note that learners should arrive at the same answer for each and every patient. (The teenage girl is obviously sexually active – as she is pregnant, and also could be susceptible to recreational drug and alcohol consumption.)

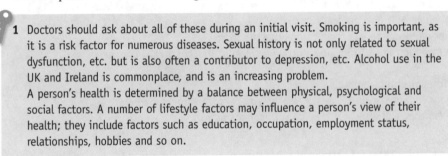

1 Doctors should ask about all of these during an initial visit. Smoking is important, as it is a risk factor for numerous diseases. Sexual history is not only related to sexual dysfunction, etc. but is also often a contributor to depression, etc. Alcohol use in the UK and Ireland is commonplace, and is an increasing problem.
A person's health is determined by a balance between physical, psychological and social factors. A number of lifestyle factors may influence a person's view of their health; they include factors such as education, occupation, employment status, relationships, hobbies and so on.

Language Note:

Recreational drugs
The term *recreational drug* is the accepted term within US/UK medical culture for an illicit (illegal) drug. This is considered a non-threatening, non-judgemental term (see Unit 8).

2 The doctor might decide to go into more detail if the patient shows evidence of alcohol abuse or recreational drug use, or if there is the possibility of a sexual health issue.

• Reassure learners that these issues will be dealt with in much more detail in Unit 8. This is a potentially complex area for the learner, regardless of gender, religious background, etc.

• Elicit the meaning of the term 'Environmental Health' as a reminder, to be sure that learners grasped the concept during the 'Think about' section.

9a

Has anyone in your household ever worked with hazardous materials that could have been brought home?*
Do you live near any factories that give off potentially hazardous fumes?

• Point out that this question* would come under the 'Environmental Health' section, as it is not directly linked to the patient's own job but to that of someone living in the same household.

9b

- Husband is unemployed, which may cause stress in the family as well as low esteem for the husband; this may have a knock-on effect for the patient, etc.
- Patient works part-time only. Cleaning work means the patient earns the lowest minimum wage. As a result, there may be financial worries for the family.
- The patient's daughter has cancer and is going through chemotherapy. This is likely to cause unnecessary stress and concern for all the family members.
- It is tiring for the patient to go back and forth to hospital every day, plus look after two other children, whom we imagine are school age – possibly primary.

Doctor's question: *How are you coping?*

- Ask learners how they would broach these concerns with a patient without appearing condescending. Brainstorm possible questions as a whole class.

Language Note:

To cope with

Note that most learners are unlikely to come up with the verb *to cope (with)* + noun / + *ing*.
Doctor's question from audio 4.3: *How are you coping?*
Ask learners a couple of questions to get them to practise the form:
How do you cope with living in the UK? How do you cope with a difficult boss? How do you cope with pain? etc.
Point out the subtle difference in meaning:
How do you manage your current situation? versus *How do you manage with your current situation?* Then tell them they will also hear *How do you manage pain?*

10a
- Point out that the aim of the case studies in this unit is NOT to encourage stereotyping but to get learners thinking about possible risk areas that they need to take into consideration when interviewing patients.
- **Suggestion:** Put 'Occupation', 'Environment', 'Finance', 'Education', 'Family', 'Lifestyle', 'Pets' up on the board and, depending on the level of the class, divide the task between small groups, each group analysing the case study according to one of these points.

Potential risk areas:
Occupation: unclear if partner is in employment or receiving welfare benefits
Environment: housing / number bedrooms in order to house two adults + three children + large, dangerous dog (in UK/Ireland, people tend to gauge size of accommodation by number of bedrooms, as opposed to total area, etc.) / facilities – toilet / running water, etc. / housing estate – could be run down / unsafe
Financial: cause of stress / lower standard of living might result in inadequate nutrition / stigma of living off welfare benefits, etc. Potential to lead to depression.
Education: three children at 22 years old (one of the children is at least five years old) indicates Sinead possibly doesn't have a high level of education and therefore access to medical education
Family: social services (formal support network) are possibly already involved with this family
Lifestyle: partner: alcohol abuse + violence have obvious consequences + negative role model for children / disruption of family life, etc. Ask patient about own drink habits – it is common for alcoholics to set up home together / domestic violence is big issue in terms of safety for woman and children.
Pets: hygiene in both cases / possible respiratory problems and allergies / potentially highly dangerous dog

10c ● Set up the role-play. Check learners understand the case study before going any further.

● Explain that the aim of this activity is to build up a bank of questions to use when asking patients about their social history.

● Depending on the level of your group, you may wish to ask each small group to compile a list of questions related to the point(s) they worked on in 10a. Then, as a group, brainstorm the first part of the interview, starting with questions related to 'occupation'.

Communication Skills

We have assumed that Sinead doesn't have a particularly high level of education. Ask learners how they might rephrase questions for her without sounding patronising. Elicit, by putting 'Let me ask … ' / 'Well, what … ' on the board and asking learners to complete the expressions. Encourage learners to use these expressions in their role play.

▶ 4.4 **10d** ● Contextualise the dialogue: Tell learners they are going to hear a GP asking Sinead Davies about her environmental health (UK English).

● Play the dialogue in one go or in parts, depending on the level of the class, to allow learners to note down the questions.

OR

Give the group control of the audio recording and allow them to listen to the extract as many times as *they* feel necessary.

Audio script >>

STUDENT'S BOOK **page 141**

Language Note:

Non-judgemental questions
Elicit the difference between using questions with *How*, *Where* and *When* as opposed to questions with *Why*. (*Why* questions can be perceived as being judgemental. See Unit 2, Question 18.)

10f ● **Suggestion:** Ask learners to put their questions under headings. Write the following on the board: 'Openers', 'Coping questions', 'Asking for permission', 'Giving a rationale', 'Facilitating questions'.

Some of the questions from Case study 1 could also be used in Case studies 2 and 3:
● **Openers**
Perhaps you could start by telling me about your current living situation?
Are you currently in a relationship?
● **Coping questions**
How does that affect you?
So, how are things there?
How do you cope with …?
Is there anything else worrying you at the moment?
● **Asking for permission**
Now, if you don't mind, I'm just going to ask you a few questions about your home life.
● **Giving a rationale**
It'll help me to better assess your present situation.
● **Facilitating questions** (picking up on cues)
You don't sound convinced?
You don't approve of the dog, I take it?

10g ● Tell learners their notes will be used later in the unit.

Summarising the encounter (verbal communication, active listening)

Rationale: to reinforce the importance of summarising and encourage learners to put it into use

> **Quotation** (Silverman et al.)
> - Divide learners into two groups and ask them to brainstorm reasons behind the importance of summarising during the information gathering process, for both the patient and the doctor.

- **Suggestion:** Elicit the benefits of summarising as a communication strategy (see Unit 3) as a reminder before learners carry out the task.
- Go through the language in the table 'Language for summarising' to check the learners' understanding of usage.

11 • **Suggestion:** In pairs, learners role-play the dialogue from audio 4.4 again (Student's Book page 141) and then continue it by using their notes and the language for summarising to summarise and check the encounter.

Patient speak (verbal communication, voice management)

Rationale: to develop skills to explain medical terminology in a patient-friendly manner, using appropriate word stress

12a • Learners will be able to use their medical knowledge to complete this task.

Suffix	Definition / Related to	Example of medical terminology	Suffix	Definition / Related to	Example of medical terminology
–algia	pain	neuralgia	–oma	tumour/growth	fibroma
–aemia	blood	leukaemia, anaemia	–osis	diseased state	endometriosis, thrombosis
–uria	urine	polyuria	–pathy	disease	uropathy
–ectomy	removal of	hysterectomy	–penia	lack of / deficiency	osteopenia
–genic	origin of	carcinogenic	–phagia	swallowing	dysphagia
–itis	inflammation	arthritis, colitis	–plasty	repair	rhinoplasty
–ology	study of	psychology	–pnoea	breathing	apnoea
–rrhoea	flowing	diarrhoea	–phobia	fear	agoraphobia

12b • **Suggestion:** Do this as a quick, whole-class activity as a means of checking the information in the table.
- Be aware that learners may come up with different examples of diseases/conditions. Simply ask learners to explain them as if to a patient.

▶ 4.5 **13a/b** • Contextualise the recording: Tell learners they are going to hear a doctor explaining medical terminology to her patients (UK English).

Audio script >>
STUDENT'S BOOK **page 142**

Out & About

Rationale: to further develop skills in explaining medical terminology in a patient-friendly manner

- Play the recording. Hopefully your learners will identify both the main and secondary stress in each. If not, elicit this from them by repeating the word *hysterectomy* several times while exaggerating the emphasis on the main and secondary stress; note it may be easier for learners to grasp in this way rather than by replaying the audio recording, as learners will be able to watch the movement of your mouth.
- **Suggestion:** Put the condition 'hysterectomy' on the board and ask two of the stronger learners to come to the board. Give them each a marker. Replay 1 and ask the learners to circle the stressed syllable or syllables as soon as they hear them – the first one to do so is the winner.
- **Suggestion:** Depending on the ability of the class, you may wish to continue with this activity as a team game. Alternatively, learners do this individually and then come together to compare as a group.

> Some of the words have a main stress and a secondary stress; here, main stress is shown by double underline; secondary stress by single underline.
> 1 hysterectomy   2 carcinogenic   3 apnoea   4 agoraphobia
> 5 leukaemia   6 arthritis   7 neuralgia   8 endometriosis

- If your learners use the same Greek terms in their own language, ask them to compare word stress patterns with those used in English.
- Reassure learners that identifying and reproducing near-native word stress is relatively difficult and may take time for them to master.
- Discuss the possible problems inappropriate word stress may cause when interviewing a patient or while speaking with a colleague (misunderstanding, the need to paraphrase or write down, etc.).

Evaluating the potential of the telephone consultation
(verbal and non-verbal communication, active listening)

Rationale: to assess the potential of this type of consultation

14 • This activity will allow you to gauge your learners' prior knowledge and use of this mode of doctor–patient communication in their own country.

15 • **Suggestion:** Brainstorm as a class and write 'Advantages' and 'Disadvantages' on the board as a reference for the next task.

> **Possible advantages:** reduce costs, reduce numbers in emergency departments, allow doctors to treat larger number of patients with minor problems, allow patients in remote areas to be treated from home, etc.
> **Possible disadvantages:** lack of human contact, possibility of misdiagnosis and increased margin of error, etc.

16b • Point out there are no right or wrong answers at this stage; learners will be able to develop their skills in the next activity.

Think about

Rationale: to ascertain learners' appreciation of the differences between face-to-face and telephone consultations

17a/b • Point out there are no right or wrong answers at this stage; learners will be able to develop their skills in the next activity. This is a means for you and them to identify potential problem areas.

Employing good telephone etiquette (verbal communication, voice management)

Rationale: to develop a framework for handling telephone consultations

18a

1 State your name
2 Obtain the caller's name and telephone number
3 Record the date and time of the call
4 Record the person's name, sex and age
5 Take a detailed and structured history
6 Provide advice on treatment or disposition
7 Advise about follow-up and when to visit a doctor
8 Summarise the main points covered
9 Request the caller to repeat the advice given
10 Ask if the person has any outstanding questions or concerns

18b

1 The patient may not have mentioned all the points he/she wishes to discuss, as in any face-to-face consultation. The most important reason for the call may not be the first point the patient mentions.
2a In the case of an emergency / good customer service (people are more stressed in such situations)
 b To ensure all the points the patient wanted to mention have been covered.

▶ 4.6 **19a** • Contextualise the dialogue: Tell learners they are going to hear a telephone consultation carried out by Dr Marsden (UK English).
 • Encourage learners to write notes, as if in an authentic situation.

Audio script >>
STUDENT'S BOOK **page 142**

Date: 26 December 2009
Tony Patchett / Tel. 01229 845143 / DOB 30/5/56
Presenting complaint: burning pains in chest
Diagnosis: indigestion
Medication: over-the-counter antacid (Gaviscon)
Follow-up: Make appointment with GP if pain not gone in 24 hours

▶ 4.6 **19c** • Remind learners that there is <u>no question for Stage 3</u> of the framework.

Stage	Language
1	Good evening, I'm Dr Marsden.
2	I wonder if you could give me your full name and telephone number, please, just in case we need to call you back at any point or we get cut off.
3	
4	… could I also have your date of birth, please?
5	So, what prompted you to call us today?
6	So, what I'm going to suggest is that you …
7	… if the medication doesn't solve the problem over the next 24 hours, then I would advise you to make an appointment to see your GP.
8	… I'd just like to briefly summarise your history to be sure I have the details correct.
9	Now, if you wouldn't mind going over the advice I've just given, Mr Patchett?
10	Now, before we finish, is there anything more you want to ask?

Non-verbal communication on the telephone (voice management, active listening, non-verbal communication)

Rationale: to encourage positive communication on the phone via non-verbal communication and appropriate voice management

20 • **Suggestion:** Put the following on the board: 'Smiling', 'Standing up', 'Lounging in a chair'. Ask learners to visualise themselves on the phone doing the above. Then ask them how these might perhaps affect a telephone consultation.

> Even though the caller is unable to see you, using non-verbal communication, such as smiling and showing warmth with the eyes, is proven to have a very positive effect on maintaining a good relation with a caller, even during difficult situations. Also, standing up while talking can lead to rushed conversation and also a feeling of superiority. On the other hand, lounging back in the chair might lead to the doctor being more casual and less attentive.

21a • **Suggestion:** Ask learners to explain their use of pausing before they listen and check.

▶ 4.7 **21b**

> Now, Mr Patchett, / I'd just like to briefly summarise your history / to be sure I have the details correct. / You've been suffering from mild chest pains since Christmas Eve / and you've experienced some acid burning. You've eaten a lot of rich food over the last days, which is unusual – / your diet's usually quite plain – / and you think this might have contributed to your symptoms. / You've no history of ulcers. / You don't have any other symptoms. / No one else in your household has these symptoms. / Is that right so far?

Audio script >>
STUDENT'S BOOK **page 142**

21c • **Suggestion:** Elicit the appropriate voice management from a stronger learner. OR

Model the passage yourself before the learners tackle this task themselves.

• **Suggestion:** Encourage learners to exaggerate the pauses at first. Then ask the learners to read out the summary as a group before they practise in pairs.

21d • You may wish to give feedback at this stage.

• Discuss the effect pausing has on the delivery of the summary.

Language Note:

Pausing (2)

Pausing at each stage enables the patient to digest the information and, if necessary, gives them the opportunity to stop and correct the doctor. This is especially important on the phone, but do remind learners that pausing should also be used in face-to-face consultations. Pausing is a communication strategy: the act of pausing encourages patient participation (see Unit 3, Exercise 5).

22 • **Suggestion:** Ask learners to refer back to Case study 1 in Exercise 10a and then as a group brainstorm possible question areas (not the questions themselves) a doctor might ask Ms Davies during the telephone consultation for situation 1.

• **Suggestion:** Depending on the level of your group, you may wish to compile a dialogue as a group, employing the framework for situation 1. Allow your learners time to practise the dialogue with a partner before getting them to select another situation to work on together.

• Remind learners to use the bank of questions they compiled in Exercise 10 and encourage learners to take notes.

• You may wish to feed back on their non-verbal communication.

Ensuring an effective telephone consultation (verbal communication, active listening, voice management)

Rationale: to introduce and practise effective skills for telephone consultations

23a

Suggested answers

Respiratory infections (smoking, ex-miner); back problems (physical activity, lifting); depression (bereavement following daughter's sudden death, leaving young children behind)

▶ 4.8 **23b** • Contextualise the dialogue: Tell learners they are now going to hear part of the telephone encounter between Richard Tomlinson and Dr Baker (UK English). Play the recording.

Audio script >>
STUDENT'S BOOK page 142

1 He is suffering from breathlessness.
2 Lifting things at work, long hours, not being able to help take care of his grandchildren. He is also possibly suffering from grief after the recent death of his daughter.
3 Could suggest Mr Tomlinson makes an immediate appointment with his GP to be examined and possibly sent for a chest X-ray.

▶ 4.8 **23c/d** • **Suggestion:** Go through the different objectives as a group to ensure learners understand what they entail; elicit possible language for 'Gathering information' and 'Picking up on cues' (see below).

• Be aware that learners may not yet understand the concept of 'Picking up on cues'. These will be dealt with in more detail in Unit 8 but there are specific examples for use over the phone (see below) that must be covered here to develop effective telephone consultation skills. Play the recording.

✓ **Establishing rapport**
(Using tone and supporting statements to ensure rapport develops)
✓ **Gathering information**
(Encouraging patient to speak – often done through non-verbal / listening actively)
✓ **Understanding the patient**
(Asking for clarification / repetition regularly throughout the interview)
✓ **Picking up on patient cues**
(Listening for change of pace and intonation in patient)

Establishing rapport
Doctor creates good rapport with patient from outset – both have grandchildren.
Doctor's tone of voice is calm and friendly and not rushed.
Gathering information
Doctor allows patient to tell his own story.
Doctor doesn't assume the patient is calling about breathlessness. (A*m I right in thinking …?*)
Doctor uses verbal facilitation and repetition to encourage the patient. (*I see, go on … / Stuff?*)
Doctor asks what patient can see (*What does it look like?*)
BUT fails to ask about hospitalisation and current medication or past occupation, all of which might have a serious bearing on the diagnosis.
Doctor fails to give patient opportunity to ask questions.
Understanding the patient
Doctor asks for clarification on a couple of occasions. (*Now, can you describe your symptoms to me in a little more detail?*)
Picking up on patient cues
Doctor picks up on effect of symptoms on lifestyle (through change of pace in patient's voice) – patient wants to spend more time with grandchildren. (*You sound a little worried by the situation?*)

• Note that the language in this section is particularly useful for developing effective telephone consultation skills.

• **Suggestion:** Deal with this language in the classroom by asking learners to write a commentary on audio 4.8 as they did in Unit 3.

23e

1 Doctor fails to ask about past work: patient indicates this is a second career (*I have my own shop now*) and, as an ex-miner, he could possibly have traces of coal dust in lungs, etc. She also misses the fact that the patient has already self-diagnosed. He recognises the symptoms, having previously suffered from bronchitis. The doctor could then have continued this line of questioning and might have arrived at a diagnosis earlier in the consultation.

2 If the cues had been picked up, the doctor would have advised the patient to visit his GP as soon as possible – diagnosis requires physical examination – and continued taking a more detailed history before summarising and giving advice.

23f • **Suggestion:** Replay the dialogue again before allowing learners to read, to give them another chance to pick out the important information for themselves.

23g • Stress the importance of communication strategies – clarification, repetition, facilitation – in telephone consultations (see Unit 2).

> **Suggested answer**
>
> Now, Mr Tomlinson, let me see if I've got this right: you've been having trouble breathing, especially when lifting or climbing stairs. You've been coughing up yellowish phlegm and you have had a couple of bouts of bronchitis in the past. You're concerned because you feel you should be helping your son-in-law more with the care of your grandchildren, but you don't always feel able to do so, and you're worried about the physical side of your job. Is that an accurate summary?
>
> Right, well, Mr Tomlinson, I'd suggest you make an appointment to see your GP. He or she will be able to carry out the relevant tests to find out the reason for your breathing difficulties.

Quotation (Silverman et al.)
- Highlight this quotation as a means of reinforcing the objectives of this section of the unit.
- Ask your learners to look back at the dialogue they wrote in Exercise 23g and check they have adhered to Silverman's advice to ensure their telephone interview was effective.

Piecing it all together

24 • Check the groups have understood the instructions for this activity.
- Ask learners A and B to sit back-to-back to replicate a telephone call situation and encourage use of the necessary communication strategies.
- Tell learners you will also be feeding back to them on both positive and negative points of their verbal and non-verbal communication, their voice management and their active listening skills.

Progress check

- Ask learners to go through the Progress check.
- Give learners some group feedback and indicate where they might need to improve.
- Give individual feedback to those who wish.

Recommended reading

- If you would like a little more information on this topic, we suggest you read the following:
  Swartz M. *Textbook of Physical Diagnosis: History and Examination.* Philadelphia: W. B. Sanders Company, 2001 (18–19)

Reading for discussion

- Go to page 151.

Unit 5 Examining a patient

LEARNING OUTCOMES

At the end of this unit, learners will be able to:

- prepare and reassure their patient during an examination
- explain examination procedures to their patient
- give effective instructions in a patient-friendly manner

DVD clip 4

Background

The physical examination is often the least pleasant part of the encounter. It can be painful for the patient concerned, or at the very least mildly uncomfortable. The patient may feel overexposed, vulnerable, humiliated – not to mention cold. He or she may be embarrassed about any number of things – being overweight, being underweight, their physical appearance. They may also be embarrassed and/or anxious about what the doctor may find. A doctor who remains respectful and takes into consideration the discomfort and embarrassment that the patient may be feeling is the one that will manage to maintain the rapport established at the beginning of the encounter. Likewise, the patient who remains relatively relaxed during an examination is more likely to comply. Doctors must also be sensitive to what they are not expecting to find – unexplained bruising or marks, etc. – which may (or may not) indicate physical or sexual abuse, for example.

When carrying out a physical examination, doctors should always bear in mind the following: cleanliness, lighting, comfort and privacy, washing hands thoroughly before touching patients, respecting a patient's sense of dignity at all times, keeping the patient draped (covering the parts not being examined with a sheet or blanket), warming their hands before touching the patient, preparing the patient, explaining different examinations to the patient, not repeating painful manoeuvres, requesting permission from the patient before removing clothes or touching him/her, explaining findings when appropriate but not discussing findings in detail with the patient until he/she is fully dressed, asking the patient to say when he/she feels pain, being aware of facial expressions which might show signs of pain or discomfort, explaining where and why they are palpating the patient, offering help to the patient as he/she gets on and off the examination table, and always keeping the patient informed of what they are doing.

Specific procedures

Read through *Techniques of the Trade* in Exercise 3a to familiarise yourself with the four most basic examination procedures.

Patient-friendly instructions

Giving patient-friendly instructions involves using indirect as opposed to direct language, informal instructions (*lie back* and not *recline*, *nose* and not *nasal passage*), the use of softeners (such as *just*), and appropriate voice management. Indirect instructions (e.g. *If you could just raise your left leg, please*) will go some way to helping the patient to relax, while more direct language (e.g. *Raise your left leg, please*) might come across more as an order.

Read through the Language Notes for each of the above (direct language, informal instructions, softeners, voice management) for information regarding form and usage.

Note: Unit 5 is more functional than the other units in the book; content is fairly minimal and the language focus relatively simple compared to other units. What is important, however, is the pragmatic aspect – the delivery, as discussed in the section above. You may wish to highlight this to your group before you start the unit.

US versus UK English

UK	US
bottom	behind
jumper/pullover (used by the older generation) (audio 5.2)	sweater

UK	US
peak flow machine	spirometer
trousers trouser leg	pants pant leg

Lead in

Rationale: to encourage learners to put themselves in the role of the patient, before and during the physical examination

- Ask learners to think about the experience from the patient's perspective; encourage learners to put themselves in the patient's shoes, as in Unit 1.
- **Suggestion:** Ask learners to visualise themselves as one of the patients (a–c) to help them to 'get into character'.
  OR
  Simply ask learners to answer the questions first individually before coming together in small groups to discuss.
- **Suggestion:** Carry out this activity yourself along with your learners to give them the patient's perspective.

> **Suggested answers**
>
> 2 Patients may be having a variety of feelings prior to the examination, ranging from mild anxiety to fear. These thoughts may be quite irrational. However, some examinations can be both painful and embarrassing. Patients might feel overexposed and, in most cases, not particularly relaxed.

- Elicit the following:
- Point out to learners that older patients brought up in a less liberal environment and those patients from certain cultural backgrounds may require extra consideration during the physical examination.

Think about

Rationale: to assess learners' own skills at this stage, considering their own experience of carrying out a physical examination in English

- **1a** • Some might not have experience of doing this in English; they should evaluate their current level of competence as they see it. It is a kind of self-assessment.
  - Be aware that learners tend to overestimate their competency. Learners may also feel the way they carry out a physical examination in English is appropriate, but this may not be the case in reality.

Procedure for physical examinations

Rationale: to raise awareness of the physical and psychological elements to be considered during a physical examination

2 • Learners will draw on their own knowledge of medical procedures to carry out this activity.
   • Point out that this is not a test of language. Learners will be quite capable of discussing these points; it will get them thinking about the communication skills required to be able to carry out this part of the encounter.

> **Suggested answers**
>
> Think about: cleanliness, lighting, comfort and privacy, respecting the patient's sense of dignity at all times, washing your hands thoroughly before touching the patient, keeping the patient covered, warming hands before touching the patient, preparing the patient, explaining different examinations to the patient, not repeating painful manoeuvres, requesting permission before removing clothes or touching the patient, explaining findings when appropriate, not discussing findings fully with the patient until he or she is fully dressed, asking the patient to tell you when he/she feels pain, watching facial expressions for signs of pain or discomfort, explaining where and why you are palpating a patient, offering help getting on and off the examination table, always keeping the patient informed.

   • Be aware that pre-experience doctors may not bring up all of these points individually.

Explaining procedures (verbal communication, active listening, cultural awareness)

Rationale: to acquire skills to explain simple procedures in a patient-friendly manner to prepare the patient

• Learners will again be able to draw on their knowledge of medical procedures to carry out this activity.

3a
> **a** Auscultation   **b** Palpation   **c** Inspection   **d** Percussion

3b • Learners in general will know the correct order of these procedures.

> **a** 4   **b** 2   **c** 1   **d** 3

4a • Encourage learners to write in spoken English as opposed to a more formal written style, as this information will form part of a dialogue later in the unit.
   • Avoid at this stage going into discussion about appropriate usage of indirect language and the softener *just* for giving instructions; these will be covered later in the unit. The aim is rather for learners to practise explaining these basic procedures.
   • Encourage learners, however, to make use of their acquired voice-management skills by including instructions for the speakers in the dialogue as they write, e.g. [intonation rises], [displays open body language], [makes eye contact], etc. You may wish to put these up on the board as a reminder while learners are writing their instructions. These will be useful when they role-play the dialogues.

Language Note:

Modal verb – *might*

Use of the modal *might* enables the doctor to keep their patient informed during the physical examination, as required under a patient-centred approach: e.g. *The stethoscope might feel a little cold*. This does not make the assumption that the patient will definitely feel cold; instead, the statement acts as a warning that this is a fairly strong possibility. In using this form the doctor is therefore preparing the patient and thus involving him/her in the examination process.

4b • **Suggestion:** Select one procedure (a–d) as a group and brainstorm an explanation, before allowing pairs to continue with the rest of the procedures.

5a

The medical instruments shown are:
- **penlight** (top left): a small electric torch the size of a pen used to examine eyes, ears, etc.
- **reflex hammer** (top right): a small hammer typically with a triangular rubber head used for testing reflexes
- **tuning fork** (bottom left): a steel instrument with a stem and two flat prongs which vibrates and produces a sound, used to assess a patient's hearing, as well as in the examination of the peripheral nervous system
- **nasal speculum** (bottom right): a speculum is a surgical instrument used for dilating orifices (such as the nasal passage), facilitating examination or operation

5b • Learners will now be used to the idea of peer evaluation and this activity should not cause them a problem.
- Explain to learners that they should feed back to their partner by rating them (a, b or c) and then by giving a few examples in support of the rating given, both positive and negative.
- Stress the need for the feedback to be constructive.

Think about

Rationale: to assess learners' own skills at this stage, considering their own experience of giving instructions in English

6a • Some learners might not have experience of doing this in English; they should evaluate their current level of competence as they see it. It is a kind of self-assessment. Learners are likely to be less competent in terms of the pragmatics of spoken communication.

6b • Point out to learners that they will come back to the instructions they have written later – once they have had more exposure to more appropriate usage – when they will have the chance to make corrections if necessary.

Verbs for giving instructions (verbal communication, cultural awareness)

Rationale: to develop linguistic competency for giving effective, patient-friendly instructions

7 • **Suggestion:** Refer learners back to the pictures on the first page of this unit. Ask them what might be causing patient (b) to be confused. (The fact that the doctor is using instructions that are confusing / medical jargon, etc.)

- Elicit the need for patient-friendly instructions and what might constitute patient-friendly instructions. It does not matter at this stage if they do not come up with all the answers to this.

> **A** 1, 10, 13, 14
> **B** 2, 4, 8
> **C** 4, 8, 13
> **D** 3, 5, 11, 13
> **E** 1, 3, 5, 6, 7, 12, 14

- Be aware that learners, even at a high level, are not necessarily aware of these verbs, although the language appears fairly simple.
- Ask learners if they know other verbs for these movements.

8a • Point out that learners can look again at cartoons E and A if necessary.

> **1** **Patient** I'm still having problems with this knee.
> **Doctor** OK, let me have a look. Can you roll up your trouser leg for me? Good, now if you could <u>recline</u> on the bed and <u>flex</u> your right knee ...
> **Patient** *[shows signs of being a little uncomfortable]*
> **Doctor** Still seems to be causing you a little discomfort, Sean.
> **Patient** Yeah, yeah, I know.
> **Doctor** Gently then, just bring your knee up to your chest. That's fine. And now <u>extend</u> your leg again ...
>
> **2** **Patient** *[wheezing heavily]*
> **Doctor** Mrs Daniels, can you <u>sit in the upright position</u> for me, please? I can see you're having difficulties today. We're going to try to make things more comfortable for you. I'm just going to listen to your chest.
> **Patient** Sure.
> **Doctor** Good. Now, I want you to <u>inhale</u> through your <u>nasal passage</u>. <u>Inhale</u> deeply ... that's it. Now <u>exhale</u>. And again ... <u>inhale</u> ... and <u>exhale</u>.
> **Doctor** Now, I want to measure your respiratory rate ... I think you've seen this little machine before. *[shows patient a peak-flow machine]*
> **Patient** *[nods]*

- Learners should not have much difficulty with this activity.

8b

> recline – lie back; flex – bend; extend – straighten sit in the upright position – sit up; inhale – breathe in; nasal passage – nose; exhale – breathe out

8c • Refer learners back to the checklist they compiled in Exercise 2 to ensure they are carrying out an effective examination, even if the aim of the activity is essentially to practise usage.

Patient speak

Rationale: to acquire appropriate language to communicate instructions specific to the examination of joint movements

9 • **Suggestion:** Learners could try to learn these in pairs – i.e. the opposite movements.

10 • Learners will now have the chance to put the instructions into practice.
• **Suggestion:** Elicit from learners, or give, a couple of examples of phrases that doctors might need to use while examining the patient, and write them up on the board; e.g. *That area seems a bit tender. Is it? There seems to be some inflammation in this part. There seems to be a lot of (stiffness in your neck). Tell me if you feel any discomfort as I (press on your abdomen). I'm sorry, I can see that caused you some discomfort.*

Using indirect language for instructions (verbal communication, cultural awareness)

Rationale: to develop use of indirect as opposed to direct language for giving instructions

▶ 5.1 **11a** • Contextualise the dialogue: Tell learners they are going to hear two consultations where the doctor instructs their patient during the physical examination (Australian English and South African English). Play the recording.

Audio script >>

STUDENT'S BOOK **page 143**

A: knee injury
B: suspected dislocated shoulder

▶ 5.1 **11b**

Consultation A
• Take off shoes and tights   4
• Try to bend left knee   2
• Stand up   1
• Lift skirt over knee   5
• Say if it feels uncomfortable   6
• Lift left leg   3

Consultation B
• Hold out right hand   5
• Stand up and put arms by side   2
• Take off shirt   1
• Bend elbow horizontally   4
• Lift right arm to shoulder level 3
• Lift and lower arm   6

▶ 5.1 **11d**

1 **If you could stand up** for me, please, Julie.
2 **You can put** your foot down now.
3 **I'd just like you to** lift your left leg as high as you can.
4 (Please,) **If you could take** off your shoes and your tights …
5 **Would you mind just lifting** your skirt over your knee.
6 **I want you to tell me** if it starts to feel uncomfortable.

Language Note:

Direct versus indirect language for instructions

Direct language: Although the instruction is grammatically correct, using an imperative *(Lift your right leg, please)* might be considered a little too direct and come across as a command rather than an instruction. This form is a little abrupt and might not be considered polite.

Indirect language: By adding a modal to the instruction, a doctor is able to soften the instruction: *If you could lift your right leg up, please*. The instruction ceases to be a command and is not aggressive. It is therefore more polite, and the patient is more likely to feel at ease and comply.

- Point out the 'Language for polite instructions' box to your learners, which contains other forms of language for indirect instructions.

11e

1 Doctors use indirect language to give instructions.
2 Indirect language is used to soften the instruction so that it comes across more as a request and less like a command. As a result, it is considered polite. Patients may be feeling anxious, frightened or agitated. Use of a more direct language could further aggravate their feelings.

- Be aware that learners will know about the use of modals and imperatives from their knowledge of general English, but it is less likely, even at this level, that they have grasped the subtleties that differentiate them.
- Point out that the activity that follows on intonation is equally (if not more) important if their instructions are to be even more appropriate to the situation.

Intonation for instructions (voice management, cultural awareness)

Rationale: to raise awareness of appropriate intonation when giving instructions

5.2 **12a** • Contextualise the dialogue: Tell learners they are going to hear three different doctors instructing their patients during a physical examination (UK English). Play the recording.

Audio script >>
STUDENT'S BOOK **page 143**

- **Suggestion:** Listen to the first doctor three times. On the third listening, pause to allow learners time to repeat, mimicking the intonation pattern.

2 Would you mind rolling over onto your stomach for me?

3 I want you to sit up with your legs stretched out in front of you.

Language Note:

Intonation for instructions

Giving polite, non-threatening instructions is not just a question of using indirect language; it is also the way in which the doctor manages his/her voice. Intonation can be a strong indicator of the doctor's attitude towards the patient – something that is difficult to counteract once the message has been conveyed. By employing an appropriate intonation, the doctor is able to soften the instruction yet further (than by simply using indirect language).

12b • Allow learners as much time as necessary to practise these examples before moving on to the next task.

12c • **Suggestion:** Give feedback directly to each learner on this; it might be a more effective, less threatening approach, as each learner will progress at a different rate with this type of task.
- Be aware that learners of all levels find acquiring appropriate intonation patterns a difficult exercise.
- **Suggestion:** Reassure your learners of this but also encourage them to persevere; native speakers of English seem less tolerant of inappropriate intonation than of inappropriate grammatical usage.

Softeners (verbal communication, cultural awareness)

Rationale: to introduce the use of softeners in English for giving instructions

13a

Language Note:

Softeners

Softeners, such as *just*, are a means of conveying warmth to speech, in this case to an instruction; they tone down or soften a particular speech act. *If you could just lift your right leg, please*, with the added softener *just*, is more polite, non-threatening, and therefore more patient-friendly than examples given in Language Note boxes appearing earlier in this unit.

- Avoid giving too much away at this stage; allow the learners to make discoveries about the usage for themselves.

The missing word in all the examples is *just*.

5.1 **13b** • **Suggestion:** Play the recording and, again, avoid any explanation; learners will be processing the language usage and making assumptions as they go through the examples.

Audio script >>

STUDENT'S BOOK **page 143**

14a

Just softens the instruction and as a result renders it more polite. It can also be used to reassure the patient or diminish the seriousness of the situation.

5.3 **14b** • **Suggestion:** Give the group control of the audio recording and allow them to listen to the extract as many times as *they* feel is necessary.

Audio script >>

STUDENT'S BOOK **page 143**

In each case, intonation rises on the word *just*.

15

The expression *just in case* means 'in the event that something may (not) happen' and is used to reassure the patient that the doctor is looking at every possible cause, even though the chance of there being a serious problem is slight.

16 • The idea of rewriting the instruction is for learners to have the chance to make improvements on their own usage, as a means of reinforcement and to aid the learning process.

> **Quotation** (Loveday)
> • Ask learners if there is an equivalent softener in their language and how doctors convey warmth when giving instructions.
> • Then ask learners to what extent the use of softeners is important in maintaining good interpersonal relations in their culture.

Out & About

Rationale: to listen out for examples of the use of softeners in learners' working/living environment

Piecing it all together

17a/b

- Point out that some of the notes recorded by the student doctor are actions and don't necessarily need vocalising (e.g. Note 3 cover genitalia).
- Tell learners you will be feeding back to them on both positive and negative aspects of their verbal and non-verbal communication, their voice management and their active listening skills.
- **Suggestion:** As a follow-up to the role-play, brainstorm ways to get the patient to use imagery if they are uncomfortable (Note 8). Be aware that some learners may not feel particularly at ease with this means of communication — i.e. getting patients to relax (*Imagine you are on a beach / in a park / in a special place, etc.*).

> **Communication Skills**
> • Ask learners to practise this type of expression: in pairs, Student A should point to a particular joint and Student B should then give an instruction, clarifying as appropriate using *as if you were trying to ...*

Progress check

- Ask learners to go through the Progress check.
- Give learners some group feedback and indicate where they might need to improve.
- Give individual feedback to those who wish.

Recommended reading

- If you would like a little more information on this topic, we suggest you read the following:
  Allan M and Spencer J. *Crash Course: History and Examination*. Oxford: Elsevier, 2004 (87–88)

Reading for discussion

- Go to page 152.

DVD clip 4

- Go to page 164.

Unit 6   Giving results

LEARNING OUTCOMES

At the end of this unit, learners will be able to:

- explain results to a patient
- encourage a patient to express his/her fears and concerns
- explain medical terminology to a patient
- give a prognosis

Background

This unit focuses on the part of the patient interview where the doctor is providing the results of tests to patients and giving patients some idea of what the likely prognosis is.

Giving a diagnosis

When a doctor explains the results of tests to a patient, the following factors need to be considered: giving the patient the correct amount and type of information; helping the patient understand and remember the information; and achieving a shared understanding, which means taking the patient's perspective into consideration.

Giving the correct amount and type of information

By using communication strategies, these objectives can be achieved. To determine how much and what type of information to give, doctors need to be able to summarise what has already been explained, check that the patient has understood, and then check the patient's current knowledge.

Helping the patient understand and remember new information

A number of steps can be taken: organising information into clear chunks; using signposting language, such as *firstly*, *secondly*; using visuals to help explain conditions or procedures; using communication strategies to check that the patient has understood; and repeating, summarising, and explaining medical terminology in a clear way. Using medical jargon can alienate a patient and cause anxiety. When medical terminology is used, a doctor should explain what is meant by it. Clearly, levels of understanding of medical terminology will vary from patient to patient, so a doctor needs to take this into account when giving information. However, even when a patient appears to be familiar with medical terminology, a doctor should check what the patient means by it, as it may not necessarily be accurate.

Giving a prognosis

This requires doctors to use the language of probability based on the results of an investigation. It is also important that doctors are able to respond to colloquial questions asked by patients regarding chances of recovery.

US versus UK English

UK	US
fighting fit	back to normal
jabs (audio 6.3)	shots

Lead in

Rationale: to highlight the importance of the explanation and planning stage of the patient interview

- Ask learners to read the quotation and then discuss the two questions in groups.

1 Gathering information about the patient can be regarded as the building blocks of the consultation.

2 It is important, after building (on) the foundations of the patient interview by discussing patient's wishes, history-taking and being knowledgeable, that you add the roof, i.e. make a joint management plan that the patient understands, feels comfortable with and is prepared to follow. (Silverman, Kurtz & Draper, 2005)

1a • Ask learners to write down criteria that they would use to evaluate how effectively a doctor provides information to a patient.

2 Do they deliver information in a way which helps the patient understand it?

3 Do they deliver the information in a way which helps the patient recall it accurately?

4 Do they deliver the information in a way which includes the patient's perspective and achieve a shared understanding with the patient?

Taken from the Calgary–Cambridge observation guide.

1b • Now ask learners to compare their criteria with the ones on page 163 of the Student's Book.

Giving and explaining new information to a patient (verbal communication, active listening, non-verbal communication)

2a • Learners should look at the table on page 60. Next to each of the guidelines, ask learners to note down two ways in which these objectives can be met.

2b • Learners should now check their answers against the table in Exercise 4.

Giving a diagnosis (verbal communication, active listening)

Rationale: to develop awareness of factors to consider when giving a diagnosis

Audio script >>

▶ 6.1   **3** • Contextualise the dialogue: Tell learners they are going to listen to a doctor explaining the results of a test to his patient (UK English).

STUDENT'S BOOK **page 143**

• Ask learners to listen out for the four objectives shown in the table and to tick the appropriate box to show how well they think the doctor achieves the four objectives. Play the recording.

	Very good	Good	Could improve
Giving correct amount and type of information	✓		
Helping patient understand and remember	✓		
Including patient's perspective	✓		

4 • Ask learners to match the examples from the audio script with the appropriate objective 1–3.

a 2   b 1   c 2   d 1   e 1   f 1   g 3   h 2   i 2   j 1, 2   k 2   l 3

Organising information (verbal communication)

Rationale: to develop use of discourse markers

5 • Ask learners to identify two other examples of signposting language from audio 6.1 (see the audio script on page 143).

> To begin with, I'm going to give you your results, and then we'll discuss where to go from there
> Let me explain.
> ... that brings me to the next point
> There are four things you need to consider

6a • Ask learners to read the extract. Ask them if the lack of signposting makes it harder to follow the sequence and timescale. Could the explanation be improved?

> Adding signposting means that the patient has a better chance of taking in what the doctor is saying, given that he/she is likely to be in a state of shock following the break.

6b • Ask learners to complete the gaps in the expanded version of the explanation using appropriate signposting from the box.

> **1** To begin with   **2** However   **3** First of all   **4** Then
> **5** When   **6** Finally

• Refer learners to the quotation on page 63. It serves the purpose of providing evidence of the importance of discourse markers in a medical context.

7 • Ask learners to look at the outline of the two scenarios. They should take it in turns to play the role of the doctor. Using the information provided, they should add appropriate signposting language to explain the results and what is going to happen to the patient next.

> **Suggested answers:**
>
> **Scenario 1**
> <u>Firstly</u>, let me give you the results of the ultrasound test. They show that you have a number of gallstones in your gall bladder. <u>In addition</u>, your bile ducts have dilated, which may mean that there are gallstones present there. We need to remove the gallstones to make you feel better. Now, <u>there are three ways</u> in which we could do this. <u>Firstly</u>, we could use drugs to dissolve the stones. <u>However</u>, this could take six months for smaller stones and around a year for larger stones. I'd like to point out that with drugs, there is a 50% chance of stones re-occurring within five years.
> <u>Moving on</u> to the <u>second</u> method, which is a surgical technique called ERCP. <u>Let me briefly outline</u> what this involves. This is where small tools are attached to an endoscope, which is a small flexible tube that is inserted into your body, to release the stones. This method has a high success rate and a low re-occurrence rate.
> <u>The final option</u> is to try open surgery, which means making an incision and removing the stones directly. However, compared with ERCP, this method is more invasive and patients tend to heal less quickly.
>
> **Scenario 2**
> <u>Let me begin by</u> giving you the results of the CT scan. You have a condition called chronic sinusitis, which is the result of a viral infection. The pain you are experiencing <u>is due to</u> tissues blocking your sinuses. <u>Now</u>, there are a number of treatments which I will outline.

<u>Firstly</u>, antibiotics, which usually clear up the condition. <u>Although</u> they don't actually kill the virus, they attack the bacteria that can make the sinuses very painful.
<u>Another option</u> is using steroid sprays or drops, which help to reduce inflamed sinuses.
<u>However</u>, if these treatments don't work, there's an operation called functional endoscopic sinus surgery, which is a very common operation and has a very high success rate. <u>Let me explain</u> what this involves. An endoscope, which is an instrument that magnifies the inside of your nose and your nasal cavities, is inserted into your nose. This allows the surgeon to see the opening of your sinus drainage channels, and any tissues blocking the affected area can be removed. <u>Following</u> the operation, the drainage of your sinus will be more efficient, and your sinus will function better.

Using *do* for emphasis and confirmation (verbal communication, voice management)

Rationale: to develop language for emphasising and confirming

8a • Tell learners to look at the statements taken from the dialogue in Exercises 3 and 4 and match the statement with the appropriate function.

> 1 b (Confirming that the patient has diabetes)
> 2 a (Stressing the need to manage the condition)

8b • Ask learners to add the appropriate form of *do* to the six sentences.

> 1 The results do confirm that he has pneumonia / The results confirm that he does have pneumonia.
> 2 As we suspected, the results do show that you have anaemia. / The results show that you do have anaemia.
> 3 I did tell you that the treatment can cause nausea.
> 4 I do think it would help if you spoke to a counsellor.
> 5 Your condition does require careful monitoring.
> 6 You do need to cut down on your alcohol intake.

8c

> 4 really, definitely, certainly
> 5 definitely, certainly
> 6 really, definitely, certainly

Rationale: to identify and practise word stress

Voice management

 9a • Learners will hear two statements taken from Exercise 8a. Ask them to mark where the main word stress is by <u>underlining</u> the word(s) that are stressed. Play the recording.

Audio script >>

STUDENT'S BOOK **page 143**

> 1 You <u>do</u> have a form of <u>pre-dia</u><u>betes</u>
> 2 We <u>do</u> need to <u>man</u><u>age</u> your con<u>di</u><u>tion</u>

• Ask learners what they notice about the word stress when *do* is used.

> The word *do* is stressed in each example.

10 • Working in pairs, learners should take it in turns practising the four scenarios listed.

> **Suggested answers**
>
> **1** The results of the investigation do confirm that you have had a mild stroke / that you did have a mild stroke.
> **2** It's important that you do keep an eye on your weight.
> **3** The X-ray shows that you did fracture a rib. / The X-ray does show that you fractured a rib.
> **4** It's important that you do take up some mild, regular exercise.

Explaining medical terminology to a patient (verbal communication)

Rationale: to develop awareness of the importance of organising language in manageable chunks

11a • Ask learners to read the extract and decide if the statements are true or false.

> **1** T   **2** F (It can also be caused by blocked bile ducts)   **3** T

11b • Ask learners to discuss what difficulties patients might have in understanding the extract, and to underline any problematic language.

> **Suggested answers:**
>
> No visuals, long sentences, little signposting, some difficult vocabulary

12 • Ask learners to match the terms taken from the extracts with their more patient-friendly alternatives.

> **1** e   **2** a   **3** d   **4** c   **5** e   **6** h   **7** f   **8** g

• Refer learners to the 'Language for explaining' section.
• Let learners look at the extract again and ask them if they can think of any other examples of signposting language that could be used.

13a • Learners should role play the following situation. The doctor should explain the medical condition in Exercise 11 to the patient, paying attention to the how the information is structured. Encourage them to draw diagrams. The doctor should invite the patient to ask questions. Point out that any medical terminology used should be followed by a brief explanation.
• Learners should give feedback to each other on their ability to explain the information.

Language Note:

Discourse markers

Discourse markers help communication by signposting the nature of the information. They have several different functions:

Adding information: *and, as well as, in addition*
Introducing qualifiers: *but, however*
Summarising: *to sum up, to recap*
Giving reasons: *this is due to, this is because*
Explaining consequences: *as a result*
Giving examples: *for example, such as, for instance*

14a

just

14b • Now ask learners to suggest why the patient became very anxious, despite the doctor using the word *just*.

> Because the doctor used the words *ulcer* and *arthritis*. In both cases, the patient had a different perception from the doctor of the seriousness of the condition.

14c • Ask learners to suggest what they could say to ensure that the patient did not become anxious.

> 1 It's just a small, harmless growth on the neck of the womb.
> 2 It just shows some wear and tear on your spine, which is normal for a man of your age.

Picking up on verbal cues (active listening, verbal communication)

Rationale: to develop listening skills and to respond to verbal signals from patients

> 6.3 **15a** • Contextualise the dialogue: Tell learners they are going to listen to the continuation of the dialogue from Exercise 3.
> • Ask learners to write down two examples that show that the patient is anxious. Play the recording.

Audio script >>
STUDENT'S BOOK **page 143**

> I hate needles. They really scare me.
> The person I was telling you about had to have his foot amputated.
> I can't lose my job. I've got my family to think of.

15b • Ask learners why the patient asks the question: *That won't happen to me, will it?*

> The patient is seeking reassurance from the doctor.

The second question shows greater anxiety.

Communication Skills

- Refer learners to the quotation. Point out that it is important that your body language mirrors what you are saying. At times, our body language may be contradicting what we are saying. For example, we may tell somebody that we are listening, but our body language may show that we are not concentrating.

Patient speak

Rationale: to expose learners to common questions asked by patients about their chances of recovery

16a • Ask learners to put the colloquial questions that a patient might ask under the appropriate heading.

> **1** B   **2** A   **3** A   **4** B   **5** A   **6** B   **7** B   **8** A   **9** A   **10** B

16b • Tell learners to work in pairs and ask each other some of the questions from 16a. The person replying to the questions may like to use the responses in 16b.

17 • Ask learners to look at the two sentences and ask them which one sounds more reassuring.

> Statement 1 is more reassuring, because it stresses the positive outcome. Eighty per cent sounds like a high figure so this is emphasised, rather than the remaining twenty per cent of operations which don't result in a complete recovery.

18 • Learners should now rank the statements provided in descending order.

> a, g, f, d, b, e, c (or a, f, g, d, b, e, c: *likely* and *probable* are near synonyms)

Cultural awareness

Rationale: to develop awareness of treating each patient as an individual
- Point out to learners that while knowledge of other cultures is important, it is also important not to stereotype people from a particular culture.
- Ask learners to read the text. Put learners into small groups and tell them to describe to the other people in the group a situation where they made the wrong assumption about a particular culture. Ask them to analyse what they based their judgement on and how they found out that they were wrong.

Piecing it all together

Rationale: to consolidate what learners have covered in this unit

19a/b • Ask learners to read the two extracts. They should underline any difficult language and suggest suitable paraphrases. They should then take it in turns to explain the condition, as if they were talking to a patient. The person playing the role of the patient should give feedback to the doctor, using the following criteria:
  - Use of signposting language
  - Giving information in manageable chunks
  - Checking the patient's understanding
  - Inviting the patient to ask questions
  • Tell learners you will give them feedback on both positive and negative points of their verbal and non-verbal communication, their voice management, and their active listening skills.

Progress check

- Ask learners to go through the Progress check.
- Give learners some group feedback and indicate where they might need to improve.
- Give individual feedback to those who wish.

Recommended reading

- If you would like a little more information on this topic, we suggest you read the following:
  Lloyd M and Bor R. *Communication Skills in Medicine*. London: Churchill Livingstone, 2005 (Chapter 4)

Reading for discussion

- Go to page 153.

> 1 That the HIV test turned out negative, even though he had skin cancer.
> 2 The patient's reaction to their results will depend on their perception of what the results mean. As in this case, the perception may not always be objective.

Unit 7 Planning treatment and closing the interview

LEARNING OUTCOMES

At the end of this unit, learners will be able to:

- explain treatment to patients
- discuss options
- describe benefits and side effects
- advise on lifestyle
- negotiate treatment
- close the interview

DVD clip 5

Background

While vast amounts of money are invested in developing new drugs, evidence shows that many patients do not collect their prescriptions or keep to treatments prescribed. Given the time invested in the consultation, it is important that patients comply with the treatment recommended by their doctor.

Achieving concordance

As part of a more patient-centred approach, doctors need to elicit patients' feelings and concerns about treatment, rather than simply prescribing a particular treatment following the case history. By doing this, there is a better chance that patients will take a doctor's advice and the prescribed treatments.

Explaining treatment and outlining options

The unit follows the stages recommended in the Calgary-Cambridge observation guide. A first stage is explaining what treatment the patient will need to undertake because of their condition, and why this is necessary. The next stages cover the various options for treatment which exist, providing detailed information on each, including the benefits and side effects. A plan of action is then agreed and the interview is briefly summarised and the plan of action repeated before closing the interview.

Advising on lifestyle

Increasingly, changes to lifestyle are becoming a major alternative option to taking drugs. However, making these changes can be very difficult, particularly where these are culturally bound. This section explores ways in which patients' beliefs and attitudes can be explored, and areas of particular concern identified and addressed.

US versus UK English

UK	US
disorientation (audio 7.4)	confusion
sick note	doctor's note (audio 7.2)
sort out (audio 7.2)	take care of
units of alcohol (audio 7.3)	drinks

Lead in

Rationale: to raise awareness of the problem of non-compliance

- Ask learners to read the quotation and then to discuss the three questions.

1 **Personal cost:** The patient does not get better and/or quality of life is not as good as it could be.

Societal cost: The time wasted by healthcare professionals in treating patients with ongoing conditions when they could be treating others. Patients may be underperforming at work, which affects others. Emotional strain on relatives/carers.

Economic cost: Cost of drugs prescribed and not used; cost of wasted time of professionals; cost of sick pay for employers.

2 The quality or the quantity of information may be insufficient.
The impact of the medication on the patient's daily life.
Physical or mental incapacity of patient.
Patient may not see the value of taking pills and prescriptions.
Social isolation.

3 Involve the patient in the decision-making process.
Find out about the patient's beliefs.
Explain clearly why it is important to follow treatment or advice.
Be supportive.

- **Suggestion:** Ask learners if they have any personal examples where they or friends did not start or finish a course of prescribed treatment.

Explaining treatment (verbal communication, active listening)

Rationale: to identify doctor-centred language

▶ 7.1

1 • Contextualise the dialogue: Tell learners they are going to listen to a doctor outlining a treatment plan to his patient (US English).

Audio script >>
STUDENT'S BOOK **page 144**

   • Ask learners to listen for whether the doctor uses any of the recommendations they noted down in the 'Lead in'. Play the recording.
   • After listening, learners should say whether they think the patient will comply with the treatment or not.

Not very likely. The doctor simply tells the patient what to do without considering the patient's perspective.

Quotation (Marinker and Shaw)
- Ask learners to read the quotation and say which model (compliance or concordance) is more common in their country.
- The quotation highlights the importance of establishing the patient's agenda. If a doctor only follows his/her own agenda (compliance), they fail to include the patient's perspective and run a greater risk of patients not adhering to treatments.
- The word *concordance* is a more commonly used term now, which fits in more with a patient-centred model, whereby the patient is consulted about how happy they are about taking a particular treatment.

Think about

Rationale: to reflect on the differences in the communication process between a compliance-based approach and a concordance-based approach

Where a doctor uses a concordance-based approach, the communication is more likely to be interactive. The doctor elicits the patient's perspective on the proposed treatments, giving him/her an opportunity to raise any concerns. If the doctor does not follow a concordance-based approach, he/she is more likely to simply tell the patient what to do, without finding out if the patient can see any difficulties in following the instructions.

Negotiating a plan of action (active listening, verbal communication)

Rationale: to provide learners with guidelines for negotiating treatment with patients

2 • Ask learners to read the seven stages recommended by the Calgary-Cambridge observation guide and to complete them with words from the box.

1 options	2 information	3 view	4 concerns
5 beliefs	6 plans	7 support; support	

3a • Ask learners to look at the script from Exercise 1 and to decide which recommendation is being missed out for each of the underlined sentences.

a 1   b 4   c 6

▶ 7.2 3b • Audio 7.2 is another version of the dialogue in 7.1. Ask learners to comment whether they think the patient is more likely to accept the recommended medication. Play the recording.

Audio script >>

STUDENT'S BOOK page 144

There is a better chance that the patient will accept the recommended medication, as the doctor has addressed the patient's concerns.

3c • Ask learners to read the script of audio 7.2 on page 144 and underline the sections that correspond to the recommended steps of the Calgary-Cambridge observation guide.

Doctor Hello, Miss Lennox. What can I do for you?
Patient The antibiotics you prescribed haven't cleared up my chest infection.
Doctor Right. Did you complete the course?
Patient Yes, I did.
Doctor And do you feel any better after taking them?
Patient No. They've had absolutely no effect, apart from giving me thrush and leaving me completely washed out.
Doctor Right. I'm sorry to hear that. <u>Sometimes antibiotics may not agree with patients.</u> *[stage 2]* What I'll do is try you with a different antibiotic and see how that goes.
Patient Isn't there something else that I could take instead?
Doctor <u>Unfortunately not.</u> *[stage 1]* It's possible that the infection may clear up on its own if we leave it, but most likely it'll drag on. A different antibiotic could really help here.
Patient I really want to get rid of it, but I'm not sure I can face another course.
Doctor <u>Is that because of the thrush and feeling washed out?</u> *[stage 3]*
Patient Yes. I've got a demanding job, and it's a struggle getting through each day at the moment.

Doctor	I can understand your concern, but antibiotics really are your best chance of getting rid of the infection quickly. Different antibiotics affect you in different ways; <u>I can also give you some cream which will sort out the thrush. If you need to, I can give you a doctor's note so you can take time off work.</u> *[stage 7]*
Patient	I can't do that. I just need to get better. OK, I'll try some different ones.
Doctor	OK, and if these don't help, come and see me again. But I'm hopeful that these will take care of the problem for you.

3d • A number of phrasal verbs appear in this dialogue. Ask learners to guess what they mean from the context. They will need to refer to the audio script again on page 144.

> 1 made better 2 tired/drained
> 3 go on for a long time 4 surviving/lasting
> 5 no longer having 6 find a solution to

3e • Ask learners to use the correct form of the phrasal verb from Exercise 3d to complete the sentences.

> 1 cleared up 2 sort out
> 3 washed out 4 drag on
> 5 getting rid of 6 get thrush

Quotation (Marinker)
• The quotation highlights the importance of giving patients sufficient information to allow them to make informed choices.

Discussing options (active listening, verbal communication)

Rationale: to develop language for discussing options

4a • Ask learners to explain what hypertension is, as if they were describing it to a patient, and to list three factors that can contribute to it.

> 1 **Suggested answer**
> Hypertension (or blood pressure) is basically the pressure of blood in your arteries. Your heart pumps blood around your body through a network of tubing called arteries. The higher your blood pressure, the greater your risk of developing narrowed arteries, which can lead to heart problems, kidney disease and strokes. (Raised blood pressure ≥160/100mmHG)
> 2 Smoking, excessive alcohol consumption, diet that is high in salt and processed foods, being overweight, lack of exercise, genetic predisposition

> 7.3 **4b** • Contextualise the dialogue: Tell learners they are going to listen to a doctor outlining different options for treating hypertension (UK English).
> • Ask learners to listen for the options the doctor suggests and to note them down. Play the recording.

Audio script >>
STUDENT'S BOOK **page 144**

> Diuretics / water pills, beta blockers, change to lifestyle

▷ 7.3 **4c** • Play the recording again and ask learners to complete the phrases taken from the dialogue.

> 1 you could consider   2 I'll outline
> 3 in turn   4 the following options
> 5 You could consider   6 Another option is taking

4d • Ask learners to work in pairs. They should look at the language for making suggestions and then take it in turns to outline the options available for treating hypertension.

Providing information on treatments (active listening, verbal communication)

Rationale: to identify language used for describing benefits and side effects of treatments

▷ 7.4 **5a** • Contextualise the dialogue: Tell learners they are going to listen to a doctor describing three possible treatments for hypertension (UK English). Tell learners to predict what treatments might be suggested. Play the recording.

Audio script >>
STUDENT'S BOOK **page 144**

> Diuratics, beta blockers and lifestyle changes

▷ 7.4 **5b** • Play the recording again and ask learners to note down the side effects or disadvantages of each treatment.

> **Side effects / Disadvantages**
> • Diuretics: frequent urination, weakness, fatigue, dizziness or muscle cramp
> • Beta blockers: nausea, dizziness, insomnia, depression or disorientation, and impotence
> • Changing lifestyle: keeping to a controlled eating and exercise plan; e.g. it can be difficult to cut out particular foods from the diet.

Explaining benefits and side effects of treatment (verbal communication)

Rationale: to develop language for describing benefits and side effects of treatment

6 • Ask learners to put the phrases under the appropriate heading.

> Benefits: 3, 6, 7, 10, 11
> Side effects: 2, 5, 8, 12
> Benefits and side effects: 1, 4, 9

Giving advice on lifestyle (verbal communication, active listening, cultural awareness)

Rationale: to practise the language of probability

▷ 7.5 **7a** • Contextualise the dialogue: Tell learners they are going to listen to the beginning of a dialogue where a doctor is advising a patient to give up something (US English). Play the recording.
• Ask learners to identify the reason why the patient says that he will find it difficult to do so.

Audio script >>
STUDENT'S BOOK **page 145**

> The patient has been smoking for a long time, and he is surrounded by people who smoke.

7b • Play the recording again and ask learners to complete the sentences.

> **1** I know, but **it's easier said than done.**
> **2** I understand that it's not easy, but **it's making your asthma worse.**

7c • **Suggestion:** Before learners read through the four treatments outlined for giving up cigarettes, ask them what treatments they are aware of and any benefits or side effects they know of.
> • Learners should now work in pairs and continue the dialogue they have just listened to by outlining the four treatments available. Each should take a turn at playing the role of the doctor. They should also use the language of probability.

Patient speak

Rationale: to recognise language used by patients to express probability

8 • Ask learners to put the ten phrases under the appropriate headings.

> Is unlikely to comply: 3, 5, 7, 10
> May comply: 1, 4, 9
> Likely to comply: 2, 6, 8

Negotiating treatment with a patient (active listening, verbal communication)

Rationale: to develop language for negotiating

7.6 **9a** • Contextualise the dialogue: Tell learners they will hear the doctor from the previous dialogue encouraging the patient to be involved in the treatment plan. Learners should identify what the patient decides to do. Play the recording.

Audio script >>
STUDENT'S BOOK **page 145**

> The patient decides not to try any of the options outlined by his doctor. He decides to use willpower.

7.6 **9b** • Play the recording again. Learners should fill in the missing words from the phrases they hear.

> **1** not really convinced   **2** How about
> **3** What's the least   **4** might be do-able
> **5** That sounds like   **6** So let's agree

9c • Learners should now practise saying the phrases aloud.

Communication Skills
• Point out to learners the importance of getting the patient to summarise what you have said. If patients are clear what is expected of them, there is a better chance of them following a plan of action.

10 • Ask learners to look at the language for *proposing* in the 'Language for negotiating treatment' box.
> • Learners should now incorporate this language into the role-play outlined.

Cultural awareness

Rationale: to develop awareness of the importance of possible cultural factors that may prevent a patient from breaking habits

11a • Ask learners to look at the two statements used by the patient in the dialogue and say how they would respond to these statements to show the patient that they acknowledge his/her situation.

> **Suggested answers**
> 1 I understand that having a few drinks with your friends is really important to you.
> 2 I can appreciate that it's going to be difficult making these changes.

11b • Ask learners to write examples of how they could respond to these statements, acknowledging the difficulty in giving up smoking.

Closing the interview (verbal communication, active listening)

Rationale: to raise awareness of stages that should be included when closing the interview

▷ 7.7 **12a** • Contextualise the dialogue: Tell learners they are going to listen to a doctor concluding the consultation from Exercise 3. The patient is a 50-year-old male, who has been advised to make changes to his lifestyle (UK English).

Audio script >>
STUDENT'S BOOK **page 145**

  • Ask learners to look at the stages outlined in the Calgary-Cambridge observation guide and tick the stages covered by the doctor in the dialogue. Play the recording.

> All the stages are covered.

12b • Learners should now look at the script for audio 7.7 on page 145 and underline any phrases that signal the closing of the interview.

> **Doctor** OK, just <u>to recap on what we have discussed</u>. [...] <u>You're are going to follow</u> the diet sheet for the next three weeks and then you'll come back and see me. You're also going to do 30 minutes exercise three times a week.
> **Patient** Yes – well, I'll give it a go, anyway.
> **Doctor** <u>Is there anybody who can give you support</u> if you're finding it difficult?
> **Patient** My wife will help if I explain why I'm doing this.
> **Doctor** That's good. <u>If you're having trouble</u> keeping to the diet <u>or you feel you need some support, you can phone me</u> at the following times during my telephone consultation hours.
> **Patient** OK, that's good to know.
> **Doctor** <u>Is there anything else you'd like to ask</u>?
> **Patient** No, it's clear what I have to do.

12c • Learners work in pairs and role-play the closing of the interview from Exercise 7. Encourage them to use as much of the language from audio 7.7 on page 145 as they can.

Out & About

Rationale: to develop awareness of how factors such as age, gender and socio-economic situation can affect attitudes to taking treatment or following advice

- **Suggestion:** Ask learners to present their findings in a mini-presentation.

Piecing it all together

Rationale: to provide an opportunity to practise the language covered in the unit

13 • Learners work in groups of three (doctor, patient and observer). Each person should play a different role so that learners all get the chance to play the different roles.
- Ask the person playing the role of the patient to comment on how they felt the doctor interacted with them before the observer gives their comments.
- Tell learners you will give them feedback on both positive and negative points of their verbal and non-verbal communication, their voice management, and their active listening skills.

Progress check

- Ask learners to go through the Progress check.
- Give learners some group feedback and indicate where they might need to improve.
- Give individual feedback to those who wish.

Recommended reading

- If you would like a little more information on this topic, we suggest you read the following:
  Marinker M and Shaw J. *Not to be taken as directed.* BMJ 2003; 326: 348–349.

Reading for discussion

- Go to page 154.

> **1** Not picking up on the rupture in the patient as it occurred.
> **2** The message from this consultation seems to be finding a balance between benefits and possible risks when explaining options for treatment.

DVD clip 5

- Go to page 166.

Unit 8 Dealing with sensitive issues

LEARNING OUTCOMES

At the end of this unit, learners will be able to:

- broach sensitive issues without bias and remain non-judgemental
- read and respond to patient cues
- employ question techniques for alcohol consumption: CAGE
- write concise and accurate notes
- update the patient note

Background

Sensitive issues

Issues that might be considered sensitive for some might seem fairly insignificant to others. Whether an issue is sensitive or not is highly subjective. The question *Are you married?*, for example, may seem fairly innocuous but could in fact constitute a potential minefield. Developing skills to enable doctors to broach sensitive issues in a manner that avoids offence and remains non-judgemental is vital if they are to succeed in taking a history of issues related to sex or reproduction, alcohol or substance abuse, etc.
Read through the table on page 78 of the Student's Book to give yourself a better idea of the type of question that could cause offence or appear judgemental – even if this is not the doctor's intention.

Sexual and reproductive health

This area of the history-taking process poses the most concern for both patient and doctor. However, it is essential that doctors acquire basic skills to enable them to do this in a way that causes the least amount of anxiety for the patient. Patients can so easily become inhibited and fail to raise their concerns, or even feel ridiculed or judged. Doctors on the other hand may feel a certain amount of embarrassment or even feel inadequately trained to deal with these issues. Doctors need to avoid making assumptions and instead challenge preconceived stereotypes and cultural differences. A doctor's own personal attitudes towards sexual practices and lifestyle could create communication barriers with the patient that need to be broken down.
Asking open questions (*what, where, when,* etc.) but avoiding questions that ask *why* can help the doctor avoid asking questions that are judgemental. At the end of the session, saying *If this does become a problem in the future, I would be happy to discuss it with you* leaves the door open for the patient to return.

Cues and responding to them

Cues are the verbal and non-verbal signs (facial expressions of anger, the clenched fist, sitting slouched in the chair, irritated tone of voice, etc.) we give out that indicate to another person what we are feeling, whether it be physically or emotionally. Quite often these betray our true feelings and emotions. What is important is that doctors are aware of the cues they give out and are able to read, interpret and respond appropriately to the cues of their patients. Emotional problems hinted at through non-verbal cues could in fact be the root cause of the patient's physical symptoms.
Read the text on page 80 of the Student's Book to gain a more in-depth understanding of this important aspect of communication.

Alcohol and substance (drug, glue, gas, etc.) abuse

A wide variety of physical symptoms could indicate alcohol abuse (e.g. abdominal pain, diarrhoea, vomiting in the morning) or drug abuse (e.g. impotence, menstrual disorders, diminished libido), as might a history of recurrent accidents. The patient's attitude (e.g. defensiveness, evasiveness and irritation), as well as certain social history issues (e.g. financial, legal and relationship problems), could also indicate alcohol or substance abuse, and a family history of alcoholism (in particular) is also a strong indicator of possible abuse. As such, a doctor needs to be constantly reading the clues.

However, while the symptoms may be fairly evident, a gradual approach to interviewing the patient will be required; most alcohol or substance abusers will be guarded or even in denial about their abuse. Familiarise yourself with the CAGE questionnaire on page 84 of the Student's Book, which is widely accepted as an effective model to enquire about alcohol abuse. Again, doctors need to remain non-judgemental and supportive to enable the patient to take the first steps in managing their abuse.

US versus UK English

UK	US
15/6/07, 15(th) June 2007	6/15/07, June 15, 2007
A&E	Emergency Room (ER)
barmaid (f) / barman (m)	bartender (m + f)
GP	family practitioner
lads (audio 8.6)	guys
mad (audio 8.6)	crazy
mates (audio 8.5)	buddies

UK	US
medication	medications
Mum (audio 8.7)	Mom
no allergies reported	denies allergies
(two) pints (audio 8.6)	(two) beers
pub	bar
spirits	liquor
STIs (Sexually Transmitted Infections) / STDs (Sexually Transmitted Diseases)	STDs (Sexually Transmitted Diseases)

Lead in

Rationale: to ascertain possible sensitive issues for both doctor and patient

a • Encourage learners to give examples they have come across, either in their own

> Any particular patient might consider any one of these issues sensitive, depending on that particular person. People's attitudes to different issues depend on background, religious or spiritual beliefs, the media, self-image, past experiences and social attitudes.

experience or among their peers and colleagues.

b • Refer learners back, if necessary, to Unit 4, where some of these issues were introduced.

Think about

Rationale: to assess learners' own skills at this stage, considering their own experience of broaching sensitive issues with a patient in English

1 • Some learners might not have experience of doing this in English; they should evaluate their current level of competence as they see it. It is a kind of self-assessment.

• Be aware that learners tend to overestimate their competency. Learners may also feel the way they approach sensitive issues is appropriate, but this may not be the case in reality.

Broaching sensitive issues (verbal and non-verbal communication, active listening, cultural awareness)

Rationale: to develop skills to enable learners to broach sensitive issues with their patient in a more effective manner that avoids offence and remains non-judgemental

Quotation (Dalton and Noble)
- Discuss the possible effects of the learners' initial assumptions on patients (1–3) in Exercise 2a. Ask your learners to elaborate on their responses.
- You may prefer to deal with this quotation after Exercise 2e instead, once your learners have had chance to work on this area a little longer.

2a
- Refer learners back to the article on cultural awareness on page 12 of the Student's Book. Ask them to read through the article again, pointing out the observation 'The potential for one person to inadvertently offend another is huge.'
- Ask learners to look at the pictures first and note assumptions a doctor might make about these patients, stressing that this is not necessarily their own opinion. Discourage learners from taking too much time over this; you want them to give an initial reaction.

Patient 1: Assumptions can be made about style of clothing and manner of the patient's appearance, relating to pre conceived ideas about particular social groups – e.g. the male gay community is known for being very fashion conscious.
Patient 2: May assume patient is already in a sexual relationship. Underage sex is common in the UK, with the highest rate of teenage pregnancies in Europe.
Patient 3: May assume patient has been attacked in some way: mugged, or abused by a carer, etc.

- Ask learners as a class to use their medical insight to brainstorm possible reasons for the visit of these three people to the doctor's surgery.

▶ 8.1 **2b**
- Contextualise the dialogue: Tell learners they are going to hear the patient's responses in each of these three consultations (UK English). Play the recording.

Audio script >>
STUDENT'S BOOK **page 145**

Patient 1: Needs proof of negative HIV test for immigration form to Australia.
Patient 2: Suffering from bad period pains.
Patient 3: Daughter concerned about his drinking.

2c
- **Suggestion:** Ask learners to close their books. Ask one learner to take the role of Patient 1 and another to take the role of the doctor, and read the response in Exercise 2c. Ask the class what assumption the doctor is making. Then ask in what situation the doctor might be justified in asking this. The answer is *none*.

▶ 8.2 **2d**

Of course. **Is there any particular reason** *you* **feel you need to have** *an HIV test?*

Audio script >>
STUDENT'S BOOK **page 145**

▶ 8.3 **2e**

Well, **if you start** *by telling me* **how you feel about your** *drinking …*

Audio script >>
STUDENT'S BOOK **page 145**

- Elicit the reason for this approach by asking what a doctor could ask the patient to ensure he/she obtained the patient's perspective of the situation. This is potentially a sensitive issue for the patient, and it is important for the doctor to establish his/her perspective on their alcohol consumption. This is also a non-judgemental question and as such all part of the patient-centred approach.
- Point out that this approach can be used to broach other potentially sensitive issues. Learners will have a chance to put this into practice a little later in the unit.

Language Note:

Emphasis

By using emphasis we are highlighting the most important word in the sentence.
In this case the word is *you,* as the doctor wishes to obtain the patient's perspective as opposed to giving his/her own opinion on the subject; the doctor wants to put the importance on what the patient has to say about the issue.

- **Suggestion:** Put the sentence *Well, if you start by telling me how you feel about your drinking...* on the board and ask learners to practise using the appropriate emphasis. Then ask what the effect is if the word <u>drinking</u> is emphasised. (The emphasis would be on the patient's alcohol consumption itself; the question would probably come across as judgemental.)

3a • **Suggestion:** Write the question 'Are you married?' on the board. Poll the group by asking how common a question this is in their culture. Then ask the group to brainstorm assumptions that might be made about the person by posing this question.
- Ask learners to read through the questions and the scenario in each case. Then go through question 3 as a class before telling learners to complete the rest of column three in the table.
- Be aware that learners are likely to find this task a little challenging and may need some guidance. (It is advisable for you to read through this table in detail before carrying out this activity in class.)

Question	Scenario	Problem with question	Improved question + rationale
1 a Are you married? **b** Are you gay?	Male/Female patient's first visit to GP	The doctor is making a judgement about the patient's sexual orientation and/or the nature of the patient's relationship by assuming the patient is married/gay.	*Are you currently in a relationship?* is a more appropriate question. Until the nature of the patient's relationship is established, doctors should refer to the patient's *partner* – a more neutral term. Also, a patient might not tell the doctor he/she is gay immediately – he/she might feel the need to gain some amount of trust in the doctor first. Patient might be in a heterosexual relationship, but not married – again, this version avoids any judgemental attitude about marriage. Avoid asking *Are you married?* Someone who is divorced, depending on the culture, might feel some stigma to this. Some may be married but separated – the doctor might need to establish this. A recent widow(er) might find the question distressing. The patient could also be bisexual, and there may at some point be a need to establish if this is the case: *Do you have sex with both men and women or just (wo)men?* This is a simple question that is not judgemental.
2 Don't you think your lifestyle is a little promiscuous?	During interview, patient divulges that he/she has several sexual partners	The doctor deems the patient's behaviour to be promiscuous.	*How do you feel about your lifestyle?* An open-ended question allows the patient to reflect and might divulge further information relative to the patient's situation. The doctor is not being judgemental of the patient's behaviour.
3 You've never had intercourse, have you?	Adult patient	Doctor assumes patient has never had intercourse.	*When was the last time you had intercourse?* (If it is reasonable to think that the patient is sexually active.) This is more positive – some adult patients may be sensitive about not having ever had intercourse. *Have you ever had sexual relations?* (If it is reasonable to think that the patient has never been sexually active.) Tag questions (see Unit 2) should be avoided, as they tend to lead the patient to a particular response.

4 Do you have a drink problem?	Patient has indicated a higher-than-average consumption of alcohol	Patient might perceive question as doctor's criticism of drinking habits.	*How do you feel about your drinking?* is a more open-ended question and takes the approach from the patient perspective first.
5 I take it your wife is aware of the situation?	Doctor knows the patient is married	Doctor assumes that the patient is only having sexual intercourse with his wife. There is also a judgemental edge to the question – *I take it ...* – assuming there is something wrong in his behaviour if he hasn't already spoken to his wife about the situation.	*Is there anyone else who needs to be aware of this situation?* The doctor cannot rule out the possibility that the patient is having extra-marital sexual relationship(s). This question also gives the chance for the patient to divulge the relevant information to the doctor, i.e. that his wife might also require treatment, etc.
6 Have you taken illegal drugs in the past?	Male/Female patient's first visit to GP	Emphasising the illegal nature of the patient's behaviour is judgemental – it is not the doctor's place to make that kind of judgement, even if it is, in effect, the case.	*Have you ever taken recreational drugs?* There may or may not be some indication in the encounter that this is an issue for a particular patient. The doctor, as part of the questions on lifestyle, has to ascertain whether or not the patient uses drugs. Although a little direct, the above question can be asked if this is the case (see later in unit).

3b • **Suggestion:** Ask the group to brainstorm an improved question for question 1 and a rationale for their choice, before getting them to complete the rest of column four of the table.

Note: it is very important that learners grasp the significance of this activity before continuing with the rest of the unit.

4 • Elicit the importance of context when broaching a potentially sensitive issue by asking learners how they feel if someone asks them a question about a sensitive topic without reason or without asking their permission. Then ask what the importance is of context when broaching a sensitive issue with a patient. (It enables the patient to better understand the reason behind the doctor's questioning, with the added bonus that the patient is then more likely to open up to the doctor, making it easier for the doctor to make an accurate diagnosis, and, in the long term, for the patient to comply with treatment, etc.)

5a • **Suggestion:** Ask two stronger learners to role-play the dialogue in front of the class. The rest of the class should have their books closed. Before the role-play begins, write up the questions in Exercise 5b on the board. Ask them to answer the questions.

5b

1 Insensitive and judgemental
2 Insensitively and dismissively
Often Dr Staples makes assumptions about the patient and his lifestyle, including in his initial question, where he automatically assumes the patient wants to discuss a sexual issue, simply because the patient looks nervous. Then at the end of the encounter, Dr Staples comes across as being disapproving of Mr Johnson's alcohol consumption, although his intention was probably simply to warn the patient of the dangers of alcohol.

• **Suggestion:** Ask learners to underline anything they feel could be considered inappropriate in Dr Staples' line of questioning.

Suggested answer

So there's something worrying you ... of a sexual nature, perhaps?
believe me, there's nothing I haven't heard already
And your wife's aware of the situation?
Ah, homosexual.
so you've had other partners, then?
Alcohol can lead to promiscuity.

• **Suggestion:** Elicit the effect of the phrase *There's nothing I haven't heard already*, by asking: *Imagine you are a patient. How would this response make you feel?*
(The doctor believes he is trying to encourage the patient to open up by minimising the symptoms and to reassure him by suggesting that nothing is new, shocking or unusual to him. Instead, the reverse is the case, and the doctor makes the patient feel he is 'just a number'; this is an impersonal approach.)

5c/d

Suggested answers

Dr Staples   There seems to be something worrying you, Mr Johnson.
Mr Johnson   [*Looks nervous, fiddling with a gold chain*]
Dr Staples   Take your time, Mr Johnson.
Mr Johnson   Right, well, it's a problem I'm having ... down there ... it's like herpes, well, I think that's what it is.
Dr Staples   I will need to ask you some personal questions, but first, I'd like to examine you. If you could just take off your trousers and underpants and pop up on the examination table. [*pause*] If you could get dressed now, thank you. [*once patient is dressed*] You were right in thinking it was herpes, what is known as herpes simplex. As I said, I'd like to ask you a few questions about your sex life, if you don't mind?

	Are you currently in a relationship?
Mr Johnson	Well, actually, I've been seeing someone new. My relationship's not that good at the moment ... I've been a little out of control recently ... had a couple of one-night stands with girls I met in the local bar.
Dr Staples	I see. And can I ask, when was the last time you had intercourse?
Mr Johnson	Just last night, I'd been drinking.
Dr Staples	Do you and your girlfriend currently have a sexual relationship?
Mr Johnson	Well, yes, off and on.
Dr Staples	And do you practise safe sex?
Mr Johnson	Not always ... well, not at all, in fact.
Dr Staples	I'd like to suggest you take a look at these leaflets on safe-sex practices ... and as you may be aware, herpes is contagious, so your girlfriend will need to be aware of the situation so that she can get herself checked out ...

- **Suggestion:** Ask two stronger learners to perform their role-play to the rest of the group. The group should stop the pair when the dialogue is not suitable, asking the pair to re-work it as necessary.

Quotation (Bickley)

- Ask the group to brainstorm possible reactions that might indicate boredom, embarrassment or disapproval.
- Check learners have understood the expression *to block communication*.
- Then ask to what extent they think this was true of Dr Staples' attitude.
- Tell learners they will now be looking at this in more detail.

Reading patient cues (active listening, verbal and non-verbal communication)

Rationale: to develop a greater awareness of patient cues and an understanding of the impact of these on the patient history

6a/b

1 Patient cues serve to indicate to the doctor any underlying concerns / the emotional aspects of the illness. They could be a short cut to the real/underlying issues for the patient, beyond the physical aspects of the illness.
2 Doctors are trained to listen for the physical aspects of the illness as opposed to the emotional. Doctors are often reluctant to deal with emotional aspects traditionally treated by counsellors or therapists.

6c

1 *Disease* refers to the purely medical aspect of what the patient is feeling, while *illness* is the impact of the illness on the patient's life as a whole.
2 Taking into consideration the doctors' own verbal and non-verbal messages is also important – sometimes more so – as patients don't ask for any confirmation of a doctor's feelings; i.e. they don't tend to check these verbally as a doctor might do with a patient, by asking clarifying questions such as *You sound stressed / You seem to be in disagreement with my analysis of the situation*, etc.
3 By asking clarifying questions, e.g. *You sound [stressed]. / You don't seem to agree with my analysis of the situation. / Your son looks a little unhappy/apprehensive about ...*

7a • Ask the group to give examples of their own experience of this.

7b/c • Point out that non-verbal cues often depend on personal traits, culture, age, gender, etc.

Out & About

Rationale: to further develop learners' knowledge of non-verbal cues within their working environment

Discussing sexual and reproductive health (verbal and non-verbal communication, active listening)

Rationale: to develop an effective means of communication that facilitates the most sensitive aspect of the patients encounter

• It is important to gauge your audience well during this section of the unit; you may find some individuals/groups more receptive to this particular topic area than others.

Think about

Rationale: to raise awareness and promote discussion of these issues within a multicultural context

8a • Depending on the dynamics of the class, you may wish to ask learners to share their thoughts in pairs before continuing with Exercise 8b.

8b • Be aware that the learner's own cultural background and beliefs may well play a strong role in the success of this activity; it is important to try and elicit as many of the points below as possible during the class discussion.

It's important to note that these will overlap.
• **The State:** In countries where there is a State religion, this would have repercussions on the legal requirements for doctors and the medical services.
In countries where there are unequal rights for women, doctors might be heavily influenced, and this may be reflected in their practice.
• **Religion:** See below
• **Media:** In countries where the media promote (actively or not) gay role models, for example openly gay TV presenters or actors etc., or allow access to discussion on these types of health issues via talk shows / e-forums, etc., the media could be said to have a particular influence on the way a doctor might think or how open he/she may be. Censorship in the media is still highly prevalent in some countries (linked to religion and State) in which case the opposite of the above might happen.
• **Professional training:** As a result of the State religion in those countries where doctors only treat patients of the same sex, these issues may be entirely new and could cause embarrassment (linked to State/religion). A predominantly Catholic country might hold certain attitudes towards certain sexual practices and reproductive health. The result of this may be that doctors may be required as part of their profession to give advice that might differ from that promoted within the UK/US medical services.

- **Family upbringing:** Regardless of national culture, the way a person is brought up and the values of the family may well differ and have a strong influence on a person's beliefs as an adult (possibly linked to religion), e.g. beliefs on traditional medicine, abortion rights, etc.

Quotation (Lloyd and Bor)
- Ask learners how easy or difficult they think it is to remain completely neutral in terms of body language when taking a sexual/reproductive health history.
- Brainstorm some possible advice for student doctors when learning to take a sexual or reproductive history.

▶ 8.4   **9a**

Audio script >>
STUDENT'S BOOK **page 145**

Dr Hanley remains objective and non-judgemental throughout the encounter, so should rate a score of 1 or 2.

9b

1 Dr Hanley uses the cone technique (as highlighted in Unit 2): beginning with open-ended questions before moving on to focused, closed questions. Dr Hanley tends to ask *when*, *how* and *where* questions.
2 *Why* questions might be perceived as being judgemental.

- **Suggestion:** Ask learners to imagine and then describe Sophie's non-verbal cues and what she is expressing by them; for example, puzzlement (furrowing of the brow when Dr Hanley announces he wants to ask some questions about her sex life), embarrassment (looking down at the floor / blushing), and slight annoyance (tone of voice in the sentence *Why would I be the only one with symptoms?*).

9c

1 There may be various reasons for your symptoms, but in order to find out more, I'm afraid I'm going to have to ask some rather personal questions.
2 Take your time, Jennifer, there's no rush. As I said, many people find this type of thing difficult to talk about.
3 Is that all right with you?
4 ... but if you'd prefer to speak to a female doctor, I can refer you to Dr Stevens.

Communication Skills
- Point this out to learners; they may find it useful.
- Ask learners the following questions: *How comfortable would you be admitting this to your patient? Have you ever admitted this to a patient? If so, how effective was it in building a more positive relationship with the patient?*
- Brainstorm possible alternatives to this sentence, e.g. *I sometimes find this topic difficult too. / I get a bit embarrassed about this kind of thing too.*

10a • Reassure learners that work covered in Units 1–4 should help them in compiling this set of questions.

Suggested answers

- Can you describe to me the symptoms you've been experiencing, Mr López?
- What seems to have brought on these symptoms?
- Is there anything that alleviates or worsens your symptoms?
- Could you tell me about any illnesses you might have had in the past?
- Any surgical interventions or hospitalisations I might need to know about?
- Do you take any medication(s)?
- Have you ever suffered from allergies to medication at all?
- Could you tell me about any illnesses that might run in your family?
- Tell me about your parents.
- Any siblings?
- Are you currently in a relationship?
- Are you working at the moment?
- Do you smoke?
- Do you drink alcohol?
- How much do you drink in an average week?
- I'm going to ask you some questions regarding your personal life, in particular your sex life, that some people find a little sensitive.
- When was the last time you had sexual intercourse?
- How regularly do you have intercourse?
- Are there any questions you would like to ask at this stage?
- I'm going to refer you to a urologist at the hospital. She's a woman, but if you'd prefer to speak to a male doctor, I can refer you to another hospital.

10b • **Suggestion:** Put up a couple of points from the table in Exercise 11a to guide learners in terms of their feedback to their partner. Don't give them all the points – you will be asking learners to give more examples later in the unit.

Quotation (Enelow et al.)

- Ask learners if they agree or disagree with this quotation and why (not).

11a • Point out that the aim of this activity is to consolidate what has been covered earlier in the unit. Learners should now have had sufficient exposure to be able to come up with most of these as a group.
- Encourage learners to compile the list of Dos and Don'ts in a table form for easy reference later on.

Do ...	Don't ...
Do contextualise the questions. Do use clear, unambiguous, open-ended questions. Do start with a general, non-threatening question. Do address relationships. Do discuss sexual behaviour by asking *how/ what/where*. Do ask direct questions (once rapport is established with patient). Do ask about sexual partners. Do establish patient knowledge about safe-sex practices (and lead into education). Do use the patient's words and language. Do remain professional. Do ask when you don't understand a sexual term or activity.	Don't make assumptions. Don't stereotype. Don't judge people. Don't use the question word *why* – it can be judgemental.

Alcohol use and abuse

Rationale: to open up discussion about alcohol consumption

12a • Learners will bring their medical knowledge to this task in order to complete the questionnaire.

1 1 unit = 10g alcohol

2 a 21 units   **b** 14 units

3 a, b, c 1 unit
  d 6–7 units
  e 32 units

4 Yes. Home-brewed beer often contains higher levels of alcohol, and certain brands of shop-bought beer are stronger than others, e.g. *Special Brew* (a brand of lager popular in the UK) has four times the level of alcohol than standard beer.

5 b (The time in which it takes the patient to consume the bottle gives doctors a more accurate idea about the possible degree of alcoholism.)

6 a (By up to 100%)

7 Armed forces, doctors, entertainment industry, publicans

12c

1 Invariably, doctors are presented with a complication of a patient's alcohol abuse, as opposed to a patient who admits he/she has a problem with alcohol. Possible complications are numerous, including: fits, falls/trauma (broken ribs, head injuries, etc.), road traffic accidents (driving under the influence of alcohol), acute pancreatitis, liver disease, pulmonary tuberculosis, chest infections, etc.

2 The time of day the patient drinks / drink pattern / whether the patient drinks alone or socially / whether the patient drinks pub or home measures / type of particular alcohol consumed / patient attitude and intentions towards alcohol / past history of related disorders + past treatment / the patient's social circumstances and family history (There is a predisposition for alcoholism if it is already present within the patient's family, especially amongst first-degree relatives (parents).)

- **Suggestion:** Ask learners to compare their thoughts about accepted levels of alcohol consumption in their country of origin as well as their thoughts on those in Ireland and the UK, as identified in the questionnaire.

Asking about substance abuse (verbal and non-verbal communication, active listening)

Rationale: to develop the use of an effective questioning technique when asking about alcohol and substance abuse

▶ 8.5 **13a** • Contextualise the dialogue: Tell learners they are going to hear Part 1 of an encounter between the patient, Dave Mullins, and his GP (UK English). Play the recording.

Audio script >>
STUDENT'S BOOK **page 146**

> From the response Dave gives in Part 1 of the dialogue, he appears to be a 'social drinker' and therefore his drinking habits are not of much concern. However, this could also be a mask, as we see in Part 2. Dave is able in Part 1 to give the 'right' responses that mask the real issue.

▶ 8.6 **13b** • Encourage learners to discuss the reasons for their decision to interview the patient further (or not) in small groups. Play the recording.
- Note there is no right or wrong answer for this – learners will use their medical knowledge to guide them in their answer.

Audio script >>
STUDENT'S BOOK **page 146**

▶ 8.7 **13c/d**

Audio script >>
STUDENT'S BOOK **page 146**

		Question	
C	Cut down	Have you ever felt the need to cut down on your drinking?	Yes (previously but not now)
A	Annoyed	Have people ever annoyed you by criticising your drinking?	Yes (girlfriend regularly gets annoyed)
G	Guilty	Have you ever felt guilty about your drinking?	Yes (missed his mum's birthday)
E	Eye opener	Have you ever needed an 'eye opener' first thing in the morning?	No (doesn't feel he's quite hit that level)

- **Suggestion:** Ask the group if they have ever used the CAGE technique and how successful it was in obtaining an accurate history for alcohol abuse. Then ask learners to discuss the methods used in their countries to ask about alcohol abuse. Ask how successful these methods are for obtaining an accurate history.

Language Note:

Auxiliaries *can* and *do*
The use of *do* in the question may create a defensive reaction and an unnecessary power struggle between doctor and patient.
Can implies a positive ability and creates a kind of alliance between doctor and patient. Therefore the doctor is able to gain the patient's confidence and is more likely to get a positive response.

13f

No, the response would probably be different. *How much do you drink?* implies there is a problem and suggests the doctor is being judgemental; the patient is likely to become defensive, which is fairly typical amongst alcoholics.

13g

Two or more positive responses on the CAGE questionnaire are said to indicate problem drinkers. Four positive responses are a definite sign of alcoholism.

Patient's feelings towards drink: Dave feels his current level of alcohol intake is fine and is not outwardly concerned about it.

His interpersonal relationships: Dave does mention his girlfriend 'might have a point'.

What happens while under the influence of alcohol: This has not yet been investigated/discussed, but Dave indicates that drinking spirits can change his personality negatively.

Any adverse effects the patient may suffer: This has not yet been investigated/ discussed, apart from the reference to missing his mother's birthday.

- **Suggestion:** Ask learners to discuss in small groups and decide how they would proceed in the treatment of this patient – that is, how they would investigate Dave's consumption in more detail and have a clearer understanding of the above points. For this, there are other question techniques (acronyms) which can be used:

'BUMP'

Black out: Have you ever had black-outs?

Unplanned: Have you ever used alcohol in an unplanned way (drunk more than you intended)?

Medicinal: Do you ever drink alcohol for medicinal reasons (cure for anxiety, the shakes)?

Protect: Do you find yourself protecting your supply of alcohol (buying enough, just in case)?

The 'FATAL DT' questions

Is there a **F**amily history of alcohol problems?

Have you ever been a member of **A**A?

Do you **T**hink you are an alcoholic?

Have you ever **A**ttempted or had thoughts of suicide?

Have you ever had any **L**egal problems related to alcohol consumption?

Do you ever **D**rive while intoxicated?

Do you ever use **T**ranquillisers to steady your nerves?

You might also decide to advise Dave Mullins on his level of consumption and indicate where and how he might be able to get help / refer him to the local chapter of Alcoholics Anonymous / give him educational materials on the subject of alcohol abuse, etc.

Patient speak

Rationale: to develop awareness of jargon commonly employed by drug users

14 • Refer learners to the appropriate pages of the Student's Book.
   • Point out the following to the group:
      • The term *junkie* originally referred specifically to someone addicted to heroin but now has a wider meaning referring to someone addicted to any kind of narcotic.
      • A *stash* also refers to the drugs in someone's possession, e.g. *The police took my stash.*

15

Language used to describe negative effects	Language used to describe positive effects
bombed	on a high
come down	spaced out
crash	stoned
have a bad trip	wasted
have the shakes	wrecked

Out & About

Rationale: to further develop learners' knowledge of jargon used within the drug culture

• Suggest possible sources of input for this activity: visual media, modern literature, etc.

16

All mean to give up drugs without any form of treatment, e.g. course of methadone, etc.

• Elicit the meaning of the expression 'cold turkey', by asking learners if they have any colloquial expressions in their language for the period of time when the patient is withdrawing from heroin. Ask if they can describe the patient's skin when they are withdrawing from heroin. (Cold turkey refers to the period of time when the patient has stopped taking heroin but is suffering the effects of the withdrawal from the drug. The patient's skin during this time resembles that of a bald turkey.)

17

A good knowledge of the jargon will help to engage with the patient and increase communication in what might be a tense and sensitive encounter. Asking the patient to repeat or explain his/her chosen form of expression might lead to unnecessary aggressive behaviour, etc.

Updating the patient note (written communication)

Rationale: to encourage accurate and concise note-taking in English

18a • **Suggestion:** Before carrying out the task, ask learners to rate their ability to write concise and accurate patient notes (as for a 'Think about').

• **Suggestion:** Write 'Both right and left ears are clear' on the board and ask the group how they could improve this entry, or why this entry might not be considered concise.

1 Both ~~right and left~~ ears are clear.
(The word *both* is sufficient to mean *left* and *right*.)

2 Cervix is pink ~~in colour~~ and smooth.
(*Pink* is obviously the colour and so superfluous.)

3 Liver is tender ~~to palpation~~.
(It is assumed the doctor palpated the liver area in order to determine it is tender.)

4 ~~Patient states there is~~ no pain over left eye.
(The reader assumes the patient is the source of information unless otherwise stated, so it is not necessary to indicate this.)

5 ~~On sight~~, patient is thin, looks distressed and generally unwell.
(As the doctor is observing the patient, it is not necessary to reiterate the fact – use of *on sight* is superfluous.)

6 Father died in 1999, aged 64. ~~He died~~ of lung cancer.
(The year of the father's death is less important than what he died of and at what age.)

7 ~~In the patient, there is~~ no history of asthma or tuberculosis exposure.
(It is taken for granted the doctor is referring to the patient.)

8 Sexual history: ~~this is~~ not appropriate ~~to the presenting complaint~~.
(It is sufficient to note that sexual history is not appropriate – it is taken as read that the doctor is referring to this particular presenting complaint.)

9 Lungs are resonant ~~to percussion~~.
(As for sentence 3.)

10 II/VI systolic ejection murmur (~~audible~~).
(A murmur is always audible, so doesn't add anything to the meaning of the entry.)

Quotation (Bickley)

• Ask the group to share examples of inappropriate entries they may have come across in their work and/or studies (possibly as case studies).

19a
This is a subjective observation of the patient's health and criticism of the patient's attitude and is therefore unprofessional, not objective, and judgemental.

19b
Patient records can be viewed by both patients and lawyers. It may be difficult to defend this type of entry in a court of law.

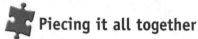

Piecing it all together

20a–d
- Encourage learners to develop their characters, noting down important points if necessary, before carrying out the role-play.
- Tell learners you will be giving feedback to them on both positive and negative points of their verbal and non-verbal communication, their voice management and their active listening skills.

Progress check

- Ask learners to go through the Progress check.
- Give learners some group feedback and indicate where they might need to improve.
- Propose individual feedback to those who wish.

Recommended reading

- If you would like a little more information on this topic, we suggest you read the following:

  Lloyd M and Bor R. *Communication Skills for Medicine.* London: Churchill Livingstone, 2004 (73–84)

  Dalton H and Noble S. *Communication Skills for Final MB: A Guide to Success in the OSCE.* London: Churchill Livingstone, 2005 (174)

Reading for discussion

- Go to page 155.

Unit 9 Breaking bad news

LEARNING OUTCOMES

At the end of this unit, learners will be able to:

- deliver bad news in a sensitive way
- reassure a patient or relative
- show empathy

DVD clip 6

Background

Breaking bad news is a skill which doctors perceive as a very important part of their role. Bad news is anything which changes the recipient's view of the future in a negative way, and examples range from bereavement to loss of a favourite pastime. Doctors acknowledge they have difficulty in this area and for this reason the unit is designed in line with best medical practice in breaking bad news.

SPIKES Model

The SPIKES model was developed to facilitate healthcare staff working with cancer patients in breaking bad news. However, it can be used as a tool to evaluate technique in delivering all types of bad news. The unit covers each of the elements in turn, providing appropriate language and activities.

Setting

Setting covers the physical location in which the news is delivered, and placement of furniture and body language need to be taken into account. Much of this should be familiar to students from earlier units.

Perception

Perception relates to what patients already know about a topic, and it is important for the doctor to determine the extent of a patient's existing knowledge and any misconceptions they may have. Unless a doctor has this information, it is difficult to judge the effect the news will have on them and whether they have understood it correctly. This section looks at ways of doing this and the appropriate language to make it possible.

Invitation

Invitation involves determining how much information the patient wants to receive and in how much detail. Not all patients will want the full picture. This section looks at various ways of determining this and appropriate ways of modifying language.

Giving Knowledge and Information

Giving Knowledge and Information is at the core of breaking bad news, and this section looks at ways of preparing the patient for what is to come and for ways of softening the language which is used to deliver the bad news. There is an opportunity for students to practise this so that they become more familiar with various permutations of the language.

Empathy

Empathy is perhaps one of the most difficult areas to teach, but it is also one of the most important areas to be aware of in breaking bad news. A wide range of language is presented and students have a range of exercises to help them to express empathy in various situations. The reading in the unit and linked activities will also help.

Strategy and Summarising

Strategy and Summarising covers the end stage of the consultation, where the doctor summarises what has happened in the session and discusses plans for moving forward. While some of the language in this stage will be appropriate for all patient interviews, additional language is introduced and there are opportunities for students to practise.

US versus UK English

UK	US
catches my chest (audio 9.2)	makes me short of breath
Down's Syndrome	Down Syndrome

Lead in

Rationale: to consider factors that can make it difficult to break bad news; this could be in a non-medical context for those learners who haven't yet worked as doctors

- Ask learners to discuss the question in small groups.

> **Suggested answer**
> Awareness that you are causing others to be disappointed or emotionally distressed.

1a • Ask learners to write a brief definition of 'bad news'. The important point to remember is to focus on how a patient may feel after receiving the news, rather than on the event itself.

1b • Ask learners to compare their definition with the quotation given.
- This quotation highlights the importance of seeing things from a patient's perspective. A doctor might give a patient news that may not seem to be bad from the doctor's perspective, e.g. telling a patient that he/she won't be able to participate in an event he/she had trained for because of a muscular injury. However, to the patient, this could be very upsetting news.

2 • Ask learners to read the examples of where a doctor has to break bad news to a patient or relatives. With a partner, learners should rate the events in order of difficulty (1= most difficult, 6= least difficult).

3 • Ask learners to discuss what makes some bad news more difficult to break.

> **Suggested answers**
> - Fear of being blamed by patients
> - Fear of not having answers to all the questions a patient may ask
> - Fear of inflicting pain on the patient
> - Doctor's own fear of illness and death
> - Lack of time to deliver the news
> - Awareness of lack of training in breaking bad news
> - Difficulty in deciding which doctor is responsible for delivering the bad news

- **Suggestion:** You could open the discussion up to a group discussion and invite learners to give specific examples from their own experience.

Preparing the patient for bad news (active listening, verbal communication)

Rationale: to provide learners with a model for breaking bad news; SPIKES is an acronym (see page 88 of the Student's Book) for key stages that should be included when breaking bad news

4a • Ask learners to come up with two factors that are important to consider when breaking bad news.

- Ask learners to refer to the SPIKES model again to check their answers and to check if the factors they came up with are included.

▶ 9.1   **4b** • Contextualise the dialogue: Tell learners they are going to listen to a doctor breaking bad news in a hospital setting (UK English). This is an awareness-raising exercise. Ask learners to note down three ways in which the doctor could improve his communication technique. Play the recording.

Audio script >>

STUDENT'S BOOK **page 146**

5a • Tell learners to read the key stages outlined in the SPIKES model for giving bad news.

▶ 9.1   **5b** • Tell learners they are going to listen to audio 9.1 again. Ask learners to identify which of the elements of SPIKES are included in the strategy.

6 • Based on what learners have already learned about communication so far during the course, ask them to discuss in small groups the ideal setting to break bad news.

7 • Ask learners to discuss the three questions in small groups.

Patient speak

Rationale: to expose learners to language commonly used by patients in response to the question *What is your understanding of the situation at this stage?*

8 • Ask learners to put the phrases under the three headings provided.

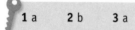

1 b   **2** c   **3** c   **4** a   **5** b   **6** b   **7** a   **8** b   **9** b   **10** c

9 • Doctors need to remember that each patient is individual, and it is important to find out how much information a particular patient wants to receive.
   • Ask learners to discuss the two questions in small groups and give specific examples. Make a note of any differences that seem to be culture-bound.

2 Age, mental health, emotional state, level of education

Softening the question (verbal communication)

Rationale: to give learners the opportunity to practise changing direct questions to indirect, or softer, ones

10a • Ask learners to look at the three questions and ask them to identify in each case which form is the softer form.

1 a   **2** b   **3** a

10b • Ask learners to discuss the difference in the language used for direct and indirect questions.

The present tense is used in the examples that are more direct. The use of the conditional makes the question softer.

Giving knowledge and information (active listening, verbal communication)

Rationale: to develop language skills for signalling to patients that bad news is coming

   • It is important that a doctor uses language to signal to the patient that bad news is to follow.

Language Note:

Structuring information

It is important for doctors to give information in manageable chunks, especially when giving bad news, as the patient or relative is likely to be in shock. The phrases below help to structure information and, if used with appropriate pausing, should give the listener time to take in what is being said:

Let me explain what has happened.
This was due to ...
This means that ...
What we need to do now is ...
After, ...

▶ 9.2 **11a** • Contextualise the dialogue: Tell learners they are going to listen to a dialogue between a doctor and a patient who is about to receive bad news (UK English). Ask learners if this is the patient's first visit to the doctor. Play the recording.

Audio script >>
STUDENT'S BOOK **page 146**

No, it isn't. The doctor refers to his previous visit.

▶ 9.2 **11b** ● Play the recording again and ask learners to complete what the doctor says to prepare the patient for bad news.

> The results are back. **I was hoping to have better news for you**, but **I'm afraid** that they were positive for HIV.

12
> **Suggested answers**
> I'm sorry to say that ...
> I'm sorry to have to tell you that ...
> Unfortunately, ...
> It's not as good as we had hoped.
> It's not the result we were hoping for.

13 ● Learners should now work in pairs and role-play the two scenarios.
● Ask learners to focus on the language needed to elicit the patient's existing knowledge and the amount of information the patient needs.
● The person playing the role of the patient should comment on how well the doctor treated him/her as an individual.

Dealing with emotions (verbal communication, active listening)

Rationale: to develop communication skills to express empathetic, exploratory and validating language

14a ● Ask learners to read through the examples of empathetic, exploratory and validating language.

▶ 9.3 **14b** ● Tell learners they are going to listen to six sentences which are examples of either empathetic, exploratory or validating language (UK English).
● Ask learners to put the examples of empathetic, exploratory and validating language under the appropriate heading. Play the recording.

Audio script >>
STUDENT'S BOOK **page 146**

> **1** c **2** a **3** b **4** a **5** b **6** c

▶ 9.3 **14c** ● Play the recording again and ask learners to note down the words the doctor stresses and where he pauses.

> **1** It's only <u>normal</u> to <u>feel</u> like that.
> **2** <u>How</u> does that make you <u>feel</u>?
> **3** I <u>know</u> this is <u>not</u> good <u>news</u> for you.
> **4** Can you <u>tell</u> me what you're <u>worried</u> about?
> **5** I <u>know</u> this must be very <u>hard</u> for you.
> **6** <u>Anybody</u> would react in the same <u>way</u>.

▶ 9.4 **15a** ● Contextualise the dialogue: Tell learners they are going to listen to the continuation of the dialogue between the doctor and the patient who has been diagnosed HIV positive (UK English). This is a continuation of the dialogue in audio 9.2 (Exercise 11).
● Learners underline examples of exploratory, empathetic and validating language in the audio script. Play the recording.

Audio script >>
STUDENT'S BOOK **page 146**

> **Exploratory:** Can you tell me how you're feeling, James?
> **Empathetic:** I can understand that.
> **Validating:** It's only natural that you feel scared. / I realise how difficult it must be for you to ask that question.

15b • Ask learners to come up with two other phrases they could say to a patient to show their support. Refer learners to the example provided.

> **Suggested answers**
> So, let's see how we can go forward from here.
> You won't be left to cope on your own.

▷ 9.4 **15c** • Play the recording again and ask learners to identify the phrases the doctor uses to reassure the patient that he will not be left to cope on his own.

> *I could arrange an appointment with our counsellor here, if you'd like to talk to somebody else?*

Agreeing strategy and summarising (verbal communication, active listening)

Rationale: to identify key words for outlining a plan of action and summarising

• Explain to learners the importance of giving patients a plan for the future and of summarising what has been discussed in the consultation.

▷ 9.5 **16** • Contextualise the dialogue: Tell learners they are going to listen to the final part of the conversation in Exercise 15.

Audio script >>
STUDENT'S BOOK **page 147**

   • Learners should answer the two questions. Play the recording.

> **1** Yes. He says they will discuss options in the next consultation.
> **2** Yes. He says he will make an appointment with the counsellor.

Case study: disregarding a constraint (active listening)

Rationale: to get learners to think about the importance of listening

17a • Ask learners to read the article and identify the constraint.

> The constraint is time.

   • Learners should then discuss the issue of time. Should doctors interrupt or allow patients to talk for as long as they want?

   • Invite learners to share any experiences they know of where doctors have deviated from the standard models and to explain the context.

Patient speak

Rationale: to expose learners to the language used by patients to talk about probability of recovering

18

> **1** c/b   **2** b/c   **3** a   **4** e   **5** d

19a • Ask learners to put the phrases listed into the correct category (Not going to recover / Some hope of recovery).

Not going to recover	Some hope of recovery
2, 4, 6, 8, 10, 11, 13, 14	1, 3, 5, 7, 9, 12

19b • Ask learners why they think patients use this kind of language.

To avoid talking directly about death and dying.

19c • Ask learners if they have expressions in their own language for dying which are expressed in a less direct way.

Communicating with relatives (verbal communication, voice management)

Rationale: to get learners to think about factors they need to consider when breaking bad news to relatives

Think about

Rationale: to consider factors that need to be taken into account when communicating with relatives

• Ask learners to suggest factors that they need to consider when breaking bad news to relatives.

Factors to be considered when communicating with relatives:
• no previous contact, therefore no existing rapport
• relatives may not understand fully the condition and the implications
• differences of opinion between relatives
• relatives may have different understandings of the patient's wishes

• Now ask learners to think about the context of breaking bad news over the phone. Ask them in what ways breaking bad news over the phone is different to doing it face-to-face.

Things to consider when communicating over the phone:
• can't read body language cues
• no time to prepare the listener – the call could come out of the blue
• voice management – pausing to give listener time to take in news, using a reassuring tone of voice, checking that the listener has a clear understanding of the situation

20 • **Suggestion:** Before learners look at the table, ask them to consider which aspects of voice are important for giving bad news. (Pausing to give listener time to take in news, using a reasuring tone of voice, stressing key words.)

• The SPIKES model can also be used for breaking bad news to relatives. In this recording, the doctor in the previous telephone conversation is now talking face-to-face with the relative. As learners listen, ask them to tick any of the stages he covers in SPIKES. Play the recording.

Setting	✓ Moves to quiet room.
Perception of the situation	Doctor does not give relative an opportunity to express her perception of the situation.
Invitation	✓ Doctor does not invite relative to indicate level of information required initially. However, towards the end, he does ask if any more information is required.
Knowledge/ information to relative	✓ Doctor does give information regarding condition and likely prognosis.
Emotions	✓ Doctor is empathetic – *I can see this is a terrible shock for you* – and validating – *It's normal to feel guilty in a case like this, but you mustn't.*
Strategy for moving on	✓ Doctor indicates that there will be further consultation when all family members are present.

▶ 9.7 **21** • Contextualise the dialogue: Tell learners they are going to listen to a dialogue between a relative and a doctor. The relative's mother has just been admitted to hospital (UK English).

Audio script >>
STUDENT'S BOOK **page 147**

• As learners listen, they should rate the doctor's voice management for each of the criteria given. Play the recording.

	excellent	good	could improve
tone	✓		
intonation	✓		
pausing			✓
speed of delivery			✓
word stress	✓		

22 • Learners should now take it in turns to play the role of the doctor. Tell learners to pay particular attention to the way they manage their voice.

Cultural awareness

Rationale: to develop awareness of cultural differences in the way bad news is given

• Ask learners to discus s the issue of telling relatives bad news about a patient before informing the patient.

Out & About

Rationale: to get learners to think about barriers to communicating bad news to patients/relatives

Piecing it all together

Rationale: to give learners the opportunity to practise all the stages of the SPIKES model

23 • Learners work in groups of three (doctor, patient and observer). Each person plays a different role and should get the chance to play each role in turn.
• Ask the patient in each case to give feedback on the doctor's performance; they should then compare their feedback with the observer.
• Tell learners you will give them feedback on both positive and negative points of their verbal and non-verbal communication, their voice management, and their active listening skills.

Progress check

• Ask learners to go through the Progress check.
• Give learners some group feedback and indicate where they might need to improve.
• Give individual feedback to those who wish.

Recommended reading

• If you would like a little more information on this topic, we suggest you read the following:
Baile WF, Buckman R, Lenzi R, Glober G, Beale EA, & Kudelka AP. *SPIKES – A six step protocol for delivering bad news: application to the patient with cancer.* Oncologist 2000; 5, 4: 302–311.

Reading for discussion

• Go to page 156.

> **1** She was a statistical abnormality in terms of surviving very malignant brain cancer.
> **2** Because she had already lived twice as long as she should have if the original diagnosis had been correct; it is unlikely that she would put much faith in the revised diagnosis.

DVD clip 6

• Go to page 168.

Unit 10 Communicating with challenging patients

LEARNING OUTCOMES

At the end of this unit, learners will be able to:

- encourage a withdrawn patient to speak
- calm an aggressive or angry patient
- assert their role as a doctor

DVD clip 7

Background

Given the considerable time constraints doctors are under with each patient interview, it is important that doctors are able to deal effectively with those patients who present challenges. Patients may be challenging for a variety of reasons, such as stress, anxiety, depression, and alcohol or drug dependency, so it is important to understand why a patient is behaving in a particular way.

Encouraging an uncommunicative patient to speak

One of the most significant communication challenges which a doctor can face is dealing with patients who speak only in monosyllables or refuse to speak completely. This section explores the use of closed questions and appropriate language to help structure a communication with a patient of this type. Questions are used to help learners understand the context of exchanges of this type and to help them develop fluency.

Calming an angry or aggressive patient

Doctors increasingly have to deal with angry and aggressive patients and do so in a time-effective way which minimises disruption. Whether anger and aggression in patients results from perceived difficulties with the service they are receiving, or from other unrelated issues, doctors need skills to try to normalise situations in which patients are angry or behave aggressively.

Asserting yourself with a manipulative patient

Many patients will attempt to manipulate their doctor in order to get what they want, if for any reason the doctor is not prepared to provide it. This can be a sick note, a renewal of or increase in a drug prescription, or a test to further explore symptoms. This section looks at ways of recognising a manipulative patient and strategies for countering this and normalising the interview.

US versus UK English

UK	US
bad chest	cough
cut up (about)	upset (about)
het up	worked up / emotional
post-natal	post-partum
(You've got to) up my prescription	(You've got to) give me stronger stuff

Lead in

Rationale: to make learners aware that it is not always possible to please all patients

- Ask learners to read the quotation.
- Ask learners as a class to identify patient types that may be difficult to warm to. They should justify their answers.

1 • Ask learners to look at the list of patient types described by Ford. Ask them how their list compares to Ford's.

   • **Suggestion:** You could also ask learners individually to rank which of these patient types would present the greatest and least challenge to them, explaining their reasons.

Communicating with an uncommunicative patient (verbal communication, active listening, voice management)

Rationale: to identify reasons why a patient may be uncommunicative and to think about communication strategies to overcome this barrier

2 • Ask learners to suggest reasons why a patient may be uncommunicative. Now ask learners to come up with two strategies they would use to draw out an uncommunicative person/patient.

> A patient might be uncommunicative because he/she is very shy, depressed, embarrassed or in pain. The following strategies may be effective: using gentle tone of voice, giving patient your full attention, giving patient time to respond.

10.1 **3a** • Contextualise the dialogue: Tell learners they are going to listen to a doctor talking to an uncommunicative patient (UK English).

   • Ask learners to listen to audio 10.1 and identify two strategies that the doctor uses to draw the patient out. Play the recording.

Audio script >>
STUDENT'S BOOK **page 147**

> He uses closed questions and facilitative language before he moves on to the next question; he shows empathy and paraphrases what the patient says: *You're worried that if you don't stay strong for the family, things will fall apart?*

   • Point out to learners that, while open questions are often used at the beginning of an interview, this technique may not be appropriate for patients who find it difficult to express themselves. In this case, patients may find it easier to respond to closed questions.

10.1 **3b** • Ask learners to listen again and this time focus on the doctor's voice, identifying two aspects of the voice that help to draw the patient out.

> The doctor pauses, uses a gentle tone of voice, and speaks quite slowly to mirror the patient's voice.

3c • Ask learners to read the transcript to the recording they have just listened to. They should underline any examples of closed questions and then comment on how effective they are in getting a response from the patient.

> The doctor uses closed questions to encourage the patient to respond more fully. The patient is depressed and doesn't respond to the open question at the beginning.
> **Doctor** Tell me, Mary, how are you feeling at the moment?
> **Patient** [*her eyes fill with tears*]
> **Doctor** [*brief silence*] <u>This is very difficult for you to talk about, isn't it?</u>
> **Patient** Yes. [*shaky voice*]
> **Doctor** <u>Are you still getting the headaches?</u>
> **Patient** Yes.

Doctor	And do the painkillers I prescribed help? [*pause*] Have you been taking them, Mary?
Patient	A couple of times, but they knock me out. I can't function properly with them. And I need to look after the family – they need me.
Doctor	I know. You have a lot on your plate at the moment, don't you? Nursing your husband, taking care of the children and looking after your mother. [*pause*]
Patient	Yes, I feel overwhelmed. [*patient begins to cry*] I'm sorry, Doctor.
Doctor	You don't need to apologise, Mary. It's perfectly normal to cry. I understand how you're feeling. You're worried that if you don't stay strong for the family, things will fall apart, aren't you?
Patient	Yes. I can't let that happen.

3d • Ask learners to highlight examples of facilitative language that the doctor uses which encourages the patient to tell her story.

> He uses closed questions appropriately, he uses silence and empathy, and he paraphrases what the patient says (e.g. *You're worried that if you don't stay strong for the family, things will fall apart*) to show understanding.

Language Note:

Indirect language

Using indirect language invites the listener to explain how they are actually feeling. Examples include:

You seem to be a little low in yourself. *You look as if ...*
You appear to be ... *Have you thought you might be a bit depressed?*

4a • The focus of this section is to give learners practice at changing open questions to closed questions. Ask learners to read the dialogue.

4b • Working in pairs, ask learners, where appropriate, to change open questions to closed questions. They should also add examples of facilitative language to encourage the patient to tell her story.

Doctor	So, Mrs Lyons, tell me, what can I do for you?
Patient	[*no response, patient stares at the floor and looks very unhappy*]
Doctor	You look very sad, Mrs Lyons. Are you finding it difficult to cope?
Patient	[*nods her head*]
Doctor	Do you have any help?
Patient	No.
Doctor	That must be very difficult for you. This is a big change in your life, and it's normal to feel overwhelmed, especially if you don't have any support. But I'm here to help you.

4c • Now ask learners to practise their amended version with their partner. They should take it in turns playing the doctor. Remind learners to focus not only on what they are saying, but how they are saying it and their body language.

Communication Skills

• Refer learners to the Communication Skills box to show other strategies for working with depressed patients.

Reading and responding to body language (verbal and non-verbal communication)

Rationale: to develop elicitation skills for drawing out an uncommunicative patient

5 • Ask learners to write down two aspects of body language that might indicate that a patient is uncommunicative.

> **Suggested answers**
>
> Staring into space, avoiding eye contact, looking at the floor

6 • Ask learners to look at the questions a doctor might ask a patient who is having difficulty expressing themselves. They should match the questions with the appropriate headings.

> **Asking why patient is withdrawn**
> 1 Can I ask what you are thinking?
> 2 What's on your mind?
> 3 You seem very distant – why is that?
> 4 You seem very far away ...
> **Encouraging patient who is trying to express themselves**
> 1 I can see that you want to say something ...
> 2 You were going to say something then?
> 3 You look as if you were about to say something?
> **Responding to strong physical signs**
> 1 I can see you are trembling – are you very anxious?
> 2 You look as if you are about to cry – are you very upset?
> **Asking how the patient is feeling**
> 1 How are you feeling at the moment?
> 2 How do you feel right now?

7 • Learners should now role-play the scenarios, each taking a turn to play the role of the doctor and patient.
  • Encourage learners to use some of the language from Exercise 6.
  • Ask learners to give feedback to each other on their performance using the following criteria:
    • Use of eye contact, doctor's body language – does it indicate concern?
    • Use of facilitative language
    • The way in which the doctor speaks – does the doctor adopt a gentle tone of voice?

Expressing emotions (verbal and non-verbal communication, cultural awareness)

Rationale: to establish how expressing emotions is viewed in the learner's culture

8 • Ask learners to read Burnard's quotation on page 98. As the quotation states, releasing emotions is good for our physical and psychological health, yet patients may be reluctant to do so because they may view this as loss of control.
  Ask learners to discuss the three questions in small groups.
  • **Suggestion:** If you have a range of nationalities in your class, you could ask learners to give mini-presentations to the rest of the class on expressing emotion in their cultures, and invite the class to comment on what is being said.

9a ▷10.2

- Contextualise the dialogue: Tell learners they are going to listen to a conversation between a doctor and an irate patient (UK English).
- Ask learners to look at the four approaches (a–d). Tell learners to listen for the approach the doctor takes and tick the correct box. Play the recording.

Audio script >>
STUDENT'S BOOK **page 148**

Quotation (Ford)

- Ask learners to think of a situation where they experienced anger which arose from some kind of loss and how they expressed their anger. Invite those learners who are happy to talk about their experience to tell the group.
- The quotation provides possible explanations why a patient may be angry. Point out to learners that it is important for doctors to try to identify why a patient is angry and to acknowledge the patient's emotions before the consultation proceeds.

9b ▷10.2

- Play the recording again and ask learners to identify two examples where the dialogue has the potential to result in communication breakdown.

When the doctor says to the patient *you're not the only one* and when he says *you've made your point, can we get on?* The doctor hasn't acknowledged the patient's feelings sufficiently.

9c

- Ask learners what steps they would take to avoid communication breaking down. Learners should share their suggestions with the group.

Acknowledge the patient's feelings, explain why you are running late.

10a ▷10.3

- Contextualise the dialogue: Tell learners that they are going to listen to the same doctor and patient as in audio 10.2. However, some of the dialogue is different. Ask learners to identify which approach the doctor takes (see Exercise 9a) and to identify three examples to justify their answers. Play the recording.

Audio script >>
STUDENT'S BOOK **page 148**

Supportive: *I appreciate the problems this has caused you / No, you're right, it isn't.*

10b

Stress, anxiety, irritability due to another reason

11 ▷10.4

Anxiety

Audio script >>
STUDENT'S BOOK **page 148**

12

- Suggestions: Learners work in groups and share any examples they have of when a patient was angry and what the underlying reason was.

13

- Learners should now read the script for audio 10.4 and write down two examples of where the doctor validates the patient's emotions and two examples of where he reassures the patient.

1 I appreciate the inconvenience this has caused you.
2 I'm doing all I can.

14a • Learners now have the chance to practise the language of validation and reassurance. Ask them to read the dialogue and then in pairs to identify where the dialogue could be improved.

> **Doctor** What can I do for you, Mr Brown? You look troubled.
> **Patient** Those antibiotics you gave me aren't doing the job.
> **Doctor** Right. Can I ask you why you think they're not working?
> **Patient** Well, they just make me feel tired and depressed, and I still have a bad chest.
> **Doctor** I'm afraid antibiotics can have that effect, but it doesn't mean that they aren't working. You still have another week to go.
> **Patient** I know, but this is the third course you've prescribed me now. I'm fed up taking them. Why didn't the other ones clear my chest up?
> **Doctor** I can understand your frustration, but sometimes we need to try different antibiotics before one hits the spot.
> **Patient** What, so I'm some kind of guinea pig? You're supposed to know what you're doing.
> **Doctor** No, you're not, Mr Brown, but I can see why you might feel that way. However, you need to understand that, with so many different infections going about, it's not always easy to choose the most effective antibiotic first time. Please bear with me.

14b • Learners should now role-play their amended version.

> **Quotation**
> • Refer learners to the quotation. Ask learners to think about a situation when they had to deal with somebody who was very angry. How quickly did they judge the patient and was it the correct judgement?

Communicating with a manipulative patient (verbal communication, cultural awareness)

Rationale: to learn how to recognise manipulative language and to respond to it in an assertive way

10.5 **15a** • Contextualise the dialogue: Tell learners they are going to listen to a conversation between a doctor and a patient with a drug-abuse problem (UK English).

Audio script >>

STUDENT'S BOOK **page 148**

• Ask learners to identify what the patient wants and to comment on the type of language the patient uses. Play the recording.

> The patient wants to increase his prescription. He tries to do this by making the doctor feel guilty.

10.5 **15b** • Play the recording again and ask learners to write down two examples of manipulative language.

> *Do you want to see me in pain? You really like seeing me in pain, don't you?*

15c ● Tell learners they are going to listen to three possible responses by the doctor, following the patient's request for a higher dose of methadone.

Audio script >>
STUDENT'S BOOK **page 148**

● Check that learners understand the words *aggressive*, *assertive* and *non-assertive* and ask which type of language they should use. Ask learners to match the doctor's response to the appropriate heading and to justify their answers. Play the recording.

> **1** a   **2** c   **3** b

● **Suggestion:** Ask learners what effect each of the doctor's responses would have on the consultation.

16a ● Learners should make appropriate changes to the three examples of aggressive language to make them less aggressive but still assertive.

> **Suggested answers**
> **1** I'm sorry you feel that she was rude to you, but I can't imagine it was intentional. Reception has been incredibly busy this morning, and it may be that she was under pressure and couldn't give you as much time as she normally would.
> **2** I've spent quite a long time explaining the situation and I can't add anything more; there are other patients waiting to be seen.
> **3** I know it's difficult for you, but there isn't anything we can do until you get your drinking under control.

16b ● Learners should compare their amended examples with a partner and then practise saying them.

Patient speak

Rationale: to familiarise learners with common phrases used by patients to describe their emotional state

17
> **a** irritable: 3, 8, 14, 18
> **b** moody: 5, 17
> **c** depressed in general: 2, 9, 11
> **d** depressed as a result of an event: 6, 13, 16
> **e** anxious: 1, 4, 7, 10, 12, 15

Out & About

● Ask learners to listen out for language which expresses different emotional states and to make a note of them, e.g. *I'm struggling to keep myself together. / I feel very weepy. / It's difficult to come to terms with.*

Piecing it all together

Rationale: to practise transferring language covered in the unit to other contexts

18 • Ask learners to work in groups of three. They should refer to their assigned roles.
   • Tell learners you will give them feedback on both positive and negative points of their verbal and non-verbal communication, their voice management, and their active listening skills.
   • **Suggestion:** Encourage learners to reflect on their performance as the doctor. The doctor should compare their self-evaluation with that of the observer. The patient should also comment on how they felt during the consultation.

Progress check

• Ask learners to go through the Progress check.
• Give learners some group feedback and indicate where they might need to improve.
• Give individual feedback to those who wish.

Recommended reading

• If you would like a little more information on this topic, we suggest you read the following:
Lloyd M and Bor R. *Communication Skills for Medicine*. London: Churchill Livingstone, 2004

Reading for discussion

• Go to page 157.

 1 On the surface, he didn't have any reason for visiting the doctor.

DVD clip 7

• Go to page 170.

Unit 11 Communicating with the elderly

LEARNING OUTCOMES

At the end of this unit, learners will be able to:

- carry out an effective interview with an elderly patient
- show sensitivity and respect to an elderly patient
- communicate with depressed elderly patients

Background

Specific challenges

As life expectancy in western countries increases, older people are requiring more medical care in their later years. In this unit, learners will focus on the specific challenges that working with older patients presents. These can include dealing with impairment of basic communication skills due to physical disability – such as deafness or conditions like dementia – or difficulties in getting the patient to express themselves when they are suffering from depression or social isolation.

Developing empathy

A major challenge for many doctors is being able to imagine themselves as old and having an insight into the everyday challenges which older people face. There are a number of exercises in the unit designed to develop empathy with older patients. Specific issues which arise when taking a medical history from an elderly patient are also covered, in particular the use of indirect language to help soften statements. There is also a focus on ways in which sensitivity and respect for older patients can be expressed during the patient interview.

Assessing an older patient's ability to live independently

Doctors are likely to encounter situations in which they will be expected to assess an older patient's ability to live independently. An appropriate model and related language are provided, along with exercises to help learners develop their fluency.

The unit also provides strategies for checking for physical factors which will affect communication, such as deafness, as well as non-physical factors such as depression, which is becoming a major issue for older patients. While dealing with sensitive issues is covered elsewhere, the issue of death is more likely to arise when dealing with older patients. This can often be a source of embarrassment and uncertainty for doctors. Language related to death is explored, including the use of metaphor, and tasks are included to help learners develop their empathy in this area.

US versus UK English

UK	US
stick	cane
waterworks	plumbing

Lead in

Rationale: the aim of this activity is for learners to focus on aspects of the ageing process

a • Ask learners to write down three common traits associated with old age.

> Problems with hearing, physical weakness / frailty, forgetfulness / being repetitive (dementia), problems with speech (dysarthria), cognitive impairment (dysphasia: problems with processing information and responding to it), depression, loneliness

b • Ask learners what aspect of ageing they think is the worst. (They should think about elderly relatives or friends if they don't have any experience working with elderly patients.)

Audio script >>
STUDENT'S BOOK **page 148**

11.1

c • This exercise is a visualisation activity. It is difficult to imagine what it is really like to grow old when you are still young. Encourage learners to close their eyes as they listen to the recording.

• Ask them how they felt as they were listening and if there were any aspects of ageing they had not considered.

Think about

Rationale: to develop awareness of barriers to taking a case history

Note: Learners will probably have mentioned some of these in the lead in activity.

1a • Ask learners to list particular barriers that doctors might experience in communicating with elderly patients.

> Problems with speech, problems with hearing, patient could be depressed, patient could be embarrassed

1b • Ask learners to briefly discuss how good communication skills can help to overcome these barriers.

> **Problems with speech:** Helped by patience, sympathy and lack of embarrassment. Doctor becomes more familiar with problem areas and speech becomes more comprehensible.
> **Problems with hearing:** Check if patient can hear you, check if hearing aid is working, check there is no loud background noise, articulate words clearly, be aware of non-verbal communication (make sure hands are away from mouth, as patient may rely on lip-reading).
> **Depression:** Identify possible causes of depression by asking about patient's routine and degree of social interaction.
> **Embarrassment:** Show sensitivity and respect.
> **Lonliness:** Establish patient's support network and contact with others.

1c • Learners work in pairs to discuss the potential problems that may come up during different stages of taking a medical history.

Interviewing an elderly patient (verbal communication, active listening, cultural awareness)

Rationale: to highlight common issues to consider when interviewing an elderly patient

▷11.2 **2a** • Contextualise the dialogue: Tell learners they are going to listen to the first part of an encounter between a GP and one of his patients, an 85-year-old widower (UK English).

Audio script >>
STUDENT'S BOOK **page 148**

- Ask learners to tick any of the problem areas that are referred to from the list provided. Play the recording.

2c

▷11.2 **2d** • Play the recording again. This time learners should write down the questions the doctor asks in the gaps.

2e • Learners discuss in small groups how the doctor deals with the problems. They should fill in the commentary boxes next to the questions they have just completed. An example is provided.

Dr Wadman	Mr Whitaker, come in and take a seat. Nice to see you. Are you comfortable there?
	Welcoming. Checks patient is comfortable.
Mr Whitaker	Yes, Doctor, thank you. Can I leave my stick just here?
Dr Wadman	Of course. **Shall I turn** the fan off, it's a bit noisy …
	Takes patient's hearing impairment into consideration.
Mr Whitaker	I'm fine, really. I'm getting used to this new hearing aid now; it cuts out most of the background noise.
Dr Wadman	Good, I'm pleased to hear it. **So, what brings you here today**, Mr Whitaker?
	Shares patient's pleasure at improvement. Poses open question. Doctor knows patient is OK with patient-centred approach.
Mr Whitaker	Oh, where shall I start? When you get to my age … it's all downhill!
	Doctor empathises with patient and laughs with him. Humour is appropriate here. This is a common expression in UK English to comment on age.
Dr Wadman	Why **don't you start with what's been bothering you** the most?
	Acknowledges possibility of multiple complaints, considering age of patient.
Mr Whitaker	Well, it's a bit embarrassing, really.
Dr Wadman	**Take your time**. Can you describe what's been happening?
	Reassures patient and encourages him to tell story in his own time.
Mr Whitaker	You can probably see – it's my hands – they're shaking all the time, I can't do much with them. It's getting worse, too. And I've got problems dribbling, too – you know, that's really embarrassing.
Dr Wadman	**How is this affecting you?**
	Asks about how condition affects daily life.
Mr Whitaker	When my Kathy was alive, we had lots of friends, always going out. We liked the good life – dinner parties, theatre …
Dr Wadman	Uh-huh.
	Facilitates patient story. Allows patient to continue, accepting reminiscence. Gives patient time to tell story in own time. Helps patient to put current situation into context.
Mr Whitaker	I was a member of the Rotary Club, you know, and I played tennis for the club team – men's doubles. Kathy wasn't much of a tennis player – but my goodness, could she dance …
Dr Wadman	Good memories?
	Demonstrates active listening.
Mr Whitaker	Wonderful memories.
Dr Wadman	And how **does this relate to the problems you've been having recently**?
	Tries to put patient back on track and structures the interview.
Mr Whitaker	It's the friends, you see, Doctor. This dribbling gets me down. I can't face them like this, can I? Don't get out much any more because of that.
Dr Wadman	I can see how that might get you down. We'll look at ways to try to control this later on.
	Empathises with patient. Ensures patient aware will return to subject later.
Mr Whitaker	It's another symptom of the Parkinson's, isn't it?
Dr Wadman	It is, yes. If I could just ask you something else at this stage … When some people cough or sneeze, they leak urine. Does this happen to you?
	Doesn't try to gloss over or give false hope.
Mr Whitaker	Yes, my waterworks are playing up a bit, too. I was about to mention that.
Dr Wadman	Right. We can also discuss how you can control this. Now, what kind of support network do you have, Mr Whitaker?
	Doctor makes reference to fact he will return to this issue – gives increased structure to interview.
Mr Whitaker	Sorry?
Dr Wadman	**Who can you call on** when you need a helping hand?
	Doctor phrases the question in a way to show patient it is OK to accept help and not diminish his sense of independence.
Mr Whitaker	My daughter-in-law's just down the road.

Dr Wadman	**And you get on well** with your daughter-in-law?
	Tries to evaluate level of informal social support.
Mr Whitaker	Oh, no, don't bother ringing her, not now my son's no longer with us, anyway.
Dr Wadman	What about neighbours?
Mr Whitaker	Maggie, she's just next door, she's great, she gets the shopping in for me – just the bits 'n' bobs I need.
Dr Wadman	Social services?
	Tries to establish formal social support system, if any.
Mr Whitaker	Don't want them coming round if I can help it. The last time they came, they took my Kathy and put her in that home, didn't they? I know they're doing their job, but ...
Dr Wadman	Some of the services they provide could make life easier for you. 'Meals on Wheels', for example. You won't have to worry so much about getting a balanced meal inside you.
	Tries to reassure patient with idea that social services provide help to facilitate and does not mean loss of independence. Patient's response already suggests he understands this, but just needs an outlet for frustrations over wife's death.
Mr Whitaker	You're right, I suppose – sometimes I'm just too tired to cook properly. Don't get me wrong, I like cooking.
Dr Wadman	**How are you coping otherwise**, Mr Whitaker?
	Re-opens discussion to see if patient has any other issues he wants to discuss.
Mr Whitaker	I don't get out much. Stick's OK around the house, but ... it just gets me down.
Dr Wadman	We'll come back to that if you like. Any other medical issues you'd like to discuss today?
	Acknowledges patient cue and sees the need to move away from subject, but confirms will return to it later in interview.

Patient speak

Rationale: to develop knowledge of common expressions used by elderly patients

3a • Ask learners to match the phrases from list A and list B to form collocations.

My hearing	is going.
	is not what it used to be.
	is playing up.
	is troubling me.
My memory	is going.
	is not what it used to be.
	is playing up.
	is troubling me.
My knee	is playing up.
	is troubling me.
My waterworks	are playing up.
	are troubling me.
I had a bit of	arthritis.
	indigestion.
	a dizzy spell.
	a funny turn.
	gout.
	rheumatism.
I have the odd	pain.
	spasm.
I have the occasional	pain.
	spasm.

I've got a touch of	arthritis.
	gout.
	rheumatism.
	indigestion.

3b • Ask learners to practise saying these phrases in turn to a partner. The doctor should use communication strategies or questions to clarify what the patient means, e.g. *When you say ... / do you mean ...? / So, just to recap ...*

Showing sensitivity and respect (verbal and non-verbal communication, active listening)

Rationale: to develop awareness of direct and indirect language

4 • Ask learners to look at the stages from the Calgary-Cambridge observation guide. Remember that this guide provides guidelines for communicating with patients in general.
  • Ask learners to focus on the third point – sensitivity – and to think about what topics might cause embarrassment or be disturbing for an elderly patient.

> Incontinence, knowing they have a hearing problem, lameness/incapacity, moving into an old people's home (US English: assisted living)

> **Quotation** (Purtilo and Haddad)
> • Ask learners what they understand by the quotation. The quotation highlights the importance of treating each patient as an individual (different patients will react in different ways) so although it is important to be aware of problems that affect elderly patients, a doctor should treat each patient and their experiences as unique.

11.3 **5a** • Contextualise the dialogue: Tell learners they are going to listen to a conversation between a doctor and an elderly lady (UK English).
  • Ask learners to rate how well the doctor communicates with his patient, using the criteria from the Calgary-Cambridge observation guide – acceptance, empathy and support, and sensitivity. Play the recording.

Audio script >>
STUDENT'S BOOK **page 149**

> Not very well.

11.3 **5b** • Play the recording again and ask learners to note down examples to justify their answer.

> • He doesn't call the woman by her name; he refers to her as *dear* or *my dear*.
> • He doesn't acknowledge how upsetting it is for her to be without her dentures.
> • He is dismissive of the patient and puts her complaint down to old age.

5c • Refer learners to the script for audio 11.3 on page 149.
  • Ask them to underline examples where the doctor shows lack of sensitivity to the patient. Learners should do this activity in pairs and compare notes. Summarise key points with the group.

Doctor	<u>Hello, my dear.</u>
Patient	Hello, Dr Griffith.
Doctor	<u>Is there something wrong with your mouth, dear?</u>
Patient	I broke my dentures, and they won't be repaired until the end of the week. I feel so foolish without them – I didn't even go to my art class today or my coffee evening cos I didn't want people to see me. It's so frus …
Doctor	Right, <u>my dear, but it's not your mouth that you've come to see me about, is it?</u>
Patient	Er, no, it's that ulcer on my ankle. It still hasn't cleared up.
Doctor	Right. You are taking your medication <u>like I told you to</u>?
Patient	Yes!
Doctor	Well, these things do take longer to clear up <u>at your age, dear</u>. Nothing to worry about, though. Is there anything else?
Patient	When do you think it's going to clear up?
Doctor	Well, like I said, it's difficult to tell <u>with somebody your age</u>. Tell you what, come back and see me in two weeks and we'll have another look at it.

Audio script >>

▷11.4 **6a** • Contextualise the dialogue: Tell learners they are going to listen to a more sensitive version of what they have just listened to in audio 11.3. Ask learners to listen to it and identify two reasons why this version is better. Write down their comments on the board.

STUDENT'S BOOK **page 149**

- He shows sensitivity when the woman speaks in an awkward way.
- He shows empathy when he asks if she is finding things difficult without her dentures.

6b • Ask learners to look at the script for audio 11.4 on page 149 and underline examples of language that demonstrates sensitivity.

Doctor	Hello, Mrs Fry.
Patient	Hello, Dr Griffith.
Doctor	<u>Your voice sounds a little different to usual. Is there something the matter?</u>
Patient	I broke my dentures, and they won't be repaired until the end of the week.
Doctor	Oh dear. <u>You must be finding it difficult without them?</u>
Patient	Yes, I feel so foolish without them. I didn't even go to my art class or my coffee evening cos I didn't want people to see me. It's so frustrating. You must think I'm very vain!
Doctor	Not at all, Mrs Fry. I remember losing two of my front teeth in a rugby match. <u>I can perfectly understand you want to look your best, and it's hard to do that without your teeth.</u>
Patient	Oh, thank you, Doctor. I don't feel as bad now.
Doctor	So, what can I do for you today?
Patient	I was just wondering about this ulcer I have on my ankle. It still hasn't cleared up.
Doctor	<u>I'm sorry to hear that.</u> Are you still taking the medication I prescribed?
Patient	Oh, yes.
Doctor	That's good. It should help with the healing. Is the ulcer still causing you a lot of pain?
Patient	Not exactly, but it feels very tender.
Doctor	Yes, it will do, <u>it's in such an awkward area.</u>
Patient	When do you think it's going to clear up?

> **Doctor** Well, it's difficult to say, but they do tend to take longer to clear up as people get older. <u>We'll keep a close eye on it</u>. Is there anything else?
>
> **Patient** No, Doctor.
>
> **Doctor** OK, Mrs Fry, shall we make an appointment for two weeks' time to see how it's responding?

7 • The aim of this activity is to identify differences in direct language and more sensitive language. Conditions such as difficulty with hearing and incontinence can cause considerable embarrassment for older patients, so it is important that doctors respond to their concerns in a sensitive way. Doctors may not be aware that they may be unintentionally too direct in English.

• Ask learners to identify why Dialogue 2 is more sensitive.

• **Suggestion:** Ask learners what they would say in their own language – would they also use less direct language?

> In the extracts from Dialogue 2, the doctor is being more objective about what has happened to the patient and about her age. By using the phrase *as people get older* rather than *somebody your age*, he is making the information more objective and less threatening for the patient.

8a • Ask learners to look at the question taken from audio 11.2. They should compare the two questions and identify what differences they notice in the language used and which is the more appropriate.

> The first is more appropriate, as referring to *some people* makes it sound like a common problem, therefore less embarrassing.

8b/c • Refer learners to the 'Language to show sensitivity' box. Ask learners to identify four examples where indirect language is used to avoid using the word *old*. Ask learners to work in pairs to identify other aspects of language that make the phrases more sensitive.

> in older age, in later life, in advanced years, older people

8d • Ask learners to rewrite the sentences to show sensitivity and respect to the patient, using phrases from the box on page 106.

> 1 Some loss of control over the bladder tends to be quite common in later life. It can be quite distressing, but there are ways to help manage it.
> 2 I can appreciate that it's difficult to remember to take medicine three times a day, but it is important.
> 3 I was noticing that you are having a bit of trouble with your saliva.

Language Note:

Indirect language

• Using indirect language can help to make it easier for a doctor to talk about sensitive issues. Tentative language (such as *I was wondering*) or modals (such as *this might be*) give the patient the opportunity to respond to suggestions, rather than simply being told what to do.

9a • The aim of this activity is to focus learners' attention on the non-verbal communication of elderly patients. At times, patients may not actually say what is on their mind or may be confused, so it is important for doctors to read such signals and respond accordingly.

• Ask learners to think of two aspects of non-verbal communication that they think are of particular significance when a doctor is talking to an elderly patient.

> Watching facial and lip movements plays an important part in understanding what others are saying. For those whose hearing is declining, it is even more important. Make sure that you face elderly patients when speaking to them, so that they can benefit from reading your lips and facial expressions.

9b • Ask learners to compare their responses with a partner.

9c • Ask learners to think about the type of non-verbal communication that might accompany the sentences in Exercise 8c. Learners should then do the same for their revised sentences from Exercise 8d.

9d • Ask learners to practise the sentences, using appropriate body language.

Communicating with patients with hearing problems (active listening, verbal communication, voice management)

Rationale: to raise awareness of problems that doctors can face when talking to elderly patients and how to deal with them

▶11.5 **10a** • Contextualise the dialogue: Tell learners they are going to listen to a conversation between a doctor and an elderly patient who has a slight hearing problem (UK English).

Audio script >>
STUDENT'S BOOK **page 149**

• Ask learners to listen for how well the doctor deals with the situation. In this example, the doctor fails to do some basic checks. Play the recording.

> **1** Moved his hands away from his face. Sometimes, particularly when discussing difficult or sensitive issues, there is an instinctive movement to cover the mouth with a hand. This is something to be aware of, particularly with patients who are hard of hearing, as it can make it more difficult for them to understand what is being said.
> **2** Checked there was no background noise.

▶11.6 **10b** • Contextualise the dialogue: Tell learners they are going to listen to a different doctor talking to a patient who has some difficulty in hearing the doctor (UK English).

Audio script >>
STUDENT'S BOOK **page 149**

• Ask learners what strategies the doctor uses to help the patient. Play the recording.

> **1** She stresses key words.
> **2** She speaks more slowly at the point where the patient misunderstood the first time.

10c • Ask learners if there is anything else they could do to help a patient with hearing difficulties.

> - Check hearing aid is working.
> - Use signposting. It is easier for patients to recognise words if they know what the context is. Tell the patient when you are moving on to a new subject. It may also be helpful to give clues that the context is changing within the conversation by pausing briefly, speaking a bit more loudly, gesturing toward what will be discussed and using gestures as much as possible to amplify what is being said.
> - Face the patient and ensure mouth is clearly visible.

11 • Learners should work in pairs and take it in turns playing the role of the patient and doctor. The patient should give feedback to the doctor on their ability to deal with their hearing difficulty.

12a • The advice highlights the importance of good articulation, especially when speaking to somebody with a hearing problem. Ask learners to explain why it is preferable to speak in a loud conversational voice, rather than shouting.

> Shouting distorts language.
> It can give the impression of anger.
> A higher-pitch voice can make it harder to hear.

12b • The aim of this activity is for learners to identify what level of volume they are comfortable with. Ask learners to work in pairs. Each pair should try to sit as far away as possible from other pairs. If the group is large, get one half of the group to do the activity first, as too much noise will result in learners having to shout.

Assessing the patient's ability to live independently (verbal communication)

Audio script >>
STUDENT'S BOOK **page 150**

Rationale: to provide learners with guidelines on how to assess a patient's ability to live independently

11.7 **13a** • Contextualise the dialogue: Tell learners they are going to listen to a student doctor giving a presentation to his class. He outlines the usefulness of the acronym BATTED for checking how well an elderly patient can carry out activities for daily living (UK English).

• Before learners listen, with a partner, they should guess what words are represented by each letter of the acronym.

> **B** Bathing
> **A** Ambulation (walking)
> **T** using the Toilet
> **T** making Transfers
> **E** Eating
> **D** Dressing

13b • Tell learners to listen and check their answers. Play the recording.

13c • As a group, ask learners to discuss how some of these functions can be measured through simple observation in the surgery.

> 🔑 Through observation during the encounter in a surgery, the doctor is able to see how mobile his/her patient is by how easy it is for them get out of the chair / how easy it is for them to dress (before/after examination) / if they require help going to the toilet.

14a • Ask learners to work in pairs and continue the dialogue provided. The person playing the role of the doctor should ask the patient questions relating to BATTED and the patient should respond appropriately.

14b • The acronym SCUMM (Shopping, Cooking/Cleaning, Using transportation, Managing money, Management of medication) is another tool used by doctors to evaluate other aspects of daily living. Learners should now swap roles and the doctor should ask the patient questions relating to these activities.

Communicating with depressed elderly patients (verbal communication, active listening)

Rationale: to practise using questioning techniques

> **Quotation** (National Institute of Ageing)
> • The quotation highlights the point that many elderly patients view mental illness as taboo. While many elderly patients may feel depressed and isolated, they are unwilling to discuss their feelings as, for this generation, admitting to suffering from mental illness was regarded as a weakness.
> • Ask learners if this situation applies to their culture.

15 • Ask learners to look at the factors likely to contribute to depression in the elderly and to discuss how easy it would be for them to recognise if an elderly person they knew was depressed.

> 🔑 **Suggested answer**
> Loneliness, poor health, not having things to look forward to

16a • Contextualise the dialogue: Tell learners they are going to listen to a doctor talking to an elderly lady who has symptoms of depression (Australian English).
• Ask learners to listen out for the patient's response when the doctor suggests she might be depressed. Play the recording.

Audio script >>
STUDENT'S BOOK **page 150**

> 🔑 She denies it. She regards depression as something shameful and doesn't want to admit it.

16b • This exercise focuses on the use of open questions to draw a patient out.
• Ask learners to look at the script for audio 11.8 on page 150 and to underline all the open questions.

Doctor	Hello, Mrs Cox. <u>What can I do for you?</u>
Patient	Oh, I don't seem to have much energy. I have this dragging feeling in my body.
Doctor	Well, we did a lot of tests last time you came in, and you seem to be fine physically. Are you sleeping OK?
Patient	No, I stay up half the night watching TV and tend to nod off for a while.
Doctor	I see ... and <u>what about your appetite?</u>
Patient	Oh, I'm not really interested in food, I just pick at the odd thing
Doctor	Right, and <u>what about your social life?</u> Do you get out and about much?
Patient	I go to church most mornings, do a bit of housekeeping and read the paper. That kind of thing. My friend takes me for a drive sometimes, but I'm not often in the mood.
Doctor	<u>What things do you look forward to?</u>
Patient	When my children come to visit. But that doesn't happen very often.
Doctor	Right. Well, from what you're saying, it may be that you're suffering from mild depression. It would explain the loss of energy, the sleeplessness and loss of appetite.
Patient	Rubbish. I'm not depressed. There's no history of <u>that</u> in *my* family.
Doctor	It doesn't have to be in your family. What I'm talking about is something that happens to a lot of people, and there are a number of treatments that can be helpful.
Patient	I don't care what you say, I'm not depressed. I keep my house and myself in order.
Doctor	Well, you've come to me because you don't have any energy and you're not sleeping or eating very well. We've done a lot of tests and you're physically in great shape. The most likely explanation for your symptoms is mild depression.
Patient	Well, if it is depression, what can I do about it?

17 • It is important to point out to learners that open questions may not always be appropriate when talking to a depressed patient. If a patient is not very responsive, closed questions are more appropriate. Ask learners to come up with other possible examples.

18a • Learners practise changing open questions to closed questions. Ask learners to rewrite the dialogue from audio 11.8, making appropriate changes to the questions. They should also include examples of empathetic and supportive language.

18b • In pairs, learners should practise their revised dialogue. They should take it in turn playing the role of the doctor and patient. They should give feedback to each other using the following criteria:
  • Showing sensitivity
  • Use of empathetic language
  • Use of supportive language

Assessing the mental state of a patient (verbal communication)

Rationale: to draw attention to the importance of taking simple steps to assess a patient's mental state, before taking a detailed clinical history

▶ 11.9 **19** • Contextualise the dialogue: Tell learners they are going to listen to the beginning of a conversation between a doctor and a new elderly patient (UK English).

Audio script >>
STUDENT'S BOOK **page 150**

• Ask learners why the doctor does not go into a detailed clinical history at the start and what he does instead. Play the recording.

> He does a quick check for any signs of mental impairment first, as there is no point in going into a detailed clinical history until he knows.

▶ 11.10 **20** • Contextualise the dialogue: Tell learners they are going to listen to a dialogue between a doctor and an elderly female patient who appears to be confused (UK English).

Audio script >>
STUDENT'S BOOK **page 150**

• The activity highlights the importance of active listening skills. Learners listen and decide if they think the patient is confused or not. Play the recording.

> No. She confuses the doctor initially, but then it becomes clear that she is not confused.

21 • Ask learners what they understand by the quotation.

> They mean that it's important to listen and allow the patient to finish what he/she was saying. The patient may not appear to answer the doctor's question immediately, but it may transpire that they do in fact give an answer, as in Exercise 20.

Quotation (Purtilo and Haddad)
• This quotation highlights the importance of listening actively to a patient, rather than concluding too quickly that the patient isn't making sense. An elderly patient may not have contextualised fully what they are saying and, as a result, may not appear to be making sense. However, by listening actively, a doctor may be able to pick up on key words and thread things together.

Talking about death and dying (verbal and non-verbal communication, active listening)

Rationale: to raise awareness of how individuals respond to death and dying

22a • The case study describes how one elderly patient deals with the prospect of dying. Ask learners to read the text and answer the questions.

> **1** It removes some of the awkwardness of the topic for her and the doctor.

• Ask learners if they agree with the question. They should discuss this point as a whole class.

22b • Ask learners to work in pairs and describe what metaphors they use for death in their own language.

Cultural awareness

Rationale: to raise awareness of the importance of treating elderly patients with respect

- Ask learners to read the quotation and elicit their response to it. You may need to explain the words *crinklies* and *crumblies*, but they should be able to deduce from the text that they are negative terms. Then, in small groups, tell learners to comment on how older people are viewed in their society and about any changes that might be taking place.

Out & About

Rationale: to expose learners to common language used for giving advice

- Ask learners to read a range of letters from popular magazines, focusing on letters written by older writers. Before they read the reply from the doctor, they should think of the language that they would use and compare their response with the one in the magazines.
- Learners could report back to the group and describe the frequency of particular language used for giving advice.

Piecing it all together

Rationale: to give learners the chance to consolidate what they have covered in the unit

- **23a** • Ask learners to come up with a list of criteria that they would use to assess a doctor's interaction with an elderly patient. Write their suggestions on the board.

- **23b** • Put learners in groups of three (doctor, patient and observer). They should now take it in turns to play each role.
  - Tell learners you will give them feedback on both positive and negative points of their verbal and non-verbal communication, their voice management, and their listening skills.

Progress check

- Ask learners to go through the Progress check.
- Give learners some group feedback and indicate where they might need to improve.
- Give individual feedback to those who wish.

Recommended reading

- If you would like a little more information on this topic, we suggest you read the following:
  Cayton H. *The alienating language of healthcare.* Journal of the Royal Society of Medicine 2006; 99: 484

Reading for discussion

- Go to page 158.

> 1 The deafness on the part of the patient was one problem; however, so too was the doctor's emphasis on whether the patient had fuel, rather than why they didn't have heat.
> 3 That it is always important not to take things at face value when dealing with the elderly.

Unit 12 Communicating with children and adolescents

Background

The first part of the unit focuses on developing communication skills for working with children. Many doctors, not just paediatricians, will routinely come into contact with children, so it is important that doctors have the necessary communication skills to interact effectively with them.

Establishing initial rapport with a child

Doctors need to be aware of differences between adult and child patients and to bear these differences in mind during the consultation. By doing so, doctors will have a better chance of gaining trust from a child and getting their co-operation.

Engaging in some small talk with a child, such as paying them a compliment and checking that they are comfortable, are important points for doctors to remember.

Developing rapport with a child

As the interview progresses, it is important for a doctor to acknowledge a child's feelings, to show empathy, and to ask a child for their permission before examining them.

Reassuring a child

Visiting the doctor's can be a daunting experience for a child so it is important that a doctor can minimise any negative perceptions the child may have, by providing reassurance throughout the interview.

Explaining procedures to a child

Doctors need to be aware that even very minor procedures can make a child uneasy, so it is important for doctors to explain procedures in simple language and to give clear instructions in order to gain a child's co-operation.

Responding to a child's verbal cues

It is important for doctors to show a child that they are actively listening to any concerns they may have and to respond appropriately. Doctors should avoid putting words in the patient's mouth or being judgemental; instead, they should elicit how a child feels and why, and show support.

Developing rapport with an adolescent

The second part of the unit focuses on developing communication skills for working with adolescents, which can present particular challenges for doctors. Apart from physical illnesses and unplanned pregnancies, doctors also need to be aware of psycho-social illnesses common to this age group, such as eating disorders and low self-esteem.

US versus UK English

UK	US
(to have) diarrhoea	(to go) diarrhea
lollies	lollipops/suckers
off her food (audio 12.1)	not eating
plaster	Band-aid

UK	US
to do a poo	to go poop / to poop
to have a wee	to go pee-pee
to open your bowels	to have a bowel movement
trainers	sneakers

Lead in

Rationale: to encourage learners to see things from a child's perspective

- Ask learners to read the quotation from a seven-year-old child and comment on its significance.

a • The quotation demonstrates one way in which child patients differ from adult

- A child does not make the decision to go to the doctor's.
- A child has a different understanding of illness, treatment and prevention.
- A child has different perceptions of a doctor, e.g. he/she may think the doctor is deliberately going to hurt him/her.
- A young child is more unpredictable.
- A child has a different vocabulary.

patients: their limited understanding of their bodies.
- Ask learners to work in pairs to come up with three other ways in which child patients differ from adult patients.

b • **Suggestion for job-experienced learners:** Identify which learners already have experience of working with children. Ask learners in turn to tell the class how comfortable they feel working with young children and to describe any specific challenges that working with young children presents for them. Ask them what benefits they have gained from the experience.
- **Suggestion for pre-experience learners:** Ask learners in turn to say how comfortable they feel about working with children. What have they learned from their experience of very young children within their family circle or with friends' children? Elicit what challenges they envisage from working with young children and what the rewarding aspects might be.

Establishing initial rapport (verbal and non-verbal communication, cultural awareness)

Think about

Rationale: to develop awareness of the importance of getting the interview off to a good start

- Point out to learners that it is important for doctors to have an understanding of how a child patient might feel about going to see a doctor. Doctors should bear these feelings in mind when they are interacting with children.

- **Suggestion:** Encourage learners to recall their own experiences of going to the doctor as a child. Do they have positive or negative memories? Ask learners in turn to share them with the class.

1 • Ask learners to suggest two things they would do to put a child patient of six years old at ease. This could include aspects of non-verbal communication.

- Be at the same physical level as the child.
- Say hello to the child and call him/her by his/her name.
- Compliment the child, e.g. admire something they are wearing or a toy they have brought with them, or praise them for something they are doing, e.g. a drawing.
- Use a gentle tone of voice.
- Repeat words used by the child to show you are listening.
- Smile at the child.

▶12.1 **2** • Contextualise the dialogue: Tell learners they are going to listen to the beginning of a consultation with a new patient. The doctor is talking to a six-year-old girl and her mother (UK English). Tell learners to listen out for any examples of good practice, including the suggestions they have made in Exercise 1. Play the recording.

Audio script >>
STUDENT'S BOOK **page 150**

2 No

3a • Ask learners to read the three stages from the Calgary-Cambridge observation guide. Focus on the third point (*Demonstrates respect and interest, attends to patient's physical comfort*) and ask learners how they could achieve this.

- Include the child in the conversation.
- Pay the child a compliment.
- Ask the child a question about him/herself, e.g. favourite subject at school, hobbies.
- Check that the child is comfortable / if child wants to sit next to the parent/carer.
- Use a friendly/gentle tone of voice.

3b • Ask learners what topics they might talk about to engage a child.

- Paying the child a compliment, e.g. admire article of clothing/toy.
- Asking about the school they go to, their favourite subject.
- Asking about hobbies.
- Questions about family, school, personal interests and career intentions can usually be relied on.

▶12.2 **3c** • Contextualise the dialogue: Tell learners they are going to listen to another doctor who is receiving a new patient. The doctor is talking to a seven-year-old boy and his mother (UK English).
- Ask learners to listen out for whether the doctor covers the three stages in the Calgary-Cambridge observation guide and if the doctor includes the mother in the small talk. Play the recording.

Audio script >>
STUDENT'S BOOK **page 150**

> **1** Yes (1 *Hello, Billy. Hello, Mrs Jones.*; 2 *My name's Dr Gordon. I'm one of three partners who makes up this family practice.*; 3 *Just let me raise your chair up a bit so you can see me. That's better. That's a great football shirt, Billy. So you're a Manchester United supporter?*)
>
> **2** Yes (*And do you support Manchester United as well, Mrs Jones?*)

Quotation (Speirs)

- The quotation draws attention to the importance of including a child in the consultation. Point out that while there is the temptation to direct the conversation at the parent when the child is very young, it is important to include the child because the child will be making judgements based on a doctor's verbal and non-verbal communication.

Making a child comfortable (verbal communication)

Rationale: to develop awareness of factors to consider when helping make a child comfortable

Audio script >>
STUDENT'S BOOK **page 150**

12.3 **4a**
- The aim of this activity is to focus on language that will put the child at ease.
- Tell learners that they are going to listen to a sentence from the dialogue in Exercise 3c and ask them to fill in the missing words. Play the recording.

> Just let me

4b
- Tell learners to work in pairs. Elicit what purpose the word *just* has in the example.

> *Just* is used for reassurance. The doctor is telling the child that there is nothing to worry about when he is adjusting the seat.

4c
- The aim of this exercise is to draw learners' attention to the different places *just* can be put in a sentence. Tell them to look at the three examples and to insert the word *just* in the appropriate place.

> I'm **just** going to clear some space for Teddy to sit.
> If I could **just** get you to sit here next to me. That's great. Are you comfortable?
> Yes, it is hot in here. Let me **just** open the window before we begin.

- **Suggestion:** You could read these sentences out loud and ask learners to focus on your intonation. By using the right intonation, the effect of using the word *just* is reinforced. Now ask learners to practise saying these sentences to each other.

Quotation (Speirs)

- Ask learners to read the quotation and discuss how a child might feel if the doctor is looking down at them (it can be intimidating).

Paying a child a compliment (verbal communication, voice management)

Rationale: to give learners examples of language that they can use to pay a child a compliment

- Refer learners to the Language Note and to the example from the recording.

Language Note:

Paying a compliment
Show learners the constructions:
That's a + adjective + noun
They're + adjective + noun
Example: That's a great football shirt, Billy

5a • Ask learners to do the matching exercise.

> **1** b/c   **2** a/d   **3** a/d   **4** b/a/b/d

- **Suggestion:** Say a couple of the examples out loud and ask learners to indicate where your voice rises and falls. Ask them to practise the examples with a partner.

> That'↑s a lovely↓ dress
> They're↑ cool trainers you're↓wearing

5b • Ask learners to think of any other expressions they could use for paying a child a compliment.

> *I like your* + noun (e.g. *I like your T-shirt*)
> *What a* + adjective + noun (e.g. *What a cute teddy bear!*)

Developing rapport (verbal communication, voice management, active listening)

Rationale: to provide guidelines for developing rapport

- Ask learners to read the stages outlined in the Calgary-Cambridge observation guide for developing rapport. These stages are general stages for any patient interaction.

6a • Ask learners to discuss how relevant the first three stages of the Calgary-Cambridge observation guide are for children.

> They are all very relevant.

▷12.4 **6b** • Contextualise the dialogue: Tell learners that they are going to listen to the continuation of the dialogue from 3c and ask them to tick the stages that the doctor covers from the Calgary-Cambridge observation guide.

Audio script >>

STUDENT'S BOOK **page 151**

> All the stages are covered.

▷12.4 **6c** • Now play the recording again and this time ask learners to fill in the missing words.

> **1** Are you   **2** can understand   **3** that is a; isn't it?   **4** must have
> **5** What I need to do   **6** Will you let me

6d • Ask learners to identify which stages the examples come under.

> Acceptance: 2   Empathy and support: 1, 3, 4   Examination: 5, 6

7a • The aim of this exercise is to focus learners' attention on constructions using the modal verb *must* to show empathy. Focus on the example from Exercise 6c: *You must have missed that, Billy.* Point out the other constructions using the word *must.* Encourage learners to come up with possible examples to complete the sentences. Then ask them to do the matching exercise.

> **1** b/d/e   **2** c   **3** e/b/d   **4** f/c
> **5** a/c/d/f   **6** a

7b • Ask learners what other expressions they know for showing empathy.

> I'm sorry to hear that / I know / I understand

7c • Now ask learners to read the two scenarios. In pairs, they should take turns in responding to the situation, using some of the phrases from 7a.

8 • Ask learners to role-play the scenario from the first dialogue in Exercise 2, making appropriate changes to create a better rapport with the child. As preparation, refer learners to the audio script on page 150 and ask them to highlight those areas that could be improved.

Reassuring a child (verbal communication, voice management, active listening)

Rationale: to dispel notions that a child might have for being responsible for their illness

9 • Ask learners to think of situations where a child patient might need reassurance.

> A child might be frightened of instruments.
> He/She might think the illness or injury is much worse than it really is.
> When you have to give a child an injection.
> He/She might think the illness is his/her fault because he/she has been naughty.
> He/She might be nervous of doctors.
> He/She may be in pain / tired / in shock.

12.5 **10a** • Contextualise the dialogue: Tell learners they are going to listen to a doctor talking to a seven-year-old girl called Jenny, who has broken her wrist. She thinks it is her fault because she didn't go to bed when her parents told her (US English).
• Ask learners to identify what steps the doctor takes to reassure the child. Play the recording.

Audio script >>
STUDENT'S BOOK **page 151**

> By telling her that her injury was an accident and that she's not to blame.

▷12.5 **10b** • Play the recording again. This time, ask learners to focus on the doctor's voice. Ask them to identify two aspects of the doctor's voice that would help to reassure the child.

> • He stresses key words.
> • He uses a gentle tone of voice.

11 • Draw learners' attention to the phrases in the 'Language for reassuring a child' box. They should then role-play the scenarios on page 122 in pairs. Ask them to give each other feedback on their performance. Move around the class, monitoring what learners are saying, taking notes of good and weak points. Then give general feedback to the class.

Quotation (Lloyd and Bor)
• Ask learners if they recall associating an illness they had as a child with bad behaviour.

12a • Ask learners to identify possible contexts in which a doctor might say the phrases to a child.

> **1** Child is worried that they are very ill.
> **2** Child feels guilty.
> **3** Child is about to be examined, perhaps with an instrument, or have an injection
> **4** Child is about to have an injection.

▷12.6 **12b** • Ask learners to listen to the phrases and ask them to identify which words are stressed in each example. Now ask them to practise saying the phrases out loud to a partner.

Audio script >>
STUDENT'S BOOK **page 151**

> **1** <u>Don't</u> look so <u>sad</u>. We're <u>going</u> to make you <u>better</u> very <u>soon</u>.
> **2** You're <u>not</u> to <u>blame</u> for this in <u>any way</u>.
> **3** <u>Don't</u> be <u>scared</u>. I <u>promise</u> this <u>won't hurt</u>.
> **4** It will be <u>very</u> quick, you'll <u>hardly</u> feel a <u>thing</u>.

13 • Learners now have the opportunity to practise the language above. Ask them to work in pairs and to take it in turns playing the role of the child and the doctor.

> **Suggested answers:**
> **1** It must have been frightening for you when you started bleeding. But please don't worry, any little bump can make your nose bleed.
> **2** I know injections aren't very pleasant, but I promise that I'll be very quick. It might help if you look at the picture on the wall over there while I do it.
> **3** So, you're worried that a tree is going to grow inside you? That won't happen because your tummy eats it up, just like the rest of the apple.
> **4** Your hand will be very sore at the moment. Don't worry, it will clear up completely. It may look bad, but the skin is protecting itself by making a blister to help it heal faster. You mustn't think it was your fault, it was an accident.

14 • Ask learners to read the quotation. Then elicit other aspects of non-verbal communication that would give a doctor an insight into how a child might be feeling.

> • Eye contact
> • Whether the child sits still or moves about
> • Facial expression
> • Proximity to adult

Examining a child (verbal and non-verbal communication)

Rationale: to demonstrate awareness and sensitivity to how a child might be feeling during an examination

• Even very minor procedures may frighten a child.
• **Suggestion:** Ask learners to think about what steps they could take to overcome this problem. (Reassure the child and explain in simple language what he/she is going to do.)

12.7 **15** • Contextualise the dialogue: Tell learners they are going to listen to a doctor giving instructions to an eight-year-old girl. The child does not co-operate (UK English).
• Ask learners to identify why the child does not co-operate with the doctor. Play the recording.

Audio script >>
STUDENT'S BOOK **page 151**

> • He does not explain what he is going to do. For example, he could shine his torch in the ear of a teddy bear first so the child can understand what is going to happen.
> • He has not reassured her that the examination is not going to hurt.
> • His voice has become agitated rather than remaining calm.
> • He is issuing commands (e.g. to keep still) rather than asking for co-operation.
> • He has not involved the parent in the preparations for the examination.

12.8 **16a** • Contextualise the dialogue: Tell learners they are going to listen to a different doctor giving instructions to a five-year-old boy (UK English).
• **Suggestion:** Before learners read the checklist for examining a child, elicit any examples from them. Then ask them to read the checklist.
• Ask learners to listen to the recording and tick any of the stages covered in the checklist. Play the recording. Refer learners to audio script to confirm their answers.

Audio script >>
STUDENT'S BOOK **page 151**

> The doctor includes all of these stages and gains the full co-operation of the boy.

16b

> **Suggested answers:**
> Are you going to let me look at (your chest)?
> I need to look at (your chest). Is that OK?
> Do you think I could look at (your chest)?
> Can I look at (your chest)?

Quotation (Lloyd and Bor)
• Point out to learners the importance of telling a child what is going to happen.

17 • In pairs, learners should role-play an improved version of the dialogue in Exercise 15. They should check that they include all the functions in Exercise 16. They should then swap roles.

• Learners should give feedback to each other, using the following criteria:
  • Explaining what is going to happen
  • Reassuring the patient that the examination is not going to hurt
  • Using a calm voice

Giving instructions (verbal communication)

Rationale: to highlight importance of using indirect language

18a • Ask learners to look at the two examples from the dialogues they listened to in Exercises 15 and 16. Ask them what differences they notice in the language used by the two doctors.

Dialogue 1: The doctor is being more forceful by using commands and *must*.
Dialogue 2: The doctor uses the phrase *I need to* and then asks the child for permission for the mother to remove his shirt. In the second sentence, she uses the phrase *I need you* to rather than *can you*.

18b • Ask learners to give instructions to each other in a more child-friendly way.

Suggested answers:

1 I need you to open your mouth a bit more so I can see better.
2 I need you to open your eyes so I can see what's causing your headaches.
3 I need you to lie as still as possible when I'm looking at your tummy.
4 I just need you to stand on the weighing machine, please.

Responding to a child's verbal cues (active listening, verbal communication)

Rationale: to make learners aware of the way in which they respond to a child

• If a child is uneasy about a doctor carrying out a procedure, it is important not to be judgemental but to find out why the child is anxious.

19a • Ask learners to match the responses with the appropriate heading.

1 b   2 d   3 c   4 a

19b • Ask learners to identify which two responses are appropriate.

Sentence 2 is appropriate, as the doctor is trying to determine what the barrier is.
Sentence 3 is also appropriate, as the doctor is validating the child's fears and offering reassurance.
Sentence 1 is not helpful, as the doctor is putting thoughts in the child's mind.
Sentence 4 is not helpful, as the doctor is putting the child under pressure by comparing her with her sibling.

Patient speak

Rationale: to expose learners to common phrases used by child patients

20 • Tell learners that it is important that doctors know how to explain medical jargon to children in simple, clear English, so that a child can process what is being said. Ask them to make appropriate changes to the questions, so that a child of ten would understand them.

> **Suggested answers**
> 1 Do you feel sleepy during the day?
> 2 Does light hurt your eyes?
> 3 Do you feel sick?
> 4 Does your tummy/stomach hurt?

• **Suggestion:** Ask learners to tell each other what words children use in their own language for different parts of the body. Ask them to feed back to the whole group.

21 • Children use a number of specific expressions for describing body parts and body functions. It is important that learners have some knowledge of common phrases. Ask learners to match the phrases that a child would use to what an adult would say.

> **1** b   **2** c   **3** a

Cultural awareness

Rationale: to raise awareness of cultural issues in consultations with a child

• Ask learners to read the text. Then invite learners to give examples of cultural differences that might affect a child's behaviour in a consultation.

> **Suggested answers**
> Cultural norms for children will influence behaviour during consultation (whether it's normal to be shy and very quiet or to be allowed to be assertive and boisterous); the role of gender in culture (girls submissive, boys aggressive); lack of familiarity with healthcare settings and procedures; language issues.

Out & About

Rationale: to raise awareness of steps taken to make a medical environment child-friendly

22 • Ask learners to read the comments by child patients and ask if they have other suggestions that might appeal to young children.

Communicating with adolescents (verbal communication, cultural awareness)

Rationale: to develop awareness of factors to consider when communicating with adolescents

> **Quotation** (Sacks and Westwood)
> • This quotation highlights the challenges of working with adolescents. Doctors need to take into account the changes that are taking place in adolescents: physiological, psychological and cognitive changes. Adolescents can be very sensitive to questioning, so it is important to adopt a supportive and non-intrusive approach.

- **Suggestion:** Elicit what potential challenges a doctor might have in communicating with adolescents.

23a • Ask learners what conversational topics they think would be suitable for adolescents.

> School, careers, hobbies, music, films, friends, pets

23b • Ask learners if they remember what barriers existed between them and their parents/carers when they were adolescents.

> Not being listened to / different interests / being over-controlled

24 • Ask learners how important they feel it is for a doctor to cover all of these areas when working with adolescents. For example, how important is it to avoid being seen as treating adolescents in a humourless way? Ask learners what difficulties they perceive in covering these areas.

> They are all relevant.

▶12.9 **25a** • Contextualise the dialogue: Tell learners they are going to listen to a conversation between a doctor and a female adolescent patient (UK English).

Audio script >>

STUDENT'S BOOK **page 151**

• Ask learners to comment on how well they think the doctor has handled the interview. Play the recording.

> Not very well, because the doctor is rather patronising, e.g. *Well, my dear, you certainly have grown since I've seen you last.*
> He is intrusive when he asks *Have you started having sex?*
> He should have used more tentative language, such as *I don't mean to pry, but …*

25b • Ask learners to match the extracts from the dialogue with the points listed in Exercise 25.

> **a** 3   **b** 4   **c** 2, 3   **d** 6   **e** 2

25c • Ask learners to look at the statements. With a partner, tell them to discuss where they could be fitted into the dialogue they have just listened to. They should refer to the audio script on page 151.

> **Doctor** OK, Catherine, if you'd like to come through to my office. Your mother can come in later. ... Take a seat, Catherine. What age are you?
> **Patient** Almost 17.
> **Doctor** Well, my dear, you certainly have grown since I last saw you. What seems to be the problem?
> **Patient** I've been having headaches and stomach pains quite a bit lately.
> **Doctor** I see. How severe are the headaches?
> **Patient** Mm, they're not too bad. I've had them regularly since I started having my periods, but they've got worse over the last six months.
> **Doctor** Mm. And the stomach pains?
> **Patient** About the same.

Doctor	**I don't mean to pry into your personal life, but I do need to know** – have you started having sex?
Patient	Um, will you have to tell my mum what I tell you?
Doctor	No. It will be between ourselves.
Patient	Oh. Um, I started to have sex with my boyfriend Tom about six months ago, when I turned 16. My parents would kill me if they knew ...
Doctor	But you're only a child ... 16 is too early to start having sex. You're not fully developed emotionally or physically yet, and you're taking a lot of risks with your health.
Patient	That's what my parents are always telling me.
Doctor	There's really nothing to laugh about, you know. It's a serious matter.
Patient	Can't you just listen to me without lecturing me?
Doctor	**I can assure you that I am listening to you**, Catherine. Now, the pains: do you think they got worse because you've started having sex?
Patient	Um ... oh, I ... I don't know.
Doctor	But you are worried about what might be causing them?
Patient	I'm not too worried about the pains, to be honest, but I think I might be pregnant.
Doctor	Do you use any form of contraception?
Patient	Sometimes we use condoms, but not always.
Doctor	**It's not my intention to lecture you, but you do really need to consider the risks you are taking.** You should always get your partner to wear a condom. Otherwise there's no telling what kind of venereal diseases you might pick up. Anyway, we can do a test to find out if you're pregnant. Is there anything else you're worried about? No? OK, I'll just ask your mother to come in, then.

Piecing it all together

26 • Learners now role-play the three scenarios.
   • Learners should give feedback on each other's performance, noting areas of good practice and where improvements could be made.

Progress check

- Ask learners to go through the Progress check.
- Give learners some group feedback and indicate where they might need to improve.
- Give individual feedback to those who wish.

Recommended reading

- If you would like a little more information on this topic, we suggest you read the following:
  Guidelines on communicating with children and young people. In Lloyd M and Bor R. *Communication Skills for Medicine.* London: Churchill Livingstone, 2004

Reading for discussion

- Go to page 159.

DVD clip 8

- Go to page 171.

Two consultations

1 Read the text and, in small groups, discuss the difference between the two visits described.

When I was 14 years old my mother took me to see a doctor about some skin lesions on my face and neck. The doctor was reputed to be one of the best in town. At his clinic, we paid the consultation fee and waited in a queue, with about ten before us waiting to see him. After about 20 minutes, somebody called out my name and asked us to enter the doctor's room. During the check up, I explained all my problems to him. He examined my lesions through a magnifying glass, quickly wrote down a prescription of drugs and, handing it to us, asked us to come for follow-up after a week. It hardly took a minute for him to see us off.

I hadn't expected such a short consultation and felt he hadn't given me enough time to explain about my problems and treatment in detail. Though he gave me a prescription, he failed to give me any assurances or encouragement. I know my mother felt the same, though neither of us spoke a word on our way back home. I used the drugs that he had prescribed, and they cured my problem. But I never went back to him for follow-up.

About a year ago, I accompanied my sick mother to another doctor for a very different consultation. Firstly, my mother explained all her problems in detail. The doctor listened carefully and, after thoroughly examining her, told us all about the disease she had and the treatment he was going to give. Finally, he asked her if she understood everything. My mother nodded happily. I could see from her face how happy and relieved she felt after this consultation.

Now I am in my final year at medical school. Looking back at those two consultations, I think they epitomise bad and good doctor-patient relationships. I see many patients daily; as a student, I can't give them anything but assurances, encouragement, hope, and my time to listen to their grievances. I know it helps them. I also see my teachers examining patients: some patients return happily after check up, whereas some look dissatisfied when they feel that the doctor hasn't given them enough time to explain all about their illness and treatment. This reinforces my belief that the best management strategy for a patient can be made even stronger when laid on a strong foundation of a good doctor-patient relationship.

Sharan Prakash Sharma, final year medical student
Institute of Medicine, Kathmandu, Nepal

BMJ 2005;330:453 (26 February), doi:10.1136/bmj.330.7489.453

2 Discuss what you see as the characteristics of a 'good' doctor.

3 Discuss your own experiences of communication when visiting a doctor and, if possible, the communication experiences of your relatives/close friends.

Unit 1

And so to the future: can we ever replace the 'human' touch?

1 Read the first paragraph of the article and discuss your *initial* reaction to this concept.

It's All a Bit 'Star Treky'

Despite looking like a cross between a vacuum cleaner and a relic from Star Wars, Britain's first Robodoc has proved a hit: the doctor with the perfect bedside manner. Performing ward rounds at St Mary's Hospital, London, the Remote Presence 6 (RP6) is one of two robots currently being trialled in UK hospitals – this is the advent of telemedicine. RP6, fitted with a video screen portraying an image of the specialist, glides from bed to bed communicating with patients in a virtual face-to-face encounter, allowing patient and doctor to see each other whatever the location of the doctor. The doctor controls the robot with a joystick which is capable not only of reading patient records and analysing test results but also asking questions.

2 Discuss these questions

1 What do you think are the reactions of patients taking part in the trial?

2 How do you think patients with dementia might react? Explain why.

3 Read the rest of the article and see how your ideas compare with the research.

But what do staff and patients think of the latest concept in patient care? Studies in the US found that patients preferred to be seen by the robot if it meant otherwise being seen by a different doctor or specialist. Here at St Mary's, Tara Fairall, recovering from a gall bladder operation, has just been 'examined' by the Robodoc. 'Its weird at first, but you soon get used to it because its like talking to a doctor. At least this way you get to talk to someone.' An elderly woman in the same ward thinks differently: 'I'd think it'd come to the end of everything if I was sent a robot. I mean, where are all the doctors?' Interestingly, patients suffering from dementia respond well – the novelty effect is somehow preferable to human contact.

The Patients Association, not surprisingly, has expressed horror at the thought of robots replacing doctors. Dr Parv Sains, leading the project at St Mary's, admits, 'It's all a bit Star Treky, but if you look at how robots are used in the military and industry there's no reason why the NHS can't move in that direction.' He adds, 'Our robots would certainly never replace doctors entirely, but they are a communication tool which allows doctors to have direct contact with their patients and may be a significant step forward in patient care.'

The Guardian

4 Discuss these questions.

1 How do you feel about Dr Sains' comparison of healthcare provision and the use of robots in the military and industry?

2 To what extent do you believe the Robodoc to be a 'significant step forward in patient care'?

5 Interacting with your patient via the Robodoc may require you to compensate in certain ways. Brainstorm strategies you might need to establish good rapport using this communication tool.

6 Discuss the idea of delivering patient care using robots with your friends and colleagues outside class. You might also want to find out more about this particular area of research. Compare your findings with the rest of the class next time you meet.

Unit 2

'Now I feel tall' – what a patient-led NHS feels like

In 2005, the UK's Department of Health issued a report in an attempt to make all those working in the NHS more aware of the importance of the need to improve patients' emotional experience, and the relevance of this in creating a patient-led NHS.

1 With a partner, discuss the meaning of the title 'Now I feel tall'.

2 Read Part 1 of the text and note information on the following:

- the current state of patient care within the NHS
- the emotional experience of the patient

Part 1

Creating a patient-led NHS

Creating a patient-led NHS requires changes in how the system works and how people behave, and in a culture where everything is measured by its impact on patients and the benefits to people's health. Changes are beginning to happen. One example of a hospital that has made patient-led changes is South Manchester University Hospital, which is trying to improve access for people with learning difficulties. Following these changes, one patient said, 'I'm only small, but now I feel tall.' However, not all patients 'feel tall', and their emotional needs are not always a high priority for the NHS. Currently, focus is on the practical and physical aspects of patient care, and there is relatively little understanding about patients' emotional responses to their experiences, and little attention is paid to the expectations of patients at an emotional level.

Defining the emotional experience of patients

What do we mean by a patient's *emotional experience*? This is about how a patient feels about their experience of using the NHS and what they value. For example, a patient kept waiting for an appointment in an outpatient clinic may have a good emotional experience if they feel someone cares about them – that is, if they are given regular information about why they are being kept waiting and an update on how long they will have to wait. The same patient left to wait without any information is likely to have a negative experience because they feel abandoned and neglected. Improving patients' emotional experience is about treating people as we would want to be treated – with dignity and respect.

The Department of Health has carried out a piece of research to explore the emotional experience of patients. It collected views of recent patients, the public and NHS staff through a series of workshops, focus groups and face-to-face interviews.

3 Read through the research that was carried out (see Part 2 below) and underline any points that are new or surprised you.

Part 2

The research

Patients and the public said that they tend to come into contact with the NHS when they are at their most vulnerable and emotional, which makes their emotions, and particularly their negative feelings, stronger. It was felt that the NHS did not always meet these emotional needs. People had different opinions and experiences, but there were some consistent themes in terms of typical positive and negative feelings. The most commonly identified negative feelings were confusion, disappointment, annoyance and frustration. The main causes were poor communication, long waiting times, patronising staff attitudes and feeling lost in the system. Most patients felt isolated, overwhelmed by the experience, and treated like a number instead of an individual. Numerous people in the study mentioned feeling scared, afraid or anxious. They often said they thought these feelings were linked to their situation and medical condition, but some felt that they were made worse by their NHS care (particularly care in hospitals). People involved in the research shared the same opinions about what a positive patient experience at an emotional level should feel like. They said patients want to feel reassured, confident, cared for, informed, safe and relaxed. Being reassured was particularly important; they wished to feel safe and 'in good hands'. Central to an ideal experience was feeling that they are important and 'special'.

Staff descriptions of the ideal situation for patients were very similar to those described by patients themselves. They appear to be aware of how patients are feeling but are limited by time, resources and the culture of the NHS itself when trying to create a more positive emotional experience. When asked for suggestions on how the ideal emotional experience may be achieved, many people were cynical about this and felt it was unlikely to be achieved but gave numerous practical suggestions on the way forward. These were based on how patients are communicated with (in terms of both quality and quantity of information) and changes to the environment (particularly waiting rooms). The final report on the results from the research says that: 'An alternative way of portraying the ideal emotional experience is separating those emotions that participants would like to feel as they go through the process, and a secondary layer – those that they would like to feel as a result of their experiences. Some key emotions do cut across both.'

Feelings during the patient journey:	Feelings resulting from patient experience:
Reassured	Satisfied
Respected	Relieved
Cared for	Cared for
Listened to	Confident (in treatment and in the NHS as a whole)
In control	Proud
Safe	
The findings were quite clear – the quality of a patient's emotional experience was a major factor in their overall satisfaction with the NHS.	

4 Now read Part 3 of the text and then in small groups discuss how you might be able to implement these points and ensure a more patient-led level of care.

Part 3

Creating a Patient-led NHS, published in March 2005, sets out the major themes for delivering a patient-led NHS. It outlines how the NHS will need to change and what services will look like.

Every aspect of the new system is designed to create a service which is patient-led, where:
• people have a far greater range of choices and of information and help to make choices;
• there are stronger standards and safeguards for patients;
• NHS organisations are better at understanding patients and their needs, use new and different methodologies to do so, and have better and more regular sources of information about preferences and satisfaction.

Where this happens, everyone involved makes sure they:
• respect people for their knowledge and understanding of their own experiences, their own clinical condition, their experience of the illness and how it impacts on their life;
• provide people with the information and choices that allow them to feel in control;
• treat people as human beings and as individuals, not just people to be processed;
• ensure people feel valued by the health service and are treated with respect, dignity and compassion;
• understand that the best judge of their experience is the individual.

Patients who are treated considerately, who are not left to endure anxiety and worry, who are treated attentively, who are given full and prompt information, who understand what they are being told, and who are given the opportunity to ask questions, are more likely to have better clinical outcomes. A good patient experience goes with good clinical care – and patients need both.

The cultural background of the doctor

1 Discuss the extent to which you believe doctors and patients with the same cultural/racial background should be matched. Then read the extract below and see if you agreed with the authors.

To summarise the main issues involved in working with patients from different cultural backgrounds:

1. It is not necessary to raise cultural or racial issues unless they are important for the patient, or unless a misunderstanding might occur if they are not addressed.

2. There is sometimes a misconception that a patient should be matched to a doctor from the same cultural or racial background in order to facilitate communication and enhance care. This may be desirable for some patients, but for others, differences in background will not be a barrier, or they may not be relevant to the treatment in any way. The patient should be able to choose whom they wish to consult and indicate how they wish to be treated; the doctor might ask, for example:

Do you feel that it would be easier for you to see a doctor from a similar background?

I can appreciate how frustrating it is to talk to someone who does not share your culture (or speak your native tongue), but perhaps you can let me know about cultural practices that are important for you to follow when you are in hospital.

The doctor acknowledges that there are communication problems and tries to work with the patient to overcome them. Alternatively, some patients may choose a doctor from a different culture, preferring not to disclose their illness to someone of their own background because they contracted it through an activity that is culturally unacceptable. For other patients, a doctor of their own gender may be more important than a doctor of their own culture. At times, matching only serves to reinforce stereotypes that groups hold about one another. Also, if a patient is matched with a doctor of the same culture, they may expect the doctor to share their values; this might place a doctor trained in a different culture system in an awkward position.

3. Patients and doctors can communicate effectively even if they are from different cultures. It is often thought that if doctor and patient are too culturally distant, they will not be able to communicate effectively. Such a belief can result in hospital staff avoiding an ethnic minority patient because they are unsure about how to communicate. In fact, differences may not always be a barrier. You can explore ways to gain information about the patient's culture that can be used in a constructive way to complement care. It is also possible that the patient is well informed about the host country's cultural practices and is willing to look beyond their own cultural viewpoint when seeking medical help.

Taken from *Communication Skills for Medicine*, Lloyd and Bor, 2004

2 Examine the reasons why the authors suggest patients might need a doctor of their own gender as opposed to their own culture.

3 Make a list of some of the key points involved in crossing cultural barriers during the patient encounter. Read the extract below to compare your answers with Lloyd and Bor's.

- Heightened awareness of cultural issues can help you to make a more accurate assessment of the patient's behaviour, to improve the therapeutic relationship and to enhance treatment.
- There are certain cultural groups, particularly new arrivals of refugees, that may have multiple psychological and physical concerns, and these may need to be discussed when there is a sense of trust and safety; i.e. assessment may take longer than with someone with full command of the language, culture and system.
- The patient may be part of a particular culture, but they will have adopted some aspects of it and rejected others. The doctor must carefully assess each patient's individual and cultural needs before deciding on an appropriate treatment.

1a Before you read, discuss the difference in meaning between the words *implicit* and *explicit*, giving synonyms if possible.

b Read the text and underline any information that surprises you

Unintentional Racism May Affect Emergency Treatment

Doctors' unconscious racial biases may influence their decisions to treat patients and explain racial and ethnic disparities in the use of certain medical procedures, according to Alexander Green from Harvard Medical School and his team. Their study, published in Springer's Journal of General Internal Medicine, is the first evidence of how unconscious race bias among doctors affects their clinical decisions.

Green and colleagues tested whether doctors showed unconscious race bias and whether the scale of such bias predicted recommendations for medical intervention to dissolve clots (thrombolysis) for black and white patients with acute coronary conditions. A total of 220 doctors from four academic medical centres in Atlanta and Boston were surveyed.

The researchers used a web-based survey tool that randomly assigned doctors to look at a picture of a black or white patient presenting to the emergency room department, alongside a brief clinical history and symptoms suggestive of a myocardial infarction. The doctors were then asked whether the chest pain was the result of coronary artery disease, whether they would give the patient thrombolysis and the strength of the recommendation on a scale of '1 – definitely' to '5 – definitely not'. The researchers used computer-based Implicit Association Tests (IATs) to measure unconscious bias. The software asked doctors whether they preferred white or black Americans and also about their beliefs concerning patients' cooperativeness in general and with regards to medical procedures in particular. Doctors' conscious racial bias was also assessed by questionnaire.

Doctors who participated reported no conscious (or 'explicit') bias for white versus black patients and reported black and white patients to be equally cooperative with medical procedures. In contrast, IATs revealed an unconscious (or 'implicit') preference favouring white Americans, and unconscious stereotypes of black Americans as less cooperative with medical procedures and less cooperative generally.

Doctors' self-reported attitudes towards patients and of stereotypes about cooperativeness by race did not influence their decision to give thrombolysis for black versus white patients. However, doctors' unconscious bias strongly influences whether or not they gave the patients thrombolsyis. As doctors' pro-white unconsciousness bias increased, so did their likelihood of treating white patients and not treating black patients.

The authors conclude that: 'implicit biases are primarily unconscious and do not imply overt racism. They do, however, remind us that implicit biases may affect the behaviour even of those individuals who have nothing but the best intentions, including those in medical practice.'

Medical News Today, 23 August 2007

2 Discuss these questions.

1 In your experience, which group in society have you found to be more or less cooperative within the medical context? In what ways? Consider age, social background, level of education, gender, culture.

2 How might a doctor ensure that their intentions towards their patient remain the best?

3 The aim of the Implicit Association Tests was to explore the automatic roots of thought and feeling. The designers of the test suggest that results should be used to prompt people to take note of the broad reach of stereotyping and to develop awareness of their own and others' automatic preferences and stereotypes. Try out the test for yourself at: https://implicit.harvard.edu/implicit/demo/.

The physical examination: points to consider

The physical examination is often considered the least pleasant part of the encounter for the patient, but although there are a number of fundamental issues that must be taken into consideration, the examination can have a therapeutic effect and even be an extension of the interview.

1a Before you read the text, think about the following:

  1 What are the fundamental issues when carrying out the physical examination?
  2 How might the physical examination be considered an extension of the interview?

b Read the text and compare your thoughts.

Engendering an atmosphere of trust and the utmost professionalism is imperative when carrying out a physical examination. The doctor who remains respectful and takes into consideration the discomfort and embarrassment that the patient may be feeling is the one who will manage to maintain the rapport established at the beginning of the encounter. Likewise, the patient who remains relatively relaxed during an examination is more likely to comply.

There is a level of intimacy and touch within the doctor-patient relationship that is only usually reserved for the patient's partner. It is important therefore that measures are taken to explain the steps of the examination appropriately and, if necessary, what information you hope to elicit from the process. This will help to avoid any misunderstanding and will reassure the patient, taking away some of the mysticism that may surround the doctor-patient relationship. Following on from this is the order in which you carry out the examination. Starting with an examination of the hands and then working ones way up the arm is more socially acceptable than beginning with any other part of the body, allowing your patient to relax and gain your trust as you do so.

The history-taking process does not stop once the physical begins; rather, it is a continuum of the interview that can in itself have a therapeutic affect for some – a kind of 'laying on of hands' (Enelow et al, 1996) during which the communication between doctor and patient can embark on a different level and questions of a personal nature can be raised that could not previously be raised. Somehow the physical examination allows for the barriers to be further broken down, and patients feel more comfortable and therefore at ease to ask questions not previously broached. It may well be at this point that their hidden agenda comes to the forefront.

Below is a case study that illustrates exactly this:
A 65-year-old woman [...] was discovered to have breast cancer several weeks earlier by her gynaecologist, [...] but the patient could not be convinced of the need for medical care. (She was eventually convinced to have a complete physical examination.) During the interview preceding the physical examination, the patient was wary, formal, closed and had no rapport with the physician. As the physical examination was coming to a close, there was a noticeable change in the patient's appearance and behaviour. She appeared to relax, no longer holding herself so rigidly. Then she gradually began to tell the story of what she had gone through since the discovery of the lump – her fear of cancer and her fear of dying. She spoke of the immense conflict she was having between following her religious beliefs (as a Christian Scientist) and accepting surgery. Finally, she spoke of what a relief it was to be able to talk about it.

Adapted from *Interviewing and Patient Care*, Enelow et al, 1996

---

2 Share with the group any experience you might have had similar to the one described in the case study.

The bad news and the bad news

1 Read the text and discuss what the 'good news' was for the patient.

I recently saw a 64-year-old man with a skin lesion on his knee that had been intermittently weeping pus over the past four weeks and had been growing in size. The lesion was well demarcated, granulomatous, and about 2x2 cm in size. He had had it for over a year, but it had never bothered him until recently. The lesion did not look infected, so I decided to remove it and send it for histology.

Four days later, I was called by a consultant pathologist, who started quizzing me about this patient. Specifically he wanted to know the patient's sexual orientation and whether he was an intravenous drug user. The patient was homosexual, and when I told the consultant so it seemed to confirm his suspicion. 'This looks like a nodular Kaposi's sarcoma,' he said, 'but I'll need to send it to an expert in London to confirm this as I'm really not certain.'

From what I knew about Kaposi's sarcoma, it was nearly always linked to HIV infection. I felt apprehensive about telling the patient of the diagnosis for several reasons: I still had no definite confirmation that this was Kaposi's sarcoma (the London expert would have the final word on that) and I would have to tell the patient he had a cancer and very possibly HIV infection as well. Talk about breaking bad news. I therefore decided not to tell the patient until I had the expert opinion.

I finally heard back from the consultant in London: 'Yes, this has all the features of Kaposi's sarcoma.' I called the patient in and broke the bad news to him. I told him that there was a good chance that this form of cancer was linked with being HIV positive, and he understood this. He explained that he had always avoided the issue of HIV testing because he was frightened. He was understandably shaken.

In our surgery we put alerts on the patient's computer records and had a "critical event" meeting to alert all staff about the "high risk patient". I talked to the regional genito-urinary medicine clinic, where the patient was seen the next day.

Then, a week later, I received some unexpected news from the clinic (the patient having given consent for the information to be sent to me): several HIV tests had been carried out, and all were negative. Everyone was most surprised. The patient had no Mediterranean or Jewish background and did not seem to be immunocompromised, so why had he developed the sarcoma? The patient telephoned me and was understandably over the moon. From thinking that he was HIV positive to having "just" a skin cancer made a huge difference to him.

This incident made me think of how rarely things are clear-cut in medicine. All the surgery staff were convinced that this patient was infected with HIV, possibly even immunocompromised with AIDS. It turned out we were all wrong. As doctors, we rely on odds and likelihood, but it is important to bear in mind that sometimes the unlikely (odd) will happen and take us by surprise.

Mark Taubert, GP registrar
Ty Bryn Surgery, Caerphilly

BMJ 2005;330:1063 (7 May), doi:10.1136/bmj.330.7499.1063

2 Where there is a possibility of a prognosis being bad, do you think this should be communicated to the patient as soon as possible? Why / Why not?

3 Discuss what conclusions can be drawn from the text about giving patients results of their tests.

Not always looking on the bright side of life

1 The article below is from a series entitled *My most unfortunate mistake*. Discuss what the unfortunate mistake was in this case.

One of my first tasks as a new Senior House Officer in vascular surgery was to get a patient's consent for elective abdominal aortic aneurysm repair. He was a slim, active, very anxious 73-year-old with a 5.6 cm asymptomatic aneurysm. He was intensely interested in the mechanics of the operation. I drew many diagrams and explained in detail the risks of surgery.

I told him there was a 5% risk of death, pausing to emphasise the gravity of the situation, and then solemnly described in painstaking detail the risks of embolisation – limb loss, paraplegia, bowel ischaemia, and cardiac and renal failure. I told him of the slim chance of survival in the event of rupture. It was a bleak picture.

He acquired a deathly pallor and, gripping the pen in trembling fingers, leant over to sign the consent form, complaining as he did so of a sharp pain in the back. He jumped up in an attempt to relieve his "muscle spasm" and then felt a little faint. He was hypotensive with bradycardia and pain on straight leg raising, a non-tender aneurysm, and a normal electrocardiogram. With reassurance from me and his wife, his pulse and blood pressure rapidly returned to normal.

I thought that his back pain must be neuromuscular. He had been leaning at an awkward angle when he signed the consent form. The sharp twinge of pain combined with suddenly rising to his feet must have induced a vasovagal attack. I returned to the ward later to find him nervously pacing the corridor with the air of a condemned man. Walking eased his back pain, he told me. Reassured, I went home.

At his operation the next day, he was found to have a large, fresh, contained aortic rupture involving two thirds of the posterior wall of the aorta and exposing the anterior longitudinal ligament of the spine. There were no complications, and he made a rapid recovery.

He was so pleased to find himself alive and still able to walk after the operation that he made light of my probably causing and then failing to diagnose his rupture. Instead, he suggested that in future I should adopt a more jovial approach to obtaining consent and that setting a few words to song might lighten the mood. I'm still struggling to find a suitable tune and something that rhymes with paraplegia. Any suggestions?

Ruth James, Research Fellow in Vascular Surgery
Nuffield Department of Surgery, John Radcliffe Hospital, Oxford

---

BMJ 2005;330:584 (12 March), doi:10.1136/bmj.330.7491.584

2 Do you think the age of a patient should make a difference in explaining the risks of a procedure?

3 Based on the knowledge that you have gained from this unit, discuss how you would deal with a similar situation.

Unit 8

Tackling Scotland's drink problem

Alcohol kills six people every day in Scotland, alcoholic liver disease has more than doubled in the past ten years, and doctors report an increase in the number of young people presenting to the NHS with serious illness resulting from alcohol misuse. Drinking in moderation can be a source of pleasure; however, the effect of excessive alcohol consumption on our health and the related social and economic impact are significant.

1a Before you read the article, think about how manufacturers, retail outlets, advertising agencies and the government might help reduce the impact of alcohol consumption in Scotland.

b Now compare your thoughts with the five-point plan proposed by the BMA in Scotland in the article below.

BMA Scotland Publishes Plan to Tackle Scotland's Drink Problem

BMA Scotland published a five point plan to tackle Scotland's alcohol problem:

1. Utilise the legislative capabilities of the 2005 Licensing (Scotland) Act, to end deep discounting of alcohol for sale in off-licences, supermarkets and other off-sales outlets. Cheap drinks promotions which encourage people to buy more alcohol, particularly in supermarkets and off-licenses, must be controlled. Some supermarkets are running alcohol products as a 'loss leader,' which in some cases has resulted in alcohol being cheaper than bottled water.

2. Undertake research into the measures by which pricing mechanisms can be used in Scotland to discourage heavy consumption of high alcohol products. Strong evidence suggests that increasing the price of alcohol may be an effective method of reducing use by adolescents.

3. End alcohol producers' sponsorship of sporting and entertainment events with a young target audience. This is an important advertising mechanism for the alcohol industry. However, the exposure of children to alcohol's linkage to entertainment events or sporting activities gives alcohol innocence by association.

4. Legislate for alcohol labelling rather than relying on voluntary agreements with the drinks industry. More than eight out of ten doctors believe that alcoholic drinks manufacturers should be compelled to clearly label their products with the number of units of alcohol in each product.

5. Reducing the drink driving limit from 80mg to 50mg will prevent around 65 deaths in the UK each year. BMA Scotland calls upon the Scottish Executive to exert pressure on the UK government to consider reducing drink driving limits. The introduction of random roadside breath testing would be a vital element in deterring people from drinking and driving, and could be implemented by the Scottish Parliament.

Announcing the plan, Dr Peter Terry, Chairman of the BMA in Scotland, said: 'Our action plan sets out a range of measures that the Scottish Executive can take forward as part of a wider strategy. Most people enjoy a drink and we don't want to end the right of individuals to have that choice; however, we want to encourage adults to drink in moderation, rather than drinking to get drunk. Worryingly, more and more teenagers are drinking at an earlier age and we must do more to combat this trend. Increasing price is one part of a strategy that can deter children from purchasing alcohol. The BMA would also like to see more done in primary schools to educate children about the dangers of drink before they are drawn in by industry advertising. After smoking, alcohol is the next big public health priority, and I want Scottish Ministers to work with doctors to end Scotland's drink problem.'

Adapted from *Medical News Today*, 26th June 2007

2 Discuss these questions.

1 Drinking in moderation vs. drinking to get drunk – where does your culture fall?

2 How does current legislation to protect the consumer in Scotland / the UK compare to what you know of legislation in your country?

3 Should the dangers of alcohol be debated with children at primary level?

A memorable patient: keep looking for a reason

1 Read the text and discuss what was memorable about this patient.

Sarah was 22 when she presented with the dreadful signs of a large space-occupying lesion deep in the dominant parietal lobe. She was drowsy with a severe headache, had severe dysphasia, and there was a significant right-sided weakness. The computed tomography said it all: a malignant intrinsic tumour at the trigone of the lateral ventricle, probably a glioblastoma.

She rallied a little on steroids overnight and so I performed a craniotomy, having suitably warned her worried family of the likely outcome and prognosis. I found a very bloody tumour that had some definition from the surrounding brain. The pathologist told me that the frozen section showed a highly malignant brain tumour, consistent with the radiologist's diagnosis. The survival from this type of tumour in this position is measured in months, and there is no evidence that surgery does much more than relieve the pressure symptoms. Consequently, I completed a cautious internal decompression, stopped the bleeding, and closed up. She was unchanged, but bled into the tumour remnant the following day and I had to reopen the craniotomy. That night I was relieved that she was no worse.

Sarah's tumour was a gliosarcoma. This is a rare and even more malignant variant of a glioblastoma, in which it is thought that the new vessel forming factors released by the primary brain tumour induce sarcomatous change in the blood vessels. The news was not good.

Surprisingly, Sarah started to get better. Her speech improved and her hemiparesis almost disappeared. She was referred for radiotherapy and underwent the full six weeks' course. The follow-up scan also looked good. She lost her job in insurance, but became a police receptionist.

Two years went by, but there was no sign of the tumour on further scans. By then, Sarah had become a good friend of the hospital, active in collecting money for the development fund and talking to the press about her treatment.

After three years, when the vast majority of patients with a glioblastoma are dead, I asked the pathologists to review the case, but despite the tumour's unusual behaviour, they could not come up with any other diagnosis.

Meanwhile, Sarah had married and was thinking of starting a family. By this time, much more sensitive magnetic resonance imaging had become more freely available, and the scan showed no recurrence. At six years, I asked the pathologist to re-review the case. By now, immunocytochemistry was much more sophisticated and, despite the mitoses and other seemingly malignant features, he was able to reclassify the lesion as a much more benign pleomorphic xanthoastrocytoma.

When I told Sarah this exciting news, I was most surprised that it seemed unimportant to her, almost to the point of disinterestedness.

She remains well almost ten years from diagnosis. Her scan is clear, but she still worries about recurrence. I worry about the possibility of radionecrosis which sometimes afflicts long-term survivors of brain irradiation.

I have learnt three things from Sarah's case. Firstly, that having lived with the diagnosis of having had cancer but being free from recurrence, being an unusual statistic with a semi-benign condition of unknown behaviour lacks meaning. Secondly, when tumours behave in highly unusual ways, keep looking for a reason. Thirdly, do not expect other patients' tumours to behave in a similarly unusual fashion – a temptation that I fell into at least once.

Michael Powell, Consultant Neurosurgeon
London

BMJ 2000;320:1187 (29 April)

2 Can you think of any reason why the patient saw the reclassification of her lesion as unimportant?

3 Discuss whether this article has influenced the way you feel about breaking bad news to patients with terminal illnesses.

A memorable patient: 'There is nothing wrong with me.'

1 Read the text discuss what was memorable about this patient.

'Next, please,' and in came a spry, fit-looking, silver haired man. In answer to the usual question, 'What can I do for you?' he replied, 'I am not complaining of anything. There is nothing wrong with me.'

There was no letter from his general practitioner. Why not? 'Because there was no point in troubling him, so I came straight to you because you are the consultant for outpatients.' There was open access in the general medical outpatients department in the Royal Infirmary of Edinburgh and one consultant physician, two registrars, and three rotating senior registrars. We would see between 80 and 100 patients each morning. This certainly gave us much experience but evidently did not give me the wisdom to advise this man.

I was unable to obtain any clinical history from him apart from an appendicectomy at the age of 18. After some resistance, because he said that I would find nothing, I examined him. He was right; I found nothing. Again with some complaint from him, I took blood for such simple screening tests as blood counts, sedimentation rate and liver function tests. All were found to be normal.

He then said, 'Now what are you going to do about me? I am a widower, aged 70, a retired lawyer with three married sons, all employed and provided for. I have no desire to carry on until I am disabled and miserable.' I probably made some encouraging or reassuring remark, which was not well received. 'Of course, I realise that the NHS can't kill people but can it afford to keep me for ten or more years of possible illness?' He left in a disagreeable mood, and I was quite shaken by the whole episode.

At lunch I told my tale to my consultant colleagues, and the new professor of psychiatry castigated me for missing acute depression, which was crying out for help. He even suggested that I encouraged the lawyer to commit suicide. This shook me even more. I have often wondered what the professor of psychiatry would have said to this educated man and how he would have managed him.

I wrote to the patient a month later and asked him to come again. There was no response. On inquiry, his general practitioner said that he had not seen him for many years and knew nothing about his visit, other than my letter reporting it. Two months later, a second letter was returned marked, "Gone away."
It was unfortunate that he saw a cardiologist.

Michael Oliver, Emeritus Professor of Cardiology
London

BMJ 1997;315 (8 November)

2 The number of patients seen by the doctors in the clinic was quite considerable. To what extent do you think time pressure might make it difficult to deal with a patient like this?

3 In the text, the author says, 'It was unfortunate that he saw a cardiologist.' To what extent you think any doctor should have been able to respond to the situation described here. How do you think the Professor of Psychiatry referred to in the text might have handled this situation?

1 Read the text and try to identify the communication problems.

'Oh dear, there's no smoke,' was my first thought as I approached the house. This was in the days of regular unannounced visits to elderly patients, and I was dropping in on Jean "while I was passing".

A lifetime of service in the local mansion had been rewarded with a retirement cottage in the grounds, one of the features of which was a permanent plume of smoke from the chimney. But on that mid-January day there was none, and I was a little apprehensive as I pushed open the front door. However, there she was, lively as ever but huddled in her overcoat and mitts in front of an empty hearth.

Over the years Jean had developed a number of eccentricities. One of the most troublesome was her manner of speech. With increasing deafness, she had adopted the habit of repeating everything said to her. Presumably this started as her way of confirming the question, but by the time I knew her it was a firmly ingrained reflex. As a result, conversations took on a surreal format:

    Me: How are you today?
    Jean: How are you today?
    Me: No, how are you today?
    Jean: No, how are you today?

And so on, all conducted at high volume. (Jean had a fine collection of NHS hearing aids, but she kept them in a drawer rather than her ears.)

    'Have you no coal?' I shouted.
    'Have you no coal?' she replied.

After much in a similar vein, she eventually seemed to get the message that I was worried about her fuel supplies. She led me out to her shed. The first door opened to reveal a pathetic pile of sticks in the corner. Problem solved, I thought, but my tour was not yet finished. The next door opened on to a pile of coal the like of which I have only seen in pictures of the Titanic's boiler room.

At this moment Jean's neighbour arrived with her shopping, and I started to inquire whether he had noticed other signs of her mental health deteriorating. Gravely we discussed the possibility of dementia and whether Jean might need help from social services or even have to give up living alone.

Meanwhile, Jean had been rummaging in her shopping bag. Suddenly, she let out a small cry of success, and, holding aloft a packet of firelighters, headed inside to get on with the business of the day.

There may be no smoke without fire, but there can be no fire without firelighters.

Sandy Sutherland, General Practitioner
Pathhead, Midlothian

BMJ 2002;325:1231 (23 November)

2 A lack of communication caused by physical impairment can sometimes be mistaken for mental impairment. How do you think it might be possible to check quickly to determine which it is? Do you have any examples of this?

3 In this case, the assumption by the doctor was that Jean's lack of a fire was due to her deteriorating mental condition. What do you think this tells us about making assumptions where older people are concerned?

4 What is the most memorable comment you have received from a patient? Share it with the rest of the group.

Unit 12 A memorable patient: the value of communication

1 Read the text and discuss what lesson the doctor learnt from this experience.

> I expect she is back in Vietnam now. I often think about her and her family.
>
> She was a pleasant child, with limited Cantonese picked up from her many years spent in a detention camp in Hong Kong. She had had a relapse of her nephrotic syndrome and had stayed with us a while until diuresis occurred, as the camps were not suitable for someone receiving high dose corticosteroids. She also had a history of asthma, which was quiescent at the time.
>
> We got on well, despite the language barrier. I guess one doesn't need many words during play. I explained her condition to her softly-spoken mother through an interpreter. I learnt that they had been in the camp for a few years and that she loved all her children very much, that they were all she had after her husband had died in a camp fight.
>
> It was coming up to a local festival, and the mother was keen to have her family together for the occasion. The wards were quiet, the child's corticosteroids had been reduced, and she was stable. I agreed that she could return to the camp for the holiday period.
>
> After the holiday, I discovered that the child had had to be admitted to the intensive care unit. She had had a severe asthma attack, required ventilation, and suffered cerebral hypoxia. No one blamed me. After all, her asthma had been under control when she left. I felt incredibly guilty, though, and I didn't want to face the mother. Nevertheless, facing up to parents was part of the job, so again I called in the interpreter and tried to explain what was being done to help, explained what could have happened, and expressed my regret at the situation. The mother just cried.
>
> The child made a surprisingly good recovery. With physiotherapy and speech therapy, she regained most of her speech and mobility. I wrote letters and made many telephone calls to camp officials, insisting that the mother be allowed daily visits to the hospital.
>
> During those weeks of recovery, the mother didn't say much to me, despite our many meetings via an interpreter. She seemed to accept the turn of events, and I was just pleased that the child was able to walk out of the hospital independently. What did it matter if the mother didn't think much of this junior doctor's management?
>
> On the day of discharge, the mother handed me a package wrapped in newspaper and thanked me for helping them. It turned out to be the most beautiful hand-knitted jumper I had ever seen. This treasured item serves as a reminder to me to be always truthful to my patients and their families, and to be sure to spend time communicating with them regardless of the disease and management outcome, because families always appreciate honesty and genuine concern.
>
> Yvonne Ou, Senior Medical Officer in Paediatrics

BMJ 2003;326:1026 (10 May)

2 In the text, the child's condition deteriorates when she is discharged to her family for their local festival. Discuss to what extent the well-being of the patient should outweigh their need to be with their family.

3 Dr Ou highlights her commitment to always being truthful to her patients. Is this always possible? Are there any situations where you have been tempted to be less truthful to patients?

The presenting complaint

Clip 1

> Kelly Turner, 23, has been referred by her doctor to the consultant, Mr Spark. She has been suffering from recurring headaches. This is her first visit to Mr Spark.

Global observations

1a Watch Clip 1 without sound and report back on one of the seven elements of non-verbal communication below:
- eye contact
- proximity
- environment
- posture
- facial expression
- clothing
- movement

1b Build up a picture of the patient and her presenting complaint from what you have seen so far.

1c Watch the clip again with sound and decide how accurate your picture of the patient was, as discussed in 1b.

1d Decide to what extent the doctor adheres to the advice given by Osler in Unit 1: *The kindly word, the cheerful greeting, the sympathetic look – these the patient understands.*

1e Write a diary entry for this patient following her visit, describing how she felt during the encounter with this particular doctor.

Clip 2

> Ted Margolis, 52, has been suffering from stomach pains and has been referred by his GP to Dr Davis, a consultant at his local hospital. Ted is a taxi driver. This is his first visit to Dr Davis.

Pre-watching

2 Clip 2 is a comparative study. What differences to Clip 1 are you hoping to see?

Global observations

3a Watch Clip 2 without sound from the start until the patient sits down (00:00>00:30). What are your initial impressions of the doctor's non-verbal communication skills?

3b Now watch the whole clip with sound and give Dr Davis a rating for any two of the points below, indicating your general impression:

Rating:　competent ✓✓✓
　　　　　fairly competent ✓✓
　　　　　needs more work ✓

	Item	Rating
1	Used a patient-centred approach throughout the consultation	
2	Began with open and moved to closed questions as appropriate	
3	Refrained from employing leading and tag questions	
4	Enquired about specific features of the condition (location, quality, severity, etc.)	
5	Asked about aggravating and alleviating factors	
6	Enquired about associated manifestations	
7	Used clear questions, avoiding complicated medical terminology	
8	Employed appropriate tone of voice	

3c In pairs or small groups, compare your overall impressions.

3d To what extent did you feel Dr Davis' non-verbal communication matched his verbal skills?

Watching for detail

Part 1: from Start to *Can we focus on the trouble you've been having with your stomach?* (00:00>01:35)

4a Watch Part 1 of the clip and take notes on EITHER Mr Margolis (his character, family life, etc.) OR the reason for his visit.

4b Share your findings with the rest of the group and build a more rounded picture of the patient.

4c Answer these questions.
1　The patients in Clips 1 and 2 have both been referred by their GPs. How does Dr Davis choose to deal with this situation?
2　What language does the doctor use to set the agenda for the interview?

Part 2: from *Can we focus on the trouble you've been having with your stomach?* to *... that's enough, innit?* (01:35>03:58)

5a Watch Part 2 of the clip. As you watch, note specific information about the patient's condition under these headings:

Attributes of a Symptom

- Location
- Quantity/Severity
- Setting
- Associated manifestations
- Quality
- Timing
- Aggravating/Alleviating
- "8th Attribute"[1]

5b There are some attributes the doctor does not ask about? Why?

5c Complete the questions Dr Davis uses to ask about some of the attributes.

1 Can I ask you _____ _____ the pain is when it _____ _____ ?

2 Have you noticed that _____ _____ _____ worse?

3 Does anything else _____ _____ ?

4 Does the pain _____ anywhere, or does it _____ _____ in that, that one _____ ?

5 Have you noticed anything else that _____ _____ with the pain?

Part 3: from *... that's enough, innit?* to End. (03:59>05:50)

6a Watch Part 3 of the clip and then answer these questions.

1 What is the doctor doing by posing the following question: *Can I ask you some specific questions about symptoms you might have had?*

2 Why does he decide to take this approach with the patient?

3 How does the doctor rephrase the question *And can I just ask if your bowels have been OK?* when it's clear the patient hasn't understood? Why is the patient more likely to understand this new question?

4 The patient uses the phrase *regular as clockwork*. What does he mean in this context?

6b Look at these questions and decide how you might improve them: *You never vomit anything up? You never vomit up blood or anything like that?*

6c Add information regarding the "8th Attribute" to Exercise 5a.

6d Why do you think the doctor doesn't try to correct the patient when he says *... they couldn't find nothing wrong when they did the EGC ...* (05:04)?

7 Watch the whole clip again. What approach does Dr Davis seem to favour to encourage Ted to tell his story in his own words: repetition, clarification or facilitation?

Over to you

You are going to role-play the scenario in Clip 1. Work in threes, taking it in turns to play the role of the doctor, patient and observer.

Doctor: before the role-play, write appropriate questions for each stage of the seven Attributes of a Symptom. During the role-play, remember to consider the patient's perspective and set an appropriate agenda.

Patient: before the role-play, use the diary entries you wrote in Exercise 1e as a starting point and give more details about the symptoms, patient's character and lifestyle, as well as any other information you think might be relevant.

Observer: during the role-play, use the checklist in Exercise 3b and give constructive feedback to the person playing the doctor.

---

[1] Asking about the patient's perspective on the symptoms, and what he/she is expecting from the doctor.

Mr Davis continues to interview Ted Margolis.

Pre-watching

1 Based on what you learnt about Ted Margolis in the previous clip, how forthcoming do you think he will be regarding questions about his family and social history? Explain your answer.

2 Look at some of the colloquial expressions used in the clip and their meanings. How many of them are you familiar with?

DIY = Do It Yourself (home improvements, etc.)
he brought it on himself = it's his own fault
cabbie = someone who drives a taxi
the Mrs = slightly derogatory term for one's own / someone else's wife
goodness knows = I really don't know

Global observations

3a Watch the whole clip and take notes on general information that might help the doctor understand more about the patient as a person (employment status, leisure time, hobbies, etc.).

3b Share your findings with the rest of the group.

3c As a non-native speaker, think about how easy it would be for *you* to understand Ted. Compare strategies you might use to better understand your patient.

Watching for detail

Part 1: from Start to *Tuesday, you know. OK, alright.* (00:00>01:52)

4a Watch Part 1 of the clip. As you watch, number the components of the PMH (Past Medical History) as you hear them. Mr Davis does not cover all of the components.

☐ Past illnesses
☐ Immunisations
☐ Accidents and injuries
☐ Pregnancies
☐ Childhood illnesses
☐ Surgical procedures
☐ Allergies
☐ Medication

4b Discuss the rationale for the exclusion of certain components of the PMH.

4c Watch Part 1 again and complete the Patient Note for this section of the interview.

PMH

DH (Drug History)

Allergies

4d What evidence is there of Mr Davis' active listening skills during this section of the interview?

4e Mr Davis asks several leading questions. Look at these examples and rewrite them so that they no longer lead the patient.

1 But you've not had any major illnesses, accidents, that sort of thing?

2 So you've not had any operations, anything like that, have you?

Part 2: from *And if I can just ask a little about your family ... to ... my own, you know, drinking.* (01:52>02:26)

5a Watch Part 2 of the clip. Which of the following is Ted susceptible to and why?

1 Lung cancer
2 Heart disease
3 Alcoholism

5b What does Ted really think about his brother's death? How do you know? How has this affected Ted and his lifestyle?

Part 3: from *Can I just ask you about that?* to *Thank you very much.* (02:26>03:10)

6a Watch Part 3 of the clip and complete the dialogue.

Doctor: Can I just ask you a bit about that? Do you _____ _____ _____ at all?

Ted: Well, I do, but I got to be careful, of course, cos of, with driving, you know. So I can only drink if I know _____ _____ _____ the next day, you know.

Doctor: OK, so how much alcohol _____ _____ _____ in a, in an average week, do you think?

Ted: Oh, probably about _____ _____ , I should think.

6b Look at the exchange above. What two questions does the doctor use to ask Ted about his drinking habits? Why does he phrase them in this way?

Part 4: from *Thank you very much* to End (03:10>03:40)

7a Before you watch Part 4, predict the points you expect Mr Davis to mention in his summary of Ted's PMH, family and social history.

7b Listen to Part 4 and check your answers to Exercise 6a.

7c Write down the question the doctor asks to check the accuracy of the summary. What is the significance of this question?

Post-watching

8 Imagine you have just been shadowing Mr Davis. What would *you* take away from this particular experience? Consider both positive and negative points.

Over to you

You are going to role-play a section of the interview (PMH, family and social history) with a patient who is very different in character from Ted. This person is not so ready to disclose information about his/her family and social history, although volunteers information about their PMH without too much persuasion.

Before you do the role-play, in pairs :

- plot the Pedigree Diagram for this patient (it could be a case you have worked on in the past or someone you know well);
- write a short description of the patient's character and their current concerns about their health. Include any other points you wish in order to give a rounder picture of the patient.

As a follow up, the doctors should evaluate their own performance, and patients should evaluate the way in which they were treated during the interview. Compare your ideas.

Examining a patient

Mr Davis carries out a physical examination of the patient.

Pre-watching

1a Now that you have a fairly detailed picture of the patient, Ted Margolis, and his symptoms, compile a list of investigations you expect Mr Davis to carry out during the physical examination.

1b Use the list you compiled for Exercise 1a to add more items to the checklist below. Include points on the medical and communication aspects of the examination.
During the physical examination, the doctor
1 washed his hands thoroughly. YES/NO
2 explained instructions clearly. YES/NO
3 kept the patient informed. YES/NO
4 palpated the area. YES/NO

Global observations

2a Watch the whole clip and evaluate the doctor's ability to carry out a physical examination effectively, using the checklist from Exercise 1b.

2b Compare your initial impressions. What might *you* have done differently?

2c How did the doctor manage his voice during the examination, and what effect did this have on the patient?

Watching for detail

Part 1: from Start to *Are you comfortable like that, Ted? Yes, that's fine.* (00:00>01:01)

3a Watch Part 1 of the clip. As you watch, concentrate on the investigations carried out by the doctor and then discuss these questions.
1 From a social as opposed to a medical perspective, why did the doctor start by examining the patient's hands?
2 Why does the doctor give a rationale for certain investigations?

3b Rewrite this instruction given by Mr Davis to make it clearer: *I'm gonna get you lying up on the couch.*

3c Is the following question suitable or unsuitable for this particular patient? Why?
... so you might feel more comfortable if you've got an empty bladder. Do you need to have a pee first of all?

3d In your culture / professional environment, how suitable would it be to use the equivalent expression in your language with an adult?

3e Rewrite the instruction in Exercise 3c, making it more suitable for this patient.

Part 2: from *So if you just look up at the ceiling for me* ... to ... *round gently.* (01:01>01:57)

4a Watch Part 2 of the clip and complete the dialogue.

Doctor: So if you just look up at the ceiling for me. That's great. If you _____ _____ _____ _____ for me now. And pop it back in again. And now _____ _____ _____ _____ feel for any glands at the _____ _____ your neck. That's fine.
Patient: What do you mean, you didn't find any?
Doctor: There are none there. No, I can't feel anything. That's fine. What I'd _____ _____ _____ now is just examine your stomach, OK? Can you tell me _____ it hurts?
Patient: It's right in there, doc.
Doctor: Alright, so I'll be _____ _____ when I'm pressing on there. What I'm going to do is just _____ _____ _____ . Could you tell me _____ _____ _____ at all?

4b Answer these questions.
1 What evidence is there that the patient trusts the doctor during this experience?
2 What is the significance of the expression *for me* and what impact might it have on the doctor's rapport with the patient?

Part 3: from *Could you tell me if it hurts at all?* to End. (01:57>03:30)

5a Watch Part 3 of the clip and complete the dialogue.

Doctor: Could you tell me if it _____ _____ _____ ?

Patient: Yeah.

Doctor: That's quite _____ , _____ _____ ? I'm gonna press a little bit harder now. So again, _____ _____ _____ it's too uncomfortable.

Patient: That's fine. Oh, oh.

Doctor: That's _____ painful, is it? I'm sorry. But alright over here?

Patient: Yeah.

5b Look at the exchanges in Exercises 4a and 5a and comment on the way the doctor demonstrates active listening skills at each stage of the dialogue. Share your thoughts with the rest of the group.

5c Answer these questions.

1 Look again at this sentence: *Could you tell me if it hurts at all?* What is the significance of the expression *at all*? Watch again and note down the intonation pattern of this expression.

2 Should the patient take the expressions *that's great / that's fine / that's good* literally? Why (not)?

Post-watching

6 How does the doctor ensure the patient's dignity is maintained right up until the end of the examination?

Over to you

The patient in this clip was very compliant; the ideal patient. Some patients find the physical examination unpleasant and need lots of reassurance and encouragement.

Compile a bank of expressions that you might find useful in dealing with different patient types, for example: the timid patient, the body-conscious patient and the aggressive patient. You may wish to think about cases you have dealt with yourself or read about.

Choose one of the patient types and take turns to role-play a difficult part of the physical examination, where you are having problems getting the patient to comply.

> Colin Shaw, 45, has come to see his GP. He's concerned about the shortness of breath he has been experiencing. The doctor has listened to his heart and has just finished taking his blood pressure.

Pre-watching

1 Based on what you studied in Unit 7, what elements would you expect the doctor to include in planning treatment?

Global observations

2 Watch the whole clip. Does the doctor cover all of the stages for negotiating treatment listed below?
1 Discuss options
2 Give information on treatment
3 Obtain patient's view for action
4 Elicit concerns
5 Consider patient's lifestyle
6 Encourage patient involvement in plan
7 Ask about support systems

3 Watch the clip again with the volume turned down and note down examples of the doctor's non-verbal communication. Evaluate these in line with models of good communication.

Watching for detail

Part 1: from Start to *Yeah, there's always a few like that, isn't there?* (00:00>01:32)

4 Watch Part 1 of the clip and answer these questions.
1 How does the patient respond to the good news that there is no problem with his heart or blood pressure?
2 How does the doctor react to the patient's response?
3 What two possible reasons does the doctor give for the breathlessness?
4 What arguments does the patient put forward for not giving up smoking?
5 How does the doctor react while the patient is giving his reasons for not giving up?

Part 2: from *Yeah, there's always a few like that, isn't there?* to *... as opposed to using just willpower on its own.* (01:32>03:30)

5 Watch Part 2 of the clip and answer these questions.
1 Towards the beginning of the clip the doctor crosses her legs. Do you think this has any significance?
2 How does the patient respond to the doctor when she tells him that it would benefit him to give up smoking? Is this significant for the doctor?
3 What options to help give up smoking does the doctor mention?
4 How does the doctor demonstrate that she is listening when the patient expresses his concerns about possible side effects?

Part 3: from *... as opposed to using just willpower on its own* to *Shall I give you a leaflet just to help?* (03:30>05:09)

6 Watch Part 3 of the clip and focus on the doctor's body language as she explains how the nasal spray will work. Identify two examples where her body language reinforces the verbal language, for example where she says *squirt it into your nose* while miming the action with her hands.

Part 4: from *Shall I give you a leaflet just to help?* to End. (05:09>06:57)

7a Watch Part 4 of the clip and focus on the doctor's body language again. Identify at least two examples of when she uses her body language to reinforce what she is saying to the patient.

7b In pairs, discuss how effective her use of body language is in helping to reinforce the message for the patient.

7c As we saw in Unit 7, the following four stages are recommended when closing the interview:
1 Summarises
2 Agrees contract with patient
3 Safety netting
4 Final checking
Watch the final 15 seconds of the clip again and circle the stages the doctor includes.

7d Suggest what the doctor could have said for the stages not covered.

8a Look at these excerpts from the clip and underline language of suggestion or negotiation.
1 Well, I would suggest you give it another try and maybe something like using the nasal spray.
2 And then gradually, over the course of weeks, we'll cut down on how much you're using and get to the point where you hardly need it and then you can just stop.
3 Well, shall we set a date to stop now then?
4 How about I give you a prescription, you can get the stuff and ...

8b How does using indirect language help the interview?

Post-watching

9 In pairs, discuss these questions.
1 What were the doctor's and patient's objectives?
2 Do you think these objectives were achieved by the end of the interview?
3 Do you think the outcome could be best described as compliance or concordance?
4 How would you describe the doctor's tone of voice? Does it contribute to the outcome?

Over to you

The patient in this scenario is very cooperative and responds well to the doctor's suggestions. Imagine you are in a consultation with a patient who needs to urgently give up smoking but is showing considerable resistance.

Work in threes, taking it in turns to play the role of the doctor, patient and observer.

Doctor: you should be more assertive in the role, as the patient is showing considerable resistance to the idea of giving up smoking.

Patient: you are worried that you'll pile on weight if you give up smoking and believe that being overweight will be equally bad as smoking.

Observer: make a note of the stages that the doctor covers from the recommended model. Observe how well the doctor uses his/her body language and voice to convince the patient. Observe how the patient responds to the doctor's suggestions.

Breaking bad news

> Debbie Turlington, 29, received 13 stitches to her ear four days ago following a dog bite. She has now presented to A&E at a different hospital because the wound has become increasingly tender. She has been told that the wound will need cleaning and has been referred to the Ear, Nose and Throat department for treatment. Ms Smithson (ENT specialist) arrives to interview the patient.

Pre-watching

1a Read the synopsis above and draw up a list of points you might need to consider when interviewing this patient.

1b Could there be any problems with the wound that the patient is not expecting?

Global observations

2a Watch the whole clip and choose one of the following tasks:
- EITHER decide to what extent Ms Smithson reassures the patient and shows empathy through appropriate voice management (pausing / speed of delivery / tone) and body language.
- OR number the stages of the SPIKES model employed by Ms Smithson as you hear them. Which does she not cover?

  ☐ Setting
  ☐ Perception
  ☐ Invitation
  ☐ Knowledge
  ☐ Emotion
  ☐ Strategy

2b Compare your findings with the rest of the group.

2c Think back to this quote from Unit 9: *Bad news is any information that changes a person's future in a negative way.* To what extent is Debbie's life likely to change? Explain why.

Watching for detail

Part 1: from Start to ... *painkillers to sort out the pain.* (00:00>02:50)

3a Watch Part 1 of the clip and pause on ... *come down and see <u>you</u>* (00:31). In pairs, look at the scene and discuss the body language employed by each of the people.

3b What language does the patient use to describe the degree of pain she is in? Why would this make the news more difficult to deliver?

Part 2: from *Alright, so ...* to ... *a bit more treatment than that.* (02:50>03:08)

4a Watch Part 2 of the clip and complete this dialogue.

Ms Smithson: Alright, so what are _____ _____ about what's _____ on?

Patient: I don't know. I guess it just needs re-stitching and cleaning up a bit, probably.

Ms Smithson: Yeah, so that's what _____ _____ _____ ?

Patient: Yeah.

Ms Smithson: OK, well I'm really sorry to have to _____ _____ it's _____ _____ _____ a bit more treatment than that.

4b Looking at the exchange above, analyse the way Ms Smithson checks Debbie's perception of the situation and how she prepares her before breaking the bad news.

4c Look at the way both the patient and Ms Smithson use the quantifier *a bit*. Why do they do this?

Part 3: from ... *a bit more treatment than that* to ... *few phone calls? Yeah, yeah.* (03:08>05:30)

5a Watch Part 3 of the clip and circle the correct responses (YES or NO).
Ms Smithson

1 invites the patient to indicate how much information (*I* in the SPIKES model) she would like. YES/NO

2 explains the procedure in a patronising manner. YES/NO

3 considers the patient's level of anxiety. YES / NO

4 uses validating language (language to reassure the patient that what they are feeling is normal) to confirm the patient's feelings. YES/NO

5b Watch Part 3 again and find examples to support your answers to Exercise 5a.

5c Write a question that Ms Smithson could have asked for the *I – information* stage (remember to soften your question).

5d What evidence is there that Ms Smithson is possibly trying to minimise the gravity of the situation? Watch Part 3 again and decide if you agree or disagree with her approach.

5e How might Ms Smithson improve the final stage of the SPIKES model: *S – summary*? Write a short summary. Use a slash (/) to indicate a pause to ensure the summary is delivered in manageable chunks. Hand it to a partner to deliver. Feed back to your partner on his/her delivery.

Part 4: from ... *few phone calls? Yeah, yeah* to ... *lesson for Jo.* (05:30>06:52)

6a Watch Part 4 of the clip and note any language that would not have been used with the patient. Why?

6b Transcribe the language Ms Smithson uses to signify to the patient the beginning and end of the dialogue with her student, and then discuss the following questions.

   1 What purpose does this serve?

   2 Why did Ms Smithson choose this point to discuss the wound with the student rather than having this discussion as soon as they entered the room?

Part 5: from ... *lesson for Jo* to End. (06:52>07:36)

7a Watch Part 5 of the clip. In your experience, or in your country, would the consultant be concerned with the practical details of a patient's admission into hospital?

Post-watching

8 Imagine you have just been shadowing Ms Smithson with Jo. What would *you* take away from this experience?

Over to you

You are faced with a similar situation. This time the patient presents three days later and the cellulitis has spread considerably; it may be difficult to save the patient's ear. Choose one of the scenarios below. Compile some appropriate language/questions for each stage of the SPIKES model and devise a checklist for an observer to enable him/her to give constructive feedback.

Scenario 1: Role-play the dialogue with the patient, explaining the situation.

Scenario 2: The patient has had the operation and has been left with cauliflower ear (a deformity of the outer ear). Role-play a dialogue with the patient's partner over the phone, giving the news.

Communicating with challenging patients

Tony Doyle, 27, is a regular attender at his GP's surgery. On this visit, he is worried that he has Multiple Sclerosis.

Pre-watching

1   Based on what you have learnt in Unit 10, what strategies should the doctor be using to deal with a patient who regularly visits his/her GP with a variety of unrelated complaints?

Global observation

2a Watch the whole clip and answer these questions.
  1 How successful do you think the interview has been for the doctor and the patient?
  2 Do you think there is communication breakdown during the interview?
  3 How do you think the doctor and patient feel at the end of the interview?
  4 How would you describe the doctor's tone of voice?

2b Watch the clip again with the volume turned down and note down examples of the doctor's non-verbal communication. Evaluate these in line with models of good communication.

Watching for detail

Part 1: from Start to *I have checked this up*. (00:00>01:59)

3   Watch Part 1 of the clip and decide whether the doctors uses any validating language.

4   Watch Part 1 again and identify at least two opportunities where the doctor could have acknowledged the patient's feelings.

5   What do you notice about the patient's non-verbal communication when the doctor suggests that he is unlikely to have MS? How does the doctor respond to these non-verbal cues?

Part 2: from *I have checked this up* to *Is there anything else going on in your life*? (01:59>02:26)

6   Watch Part 2 of the clip and complete the dialogue.

Patient: I'm pretty sure I have got MS. I have checked this up.
Doctor: Mr Boyle, _____ _____ _____ what you say, but I feel that I would really like to explore other options to make sure that we haven't, that we don't miss anything—
Patient: What? Well are you saying you don't believe me?

Doctor: _____ _____ to what you have to say—
Patient: I'm telling you the truth!
Doctor: But I'm _____ trying to explain to you that MS is not the only diagnosis. Just _____ _____ me a moment.

Part 3: from *Is there anything else going on in your life?* to End.

7   Watch Part 3 of the clip and complete the examples below where the doctor empathises with the patient.
  1 Patient: ... I lost my job three months ago.
     Doctor: That _____ _____ _____ pretty difficult.
  2 Patient: ... she's gone to stay with her mum.
     Doctor: So _____ _____ _____ for you. So things are looking _____ _____ .

8   Why do you think the doctor uses validating language in this part but not the previous one?

9   Towards the end of the clip, when the patient is responding to her question about neck pain, what non-verbal indication does the doctor give to show that she is listening? How could this be improved on?

Over to you

The patient's belief that he has MS is a key issue in the consultation. The doctor does not challenge him directly on this belief, although there are a number of opportunities.

You are faced with a similar situation. How would you take steps to challenge the patient's claim in a calm but assertive way?

Work in threes, taking it in turns to play the role of the doctor, patient and observer.

Doctor: you should take steps to challenge the patient's claim that he has MS in the early stages of the interview.

Patient: you are willing to accept what the doctor says, providing you are given a clear explanation of why you do not have MS.

Observer: make a note of the stages that the doctor covers from the recommended model. Observe how well the doctor uses his/her body language and voice to convince the patient. Observe how the patient responds to the doctor's suggestions.

Communicating with children

> *Sarah Prescott, 9, has come with her mother to see her GP because of a laceration on her arm.*

Pre-watching

1 With reference to Unit 12, what elements of good communication should the doctor consider to minimise the child's anxiety in these stages:
   - Establishing initial rapport with a child
   - Developing rapport with a child

Global observations

2a Watch the whole clip and tick the stages that the doctor covers.

Establishing initial rapport
- ☐ greets patient
- ☐ demonstrates respect and interest
- ☐ pays child a compliment
- ☐ checks child is comfortable

Developing rapport
- ☐ acknowledges child's feelings
- ☐ shows empathy and support
- ☐ shows sensitivity
- ☐ shares thoughts with patient
- ☐ explains why examination is needed
- ☐ asks for permission to examine child

2b Overall, how effective do you think the doctor's communication has been?

2c Do you think the doctor's tone of voice helps to put the child at ease? Note down two examples to justify your answer

2d Watch the clip again with the volume turned down and note down examples of the doctor's non-verbal communication. Evaluate these in line with models of good communication.

Watching for detail

Part 1: from Start to *No, I think that's all right.* (00:00>01:23)

3 Watch Part 1 of the clip and complete the following examples where the doctor shows empathy and support.

Patient: ... I scraped my arm on a nail.
Doctor: Oh dear. Well, _____

_____ , _____ _____ .

Accidents happen all the time. It _____

_____ _____ .

...

Doctor: [puts gloves on] Right, let's—oh no, that _____ _____ nasty. I _____ _____ hurts. Does it? You're being very _____ .

Part 2: from ... *but what I need to do* to End. (01:23>02:48)

4 Watch Part 2 of the clip. When the doctor says *What I need to do is give you an injection*, the child reacts quite negatively. What softeners could he have used to reduce her anxiety?

5 Answer these questions.
   1 What do you think of the doctor's explanation for giving an injection?
   2 How effective do you think the doctor's distraction technique is when he asks her to imagine she's lying on a beach?
   3 Do you think the doctor closes the interview well?

Over to you

Role-play the scenario you have just watched. Work in threes, taking it in turns to play the role of doctor, patient and observer.

Patient: you should show greater resistance to having an injection than the child in the clip.

Doctor: pay particular attention to your tone of voice and body language.

Observer: give feedback on the doctor's tone of voice, non-verbal communication and degree of empathy shown.

Clips 1 and 2

1a

Eye contact
The doctor uses very little eye contact, spending much of the time either reading the GP's referral or writing his notes.

Proximity
The doctor is seated across his desk from the patient, which is not conducive to creating good rapport, and he doesn't offer a different seating arrangement.

Environment
The environment is not very inviting for a patient – the office is fairly untidy (empty cups and old files on the desk, posters falling off the walls, untidy shelving).

Posture
The doctor's posture starts off quite well – he is sitting upright in his chair at a comfortable distance from his desk and the computer, but this deteriorates.

Facial expression
He doesn't smile as the patient enters; in fact, he looks slightly annoyed; he frowns quite a bit.

Clothing
His clothing is professional: smart, clean, ironed shirt.

Movement
His movements are quite aggressive at times, for example when he is describing the symptoms. He doesn't stand up and attempt to shake the patient's hand when she enters, but he does motion to the patient sit down. Furthermore, he puts his head in his hand, wipes his nose with his hand and scratches his head.

1d
The doctor doesn't heed any of the advice given by Osler; he achieves none of these things.

3a

Suggested answer
This doctor is far more patient-centred. His non-verbal communication is open, he welcomes his patient with a smile and a handshake and uses eye contact. He stands up as the patient enters the room. The patient, although in some pain, responds with a smile. The seating arrangement is more appropriate in terms of creating rapport with the patient.

3b

1	Used a patient-centred approach throughout the consultation (This is very patient-centred, especially compared to the approach of the doctor in Clip 1.)	✓✓✓
2	Began with open and moved to closed questions as appropriate (He allowed and encouraged the patient to express himself in his own words, moving from open to more specific questions in order to obtain precise details.)	✓✓
3	Refrained from employing leading and tag questions (He used tag questions when enquiring about the specifics of the condition instead of simple closed questions that would not lead the patient.)	✓
4	Enquired about specific features of the condition (location, quality, severity, etc.)	✓✓
5	Asked about aggravating and alleviating factors	✓✓✓
6	Enquired about associated manifestations (He asks permission before asking specific questions about the associated manifestations, which would be appropriate at this stge – the doctor is trying to eliminate the presence of certain symptoms.)	✓✓✓
7	Used clear questions, avoiding complicated medical terminology (He did not use any medical terminology with the patient)	✓✓✓
8	Employed appropriate tone of voice (Yes, throughout the whole interview)	✓✓✓

3d
His verbal and non-verbal skills match perfectly.

4a

Suggested answer
Mr Margolis, who prefers to be called Ted, is a family man, married with daughters. He has been trying to organise an evening at a restaurant to celebrate his wife's birthday but is having difficulty convincing his daughters to take part. He seems a fairly laid-back person, a jovial character who is able to laugh at himself.
Ted has presented with pains in his upper quadrant and chest and is also having problems sleeping.

4c
1 Dr Davis explains to the patient that he has read the referral letter and the patient note but invites the patient to give an account from his side.
2 *Can I come back to the sleeping problem? Can we focus a little bit on the trouble you've been having – I mean, with your stomach.*

5a

Location
Mentioned in Part 1 – patient indicates position of pain with his hand. Patient volunteers the information.

Quantity/Severity
8 on a scale 1–10 = quite severe at times

Setting
He tends to get the symptoms when he hasn't eaten for a while.

Associated manifestations
None – no vomiting, no blood

Quality
Sharpish pain and feeling full

Timing
Had symptoms for over a year

Aggravating/Alleviating
Aggravate = fruit and juices, hot liquids
Alleviate = eating

"8th Attribute"
See Exercise 6c below

5b
He doesn't ask about Location. This information was volunteered by the patient in Part 1 – he indicates the location of the pain with his hand. The "8th Attribute" has also not been asked about at this stage. Maybe the doctor wishes to get a more complete picture first before asking the patient's perspective on the situation.

5c

1 Can I ask you **how bad** the pain is when it **comes on**?
2 Have you noticed that **anything makes it** worse?
3 Does anything else **relieve it**?
4 Does the pain **move** anywhere, or does it **just stay** in that, that one **spot**?
5 Have you noticed anything else that **comes along** with the pain?

6a

1 The question serves as a signal to indicate a change in approach for the interview.
2 The doctor is indicating he will now ask some specific closed questions to establish a more accurate diagnosis. He is also indicating that he will take charge of this section of the interview – i.e it ceases to be patient-centred at this point.
3 *You're going to the toilet alright?* This question avoids the medical term *bowel*.
4 That is is going to the toilet regularly.

6b

Suggested answer
Use simple Yes/No type question as opposed to leading questions: *Have you ever vomited up anything? Have you ever vomited blood?*

6c

The doctor asks about the patient's perspective: *You must have your own idea about what might be causing it.* He asks what he hopes they can achieve together during this visit: *What were you hoping that we would, we would do for you today?*

6d

The doctor doesn't want to stop the flow of the story unnecessarily, especially as he understands what the patient is trying to say from the context. Correcting the mistake might also humiliate or intimidate the patient, jeopardising the good rapport that they have.

7

Mr Davis tends to prefer repetition but seems to use it as a means of clarification as opposed to encouraging the patient to express himself. The patient is pretty chatty and as such does not need much encouragement to speak.

Clip 3

1

Suggested answer
Ted seems quite an open person. Unlike some patients, he gives the impression he will be fairly open about his family and social history

and discuss these without too much problem. However, one cannot make assumptions; the doctor needs to be ready to read the patient cues.

3a

Ted has been working as a taxi driver for 15 years; he likes a drink but not to excess; he went with his family to Tunisia last year; he does a fair amount of DIY, but he seems to be accident-prone and has been to A&E several times due to minor injuries.

4a

1 Past illnesses
2 Accidents and injuries
3 Surgical procedures
4 Medication
5 Allergies
6 Immunisations

4b

Mr Davis doesn't ask about pregnancies, which is normal as the patient is male. He also doesn't ask about childhood illnesses. It might have been useful for the doctor to investigate this a bit further – it is easy for a patient to forget illnesses from their childhood. Mr Davies is probably assuming there is nothing significant.

4c

PMH
Bronchitis
Several DIY accidents
DH
Rennies, paracetamol
Allergies
Penicillin

4d

Doctor and patient are able to share a laugh together (the DIY story); he encourages the patient to tell the story in his own words and at his own pace, using facilitating techniques (*nothing else?, did you?*); he empathizes with the patient when he talks about his wife sending him to the appointment for his vaccinations (he gives a knowing smile).

4e

1 Can you tell me about any major illnesses or accidents you might have had in the past?
2 Have you ever had an operation?

5a

Heart disease and alcoholism. His father and grandfather both died after a heart attack. Alcoholism is evident in the family – his brother died from liver disease as a result of heavy drinking. Ted may also be susceptible to both of these.

5b

He feels it is his own fault (*he brought it on himself*). Ted's tone of voice also

suggests this. Ted has rethought his own drinking habits and now only drinks six pints on average per week, although his total consumption might be in the same night. He only drinks alcohol if he is not driving the next day.

6a

Doctor: Can I just ask you a bit about that? Do you **drink any alcohol** at all?
Ted: Well, I do, but I got to be careful, of course, cos of, with driving, you know. So I can only drink if I know **I'm not driving** the next day, you know.
Doctor: OK, so how much alcohol **would you drink** in a, in an average week, do you think?
Ted: Oh, probably about **six pints**, I should think.

6b

Do you drink any alcohol at all? and *OK, so how much alcohol would you drink in a, in an average week, do you think?*
In the first question, the doctor is making a point of asking whether or not Ted does in fact drink, rather than simply assuming he does and asking how much. The use of *at all* makes the question sound less blunt. When addressing the sensitive issue of how much Ted drinks, the doctor uses an indirect question, again making the question sound less blunt.

7c

Is that a fair summary of what we've discussed so far?
Mr Davis wants to give Ted the chance to correct inaccurate information, add missing details and recall new information. Summarising is an important stage of the patient-centred interview, allowing the patient to fully participate in the history-taking process.

Clip 4

2c

Dr Davis managed his voice to good effect during the whole physical examination. He maintained a tone of voice that was calm and reassuring, softly spoken but clear at all times. This ensured that the patient complied throughout the examination.

3a

1 It is important to start by examining the hands; it is a socially more acceptable approach that gives time for the patient to develop trust in his/her doctor.
2 It is important to explain investigations to the patient so that they have a better understanding of

why they are being carried out. Some investigations (in this case hands and eyes) may not be obvious to the patient considering the symptoms they have presented with.

3b
Suggested answers

I would like you to lie on the couch. / Could you please lie on the couch? / If you could just lie on the couch, please. / If you wouldn't mind lying on the couch, please.

3c

This language would not be suitable for this patient. He appears to be a little embarrassed by the question *Do you need to have a pee first of all?* This language is more appropriate for a child or someone who has indicated they did not understand the more clinical expression 'empty your bladder'. Note 'empty your bladder' is very widely used in English.

3e

Do you need to empty your bladder first? / Do you need to visit the toilet before we start the examination?

4a

Doctor: So if you just look up at the ceiling for me. That's great. If you **stick your tongue out** for me now. And pop it back in again. And now **I'm just going to** feel for any glands at the **base of** your neck. That's fine.

Patient: What do you mean, you didn't find any?

Doctor: There are none there. No, I can't feel anything. That's fine. What I'd **like to do** now is just examine your stomach, OK? Can you tell me **whereabouts** it hurts?

Patient: It's right in there, doc.

Doctor: Alright, so I'll be **especially careful** when I'm pressing on there. What I'm going to do is just **press round gently**. Could you tell me **if it hurts** at all?

4b

1 The patient complies with the investigations without any signs of resistance.

2 *For me* is used to encourage the patient to comply with the doctor's requests during the examination. It is often used with children but can be used with adults in this context.

5a

Doctor: Could you tell me if it **hurts at all**?

Ted: Yeah.

Doctor: That's quite **tender, is it**? I'm

gonna press a little bit harder now. So again, **tell me if** it's too uncomfortable.

Ted: That's fine. Oh, oh.

Doctor: That's **quite** painful, is it? I'm sorry. But alright over here?

Ted: Yeah.

5b

There are plenty of examples where the doctor demonstrates active listening skills, for example relieving pressure on areas of pain and apologising, and responding to questions related to investigations the patient doesn't understand.

5c

1 *at all* is a softener placed at the end of a sentence to add politeness. The intonation rises on this expression.

2 Expressions like *that's great/fine/ good* should not be taken literally; the doctor uses these to indicate a transition from one stage of the physical examination to the next.

6

The doctor maintains dignity by ensuring that areas not being examined are covered by a blanket. At the end of the examination he suggests the patient dresses first before they discuss the findings of the examination. (The patient is less vulnerable once dressed and more able to participate on an equal level with the doctor.)

Clip 5

1 Suggested answers

Obtain patient's view of need for action.
Elicit any barriers to implementing a plan.
Take patient's lifestyle into account
Encourage patient to be involved in plan.
Ask about support networks.

2

Yes, he does.

3

The doctor's non-verbal communication is in line with good practice. She leans towards the patient, she maintains good eye contact throughout the interview, she reads the patient's body language and responds appropriately, she uses her hands to explain the different options, she smiles and laughs in response to the patient's comments (grandad's smoking, chewing gum), she tries to enthuse the patient about the benefits of brisk walking by using her arms and contrasting this to slow walking with a dog.

4

1 He says *oh* and looks down at the floor.

2 She gives him an opportunity to express his feelings by saying that he still looks worried.

3 Being pretty overweight and smoking heavily

4 He's been smoking for 30 years, he enjoys the social aspect of smoking, his grandfather was a heavy smoker and lived until he was ninety, smoking helps him to deal with stress.

5 She nods a lot and smiles at times to show that she understands what the patient is saying.

5

1 Crossing ones legs is often a subconscious response and is seen as a protective gesture. In this case it coincides with a change of focus from sharing a laugh about the patient's grandfather to listing the dangers of smoking, which could invite an unwanted reaction from the patient.

2 He makes no verbal response and his body language does not indicate whether he agrees or disagrees. Yes, it is significant, as it allows the doctor to proceed as if he agrees and then to bring up the question about how he might give up smoking.

3 Inhalator, patches and nasal spray

4 She acknowledges that there are side effects, outlines what they are, and then points out that the benefits of using nicotine replacement still outweigh any side effects.

6

Her body language reinforces her message when she says the following: *Gradually, over the course of weeks …*
… cut down on how much you're using …
… get to the point where you hardly need it.

7a

Upping the amount you walk – raises her hand
Getting the heart rate up – raises her hand more vigorously
Really brisk walk – mimes walking movement
Do fast walking – mimes walking more vigorously
Pootling along slowly with the dog – mimes holding a dog lead without much enthusiasm
Get on your trainers – very vigorous miming of exercising

7b

Her body language is very effective in terms of reinforcing what she is saying on a visual level, mirroring the enthusiasm in her voice, and demonstrating that vigorous exercise can be enjoyable.

7c

She doesn't include stages 3 or 4.

7d

Stage 3: If you find you are struggling with what we've agreed, call us and we can try to help you.
Stage 4: OK, if there is anything else you'd like to ask in relation to the plan …

8a

2 *Well, I would suggest* you give it another try.
3 And then gradually, over the course of weeks, <u>we'll cut down</u> on how much you're using …
4 Well, <u>shall we set a date to stop now then?</u>
5 <u>How about I</u> give you a prescription, you can get the stuff, and …

8b

It allows the patient to be involved in the treatment plan.

9

1 Doctor's objectives: to highlight dangers of smoking and to get the patient to agree to take steps to stop. Patient's objectives: to find out what is causing the breathlessness and to seek appropriate treatment.
2 Yes, both doctor and patient appear to have achieved their objectives.
3 Concordance: the doctor respects the wishes of the patient and allows the patient to set the terms of the treatment.
4 The doctor speaks in a gentle and concerned way. She reassures patient by stressing the word *fine* at the beginning of the scenario: *Your heart is fine.* She also shows enthusiasm in her voice when she encourages the patient to do some brisk walking.

Clip 6

1b

Suggested answers

Risk of poisoning, damage to eardrum or cartilage around the ear, scarring to the face, facial nerve damage

2a

1 Permission
2 Setting
3 Knowledge
4 Explain
5 Strategy
Ms Smithson does not cover
I – invitation or S – summary.

2c

The patient will be required to stay in hospital for two days and therefore take time off work, which could cause some inconvenience as she is covering

for colleagues and is very busy. The wound is not particularly severe, and, as such, her life is unlikely to change dramatically.

3a

Ms Smithson: smiling / good eye contact / warm / proximity: close but not overbearing / non-threatening posture – slightly forward
Student: attentive / proximity: giving space
Nurse: proximity: giving space

3b

It just feels a bit tender, that's all. / It's a bit, sort of tender. / I feel fine.
Patient minimises the pain, and so it will be quite a shock that she will be admitted to hospital, given that she is not in severe pain. Also, she has been told by A&E the wound simply needs cleaning and maybe re-stitching.

4a

Ms Smithson: Alright, so what are **your thoughts** about what's **going** on?
Patient: I don't know. I guess it just needs re-stitching and cleaning up a bit, probably.
Ms Smithson: Yeah, so that's what **you are expecting**?
Patient: Yeah.
Ms Smithson: OK, well I'm really sorry to have to **tell you** it's **going to involve** a bit more treatment than that.

4b

Ms Smithson uses an open question: *So that's what you're expecting?* so as not to lead the patient. She confirms the patient's perception before moving on to prepare her for receiving the bad news.

4c

Both use it to minimise the situation. The patient is expecting a more simple procedure, which is what A&E have led her to believe (*re-stitching and cleaning up a bit, probably*). The doctor tries to minimise the impact of the bad news (*a bit more treatment than that*).

5a

1 NO
2 NO
3 YES
4 NO

5b

1 Ms Smithson doesn't consider I in the SPIKES model.
2 Her explanation is clear and appropriate to the level of education of the patient but avoids medical jargon

3 She uses the words *I can see you're getting a bit anxious.* She is able to read patient cues and respond appropriately.
4 Using validating language to show that the patient's feelings are normal is not necessary here, considering the degree of the bad news as presented by the doctor.

5c

How much detail would you like me to go into? / Are there any areas you would rather I didn't go into?

5d

Cos you don't want to be left with any nasty scaring, do you?
This hints that the infection is more serious than she has described to the patient. You may believe in giving the worst case scenario so that the patient has all the facts.

6a

Cellulitis (used with patient but explained) / soft tissue / intravenous / structures / parotid gland / facial nerve

6b

Are you alright if I just show Jo the wound and explain to her medically what's going on? So that was just a little anatomy lesson there for Jo.
1 It keeps the patient informed and asks the patient's permission; if the patient refuses, this can be done later.
2 This is the best moment, as the doctor has already explained what is going on to the patient. Listening to the discussion with the student could be alarming for the patient if they are not aware of the situation already. This approach is in line with the patient-centred approach.

7a

It is more likely that the nursing staff would deal with this. The doctor in this clip shows concern for the patient as a whole and takes into consideration the impact of her treatment on the rest of her life.

Clip 7

1

Be prepared to probe for the source of anger, while being supportive of the patient's feelings.
Avoid provoking the patient.
Be prepared to be assertive to deal with manipulative behaviour, while making sure that any aggression is minimised.

2a

1 The encounter has not been particularly successful for either patient or doctor. The patient's objective is to get the doctor to acknowledge that he has got MS.

The doctor does not do this and has pointed out alternative diagnoses with which the patient is not comfortable. The doctor's objective appears to be to identify possible reasons for the patient's symptoms and to act to resolve these. While she appears to have identified a possible cause for the symptoms, she is unable to get the patient to agree with her diagnosis; he remains quite convinced of his own diagnosis.

2 There is communication breakdown, as the doctor fails to successfully challenge the patient on his self-diagnosis. As a result, the issue keeps recurring and prevents discussion of a more likely diagnosis.

3 The doctor seems to have identified the cause of the patient's symptoms but is unable to get the patient to accept her diagnosis, so is likely to feel frustrated that the patient is not willing to cooperate. The patient is also likely to feel frustrated because he has not achieved his objective

4 The doctor's voice suggests that she doubts the validity of what the patient is saying, particularly when she says *really* in response to the patient stating that he has MS; her intonation rises and then falls when she says the word. In general, she adopts quite a firm and assertive tone.

2b
Suggested answer
The doctor's facial expressions indicate that she is not convinced about what she is hearing – she raises her eyebrows a lot, grimaces, frowns and bites her lip at one point. Her posture is quite rigid, and there is little movement in her hands. The seating arrangement is not ideal, as the doctor and patient are facing each other directly

3
Up to this point, she doesn't use this kind of language.

4
When the patient says: *I'm a bit scared / I'm feeling very tired / And then I've got pins and needles and then dropping things*

5
The patient's eyes narrow, and he frowns, suggesting annoyance. The doctor picks up on this and quickly moves on to her next question to let the patient's feelings subside.

6
Mr Boyle, **I do hear** what you say, but I feel that I would really like to explore other options.
I'm listening to what you have to say.

But I'm **simply** trying to explain to you that MS in not the only diagnosis. Just **bear with** me a moment.

7
1 That **must have been** pretty difficult.
2 So **that's another blow** for you? So things are looking **pretty rough**?

8
Because the doctor is now discussing the issue of depression and feels that events in the patient's life have led to depression.

9
The doctor nods. However, the nodding could be more emphatic and consistent. In addition, smiling and moving her hands apart would indicate that she is listening.

Clip 8
1
Suggested answers
Establishing initial rapport: greet patient, demonstrate respect and interest, consider paying the child a compliment, check child is comfortable
Developing rapport: acknowledge child's feelings, show empathy and support, show sensitivity, share thoughts with patient, explain why examination is needed, ask for permission to examine child

2a
Establishing initial rapport
He greets the child.
He doesn't show much interest in the girl apart from telling her that she has grown.
He checks she is comfortable by asking *Are you going to be comfortable there?*
Developing rapport
He acknowledges the child's feelings. He says *Oh dear* in response to the child saying her arm hurts.
He shows empathy when he says *Nails shouldn't be sticking out of the wall, should they? That's horrible* and when he says *I bet that hurts, doesn't it?*
He shows support when he says *You're being very brave* and when he reassures her that it wasn't her fault.
He shares his thoughts with the child and mother when he says there shouldn't be any scarring.
He doesn't explain why he needs to look at the child's arm.
He asks for permission to look at her arm: *Can I have a little look?*

2b
Moderately effective; he succeeds in getting the patient to cooperate with him, and he covers most of the

recommended stages. However, at times he lacks sensitivity, for example when he tells the girl she has to have an injection and comes across as a little patronising. He also calls the mother *mummy*.

2c
While the doctor sounds quite friendly, he doesn't really adapt his voice sufficiently for dealing with a clearly anxious child. Examples include:
• When the doctor says he has to give the girl an injection to stop her arm hurting; he comes across as impatient.
• When the doctor says *Now what we need to do, mummy, is to clean this, and you must make sure you keep it clean* he comes across as patronising.

2d
Good points: At the start of the interview he smiles at the mother. He leans forward and makes eye contact with the girl. When seated, he makes a clear effort to place himself at the same level as the girl by hunching over
Weak points: He doesn't smile at the girl at the beginning. He looks slightly irritated when the girl says she doesn't like injections. He doesn't smile during the consultation, apart from after giving the injection.

3
Oh dear. Well, **don't worry don't worry**. Accidents happen all the time. It **wasn't your fault**.
... oh no, that **does look** nasty. I **bet that** hurts. Does it? You're being very **brave**.

4
... a **little/tiny** injection.
... **just** give you ...

5
1 It could be better. Apart from paying more attention to his tone of voice, the doctor could have explored why the child was afraid of injections and explained that the injection was important to get rid of any dirt in the arm, which was part of the reason why her arm was hurting.
2 It would be more effective if he used a gentler tone of voice. He could have reminded her to keep her eyes focused on the picture (she seems to stare into space) and then asked her a couple of questions about the seaside to distract her.
3 Yes. He makes a practical suggestion to dispose of the nail, which the girl seems to approve of. He praises her again for being good.